Affective Communities

POLITICS, HISTORY, AND CULTURE

A series from the International Institute at the University of Michigan

Series Editors: George Steinmetz and Julia Adams

Sponsored by the International Institute at the University of Michigan and published by Duke University Press, this series is centered around cultural and historical studies of power, politics, and the state—a field that cuts across the disciplines of history, sociology, anthropology, political science, and cultural studies. The focus on the relationship between state and culture refers both to a methodological approach—the study of politics and the state using culturalist methods—and a substantive one that treats signifying practices as an essential dimension of politics. The dialectic of politics, culture, and history figures prominently in all the books selected for the series.

Leela Gandhi

AFFECTIVE COMMUNITIES

Anticolonial Thought, Fin-de-Siècle Radicalism, and the Politics of Friendship

Duke University Press

Durham & London

2006

Designed by C. H. Westmoreland

Typeset in Adobe Caslon

by Keystone Typesetting, Inc.

Library of Congress Cataloging-in-Publication Data

Gandhi, Leela, 1966–

Affective communities : anticolonial thought, fin de siecle radicalism, and the politics of friendship / Leela Gandhi.

p. cm. — (Politics, history, and culture)

Includes bibliographical references and index.

ISBN 0-8223-3703-7 (cloth : alk. paper)

ISBN 0-8223-3715-0 (pbk. : alk. paper)

1. Radicalism—England—History—19th century. 2. Radicalism—England—History—20th century. 3. Anti-imperialist movements—England—History—19th century. 4. Anti-imperialist movements—England—History—20th century. I. Title. II. Series.

HN400.R3G36 2006

320.530942′09034—dc22

2005025992

For Pauline Nestor and Bronte Adams

CONTENTS

Acknowledgments ix

1 INTRODUCTION
Affective Communities 1

2 MANIFESTO
Anticolonial Thought and the Politics of Friendship 13

3 SEX
The Story of Late Victorian Homosexual Exceptionalism 34

4 MEAT
A Short Cultural History of Animal Welfare at the Fin-de-Siècle 67

5 GOD
Mysticism and Radicalism at the End of the Nineteenth Century 115

6 ART
Aestheticism and the Politics of Postcolonial Difference 142

7 CONCLUSION
An Immature Politics 177

Notes 191
Index 237

ACKNOWLEDGMENTS

Several individuals and institutions have supported and accompanied the making of this book. A generous grant from the Australian Research Council directly facilitated research and helped release invaluable writing time. La Trobe University was likewise supportive in crucial ways, extending financial assistance, allowing for periods of leave from teaching, and, most of all, providing a uniquely collegiate and intellectually sustaining milieu. So too, the business of actual research was eased considerably through the assistance and patience of staff and archivists at the following libraries: St. Stephens College, Teen Murthi, the Bodleian, La Trobe University, Monash University, and Sri Aurobindo Ashram.

Over the last few years I have benefited greatly from scholarly hospitality at the Universities of Lisbon, Evora, Trento, Oxford, Massachusetts, Monash, Melbourne, Sydney, New South Wales, and Delhi, and the Centre for Cross-Cultural Research in Canberra. For affective accommodation at these institutions as well as for their intellectual and personal generosity, I wish to thank especially Maria Alzira Seixo, Tapan Basu, Liana Borghi, Brinda Bose, Barbara Caine, Giovanna Covi, Ros Diprose, Alison Donnell, Simon During, Debjani Ganguly, Costanza and Mario Garavelli, Paola Giacomoni, Chris Healy, Victor Mendes, Suroopa Mukherji, Michele Nicoletti, John Noyes, Ira Raja, Manav Rati, Linnell Seacomb, Lalitha Subbu, Rajeswari Sunder Rajan, Ferdinando Targetti, Jurgen Todesco, and Joy Wang. I owe additional thanks to Robert Young, who has also been the most supportive and stimulating of readers for this work. At a delicate stage of writing I received invaluable support and editorial feedback from Julia Adams, George Steinmetz, and others involved in the Politics, History, and Culture Series for Duke University Press. At the press itself, I received particular support from my editor Valerie Millholland and from Fred

Kameny, who has been the most painstaking of copy editors. It is a rare luxury to have a book shepherded toward completion and one for which I remain very grateful. Ample thanks are also due to the Humanities Research Centre at the Australian National University for a month-long fellowship that enabled me to prepare the final manuscript in the most congenial setting.

Dipesh Chakrabarty and Ashis Nandy have been instrumental as mentors for this and other work: sympathetic, impatient, enthusiastic, tough, always encouraging. Communities of friends, debts to whom are inevitably somewhat unaccountable, have helped, thus, in incalculable ways: Daniel Alexander, Julia Briggs, Marion Campbell, Terry Collits, Kate Cook, Michael Dutton, Joanne Finkelstein, Ramin Gray, Mani, Smriti, and Siddharata Iyer, Vinay Kumar, Caroline Lewis, Amanda Macdonald, Hilary Mcphee, Sunam Mukherjee, Claire Murray, Raju Pandey, Nishad Pandey, Ratna Raman, Arvind Rane, Mahesh Rangarajan, Nimmi, Elizabeth Rubin, Sanjay Seth, Ruth Vanita, Don Watson. It is with appreciative pleasure that I acknowledge all of the above here along with my goddaughter Helena and her brother Ruben. My parents Ramachandra Gandhi, Indu Gandhi, and Veenapani Chawla have consistently been sources of insight, comfort, and conversation. My greatest debts are to them as well as to Pauline Nestor and Bronte Adams for such love and presence as never allows even the most intense periods of work and absence to seem like a privation. For their matchless gifts of humor, compassion, loyalty, and fierce and unyielding intelligence, then, my deep gratitude.

1

INTRODUCTION

Affective Communities

Over the last few decades postcolonial scholarship has tended to designate anti-imperialism "proper" as an action performed solely by the putative non-West upon the putative West, through gestures of either oppositionality (culturalism, nativism, fundamentalism) or infiltration (hybridity, mimicry, reactive interpellation, "the journey in"). Supplying us with complex theoretical means through which to diagnose the oppositional energies of nonwestern anti-imperialism, especially when expressed in the form of anticolonial nationalism, postcolonialism has however remained tentative in its appreciation of individuals and groups that have renounced the privileges of imperialism and elected affinity with victims of their own expansionist cultures. It is to such western "nonplayers" in the drama of imperialism that this book devotes its attention, thus seeking to shed greater light on some "minor" forms of anti-imperialism that emerged in Europe, specifically in Britain, at the end of the nineteenth century.

The exhumation of these "internal" and subjugated forms of anti-imperialism, I submit, productively complicates our perspective on colonial encounter. It brings, as David Cannadine and Jonathan Schneer among others have urged, the history of the British Empire into closer proximity to the history of the British nation, showing how imperial messages were frequently intercepted, refused, and diluted from within the imperial metropolis well before they reached the colonial periphery.[1] As Schneer writes, "The imperial drumbeat was steady and all-enveloping in turn-of-the-century London . . . Nevertheless, because London was an imperial metropolis it was cosmopolitan and because it was cosmopolitan it contained anti-imperialists and critics of empire. These men and women did not attain the influence of their imperial counterparts, but neither were they a negligible force. Moreover just as the champions of empire helped to shape the imperial metropolis, so too did they."[2] Lending its voice to stories of such long-forgotten nineteenth-century metropolitan anti-imperialists, this book is at one level a work of straightforward historical redressal. At another level, and in its heart, it is also an inquiry into the onerous politics of "betrayal," "departure," "flight," "treason" exemplified by metropolitan anti-imperialists. What ethical imperatives, I wish to ask in the following pages, rendered some Europeans immune to the ubiquitous temptations of an empire described by Schneer as a machine or factory "for making imperialist-minded citizens"?[3] Which were the intolerable domestic pressures exercised by empire upon its own citizenry, such that some among it chose to betray the claims of possessive nationalism in favor of solidarity with foreigners, outsiders, alleged inferiors? How might we recognize as political the disaggregated forms of a dissent engaged for its own sake, bearing no practical investment in the *telos* of the anticolonial nation-state and certainly gaining no apparent material advantage from the economic and political diminution of imperial power? What part, if any, did western critiques of empire play in the dissolution of the tired and violent deadlock between colonial power on the one hand and anticolonial resistance on the other? How "successful" were they? How did they blur the rigid cultural boundaries between West and non-West, colonizer and colonized? These are some of the questions to be canvased in the course of the following discussion as we endeavor to glean one paradigmatic narrative of metropolitan anti-imperialism from the annals of late Victorian radicalism.

Although departing from postcolonial theory in an emphasis on internal rather than external critiques of empire, my arguments nonetheless take their cue from premises fundamental to that larger body of thought, especially insofar as they pose an inquiry into the cultural osmoses occasioned by colonial encounter. To recall, the scholarship variously liberated by the epochal publication of Edward Said's *Orientalism* (1978) and his later *Culture and Imperialism* (1993) finds its theoretical moorings in three assumptions also central to my concerns here: first, that colonialism was a hierarchically aligned system of division or binary opposition designed, in the main and through the discourse of "orientalism," to sequester the West from the psychic contagion of nonwestern alterity; second, that as such a project of division, partition, and separation, colonialism failed its informing orientalist enterprise largely on account of the irremediable leakiness of imperial boundaries; and third, if postcolonial thought is to lay claim to political and ethical import it must use the analytic advantage of historical hindsight scrupulously to disclose the failure of imperial binarism. Said names this third procedure the "contrapuntal perspective" of postcolonial thought, committed in its best moments to revealing the "overlapping territories" and "intertwined histories" of colonial encounter. The law of division, as he writes, may well have been germane to imperial subjectivity and epistemology: "Throughout the exchange between Europeans and their 'others' that began systematically half a millennium ago, the one idea that has scarcely varied is that there is an 'us' and a 'them,' each quite settled, clear, unassailably self-evident. As I discuss it in *Orientalism*, the division goes back to Greek thought about barbarians, but, whoever originated this kind of 'identity' thought, by the nineteenth century it had become the hallmark of imperialist cultures as well as those cultures trying to resist the encroachments of Europe." Yet, Said avers, it is precisely such "identity thought" that postcolonial revisionism has exposed to be fictional and illusory: "Gone are the binary oppositions dear to the nationalist and imperialist enterprise . . . new alignments are rapidly coming into view, and it is those new alignments that now provoke and challenge the fundamentally static notion of *identity* that has been the core of cultural thought during the era of imperialism."[4]

In the course of its discursive and disciplinary transmission the theme of Saidian "contrapuntality" has reached its apogee and possibly received its most inspired elaboration through the tropes of "hybridity," "interstitiality," "mimicry" and the "in-between," each closely associated with Homi Bhabha's oeuvre and each announcing the epistemic and existential impossibility of colonial division. Imperialism, Bhabha reiterates in his influential essays, never fulfills its fantasy of discrete binarization. Its yearning for secure psychic quarantine is always complicated by a perennial osmosis through which colonizer and colonized mutate unawares but inexorably into each other in the countless hybrid and interstitial sites of imperial antagonism: "the primitive Manicheanism of the settler—black and white, Arab and Christian—breaks down in the present of struggle for independence. Polarities come to be replaced with truths that are only partial, limited and unstable."[5] That is to say, it is precisely as a project of pure division that colonial fantasy carries elements of its own inevitable disappointment; precisely its craving for the hygiene of oppositionality that renders it susceptible to contagion from a field where, à la Marx, "everything seems pregnant with its contrary."[6] Or, as Bhabha contends in characteristic complication of this theme: "Reading from the transferential perspective, where the Western ratio returns to itself from the time lag of the colonial relation, then we see how modernity and postmodernity are themselves constituted from the marginal perspective of colonial difference. They encounter themselves contingently at the point at which the internal difference of their own society is reiterated in terms of the difference of the other, the alterity of the postcolonial site etc."[7]

Over the last few decades postcolonialist scholars have carefully worked through the obligations of a "contrapuntal perspective," breaking down the stern binary of colonial encounter by refusing the myths of cultural purity, origin, inauguration, and initiation both to the imperial West and to its opposite, anticolonial nationalism or nativism. Generally speaking, one set of scholars has sought to dissolve colonial division within the territorial and subjective geography of empire itself, showing how the substance of imperial self-articulation was in fact furnished by the materials of nonwestern difference: thus the nineteenth-century English novel obtained its narrative and domestic detail from the cornucopia of the imperial periphery; the seemingly patriotic "culture" of English Studies was first developed in the pedagogic laboratories of colonial India, and so on.[8] Here we might also record the theme, ubiquitous in postcolonial theory and fiction, of the "voyage in," surmising the historical failure of colonial separation from the present admixture of the imperial metropole, its mixed and vexed demography invoked as testimony to the complicating veracity of previous imperial contact zones.

Further to this project, another set of scholars has attempted to dissolve the logic of imperial manicheanism by nagging at its inversion and reinstatement in the narrative of anticolonial nationalism—eschewing, to this end, the oftentimes pernicious consolation of "a rhetoric of blame."[9] Seeking instead, as Bhabha puts it, "a critical position . . . free of the 'inverted' polarities of a 'counter-politics of exclusion,' " work in this area proceeds deconstructively, drawing attention to the adulterants of occidental modernity secreted within every dream of anticolonial nationalist purity. So, close cultural readings reveal in place of anticolonial nationalism's confident claim to edenic premodern antiquity a fictive and orientalist-inspired "invention of tradition," in place of its bombastic assertions of radical difference and originality a "derivative discourse," contingent upon the oppressive forms of imperial nationalism.[10] In a similar vein, historiography inspired by the work of the Subaltern Studies collective highlights, in lieu of its claims to anticolonial oppositionality, élite nationalism's self-defeating collusion, collaboration, and implication in the imperial project, its reliance on the infrastructure and grammar of empire to disqualify elusive and disruptive forms of popular resistance (such as peasant rebellions in South Asia) internal to the anticolonial nation-state.

At its core, this book is thus deeply indebted to the impulse against imperial binarism amplified in the postcolonial critiques, summarized above, of both colonial and anticolonial nationalisms. Nonetheless, it dramatizes a complaint against the subtle determinism to which postcolonial orthodoxy is susceptible because of its reliance on a concealed rhetoric of historical dialecticism in which the dissolution of colonial division is seen as in some ways inevitable: a matter of temporal unfolding, an evolutionary effect of the laws of biological mutation. "I attempt," as Bhabha writes of his theoretical project, "to represent a certain defeat, or even an impossibility, of the 'West' in its authorization of the 'idea' of colonization . . ."; the "fetishized colonial culture" is always "potentially and strategically an insurgent counter-appeal"; the territorial transmission and imperial projection of the "Western sign" invariably "inscribes an ambivalence at the very origins of colonial authority."[11] Without arguing the case for an elision of agency in such thought, I would however point to its relative neglect of, or disinterest in, anticolonial actors, especially such as might have performed their political vocation impatiently from within imperial culture, unwilling to wait for its eventual hybridization, actively renouncing, refusing, and rejecting categorically its aggressive manicheanism.[12] The naturalist theatre of "interstitiality" and "in-between-ness" is, I maintain, an inadequate setting for the aspirational energy of this latter endeavor, its politics demanding, in addition to those improvisational gestures of "slyness" and "mimicry" catalogued by Bhabha, scope for greater inventiveness, and manifesting a desire not only for dissolution but for the inauguration of new and better forms of community and relationality hitherto unimaginable within the monochromatic landscape of imperial division, where all opposition is tediously condemned to the logic of repetition and resemblance.

Faced with an ultimately unsatisfactory theoretical choice between the oppositional but repetitive forms of cultural nationalism on the one hand and the subversive but quietist discourse of hybridity or contrapuntality on the other, some postcolonial scholarship over the last decade or so has begun the task of reengaging the colonial archive for more selfconsciously creative forms of anti-imperialism, especially in its western or metropolitan articulation. So, for instance, Kumari Jayawardene's *The White Woman's Other Burden* (1995) offers an instructive discussion of western women who defied both imperial and anticolonial orthodoxy in fulfilling their feminist allegiance with their nonwestern counterparts. In a similar vein, Ramachandra Guha provides a compelling account of the "other side of the Raj" in *Savaging the Civilised* (1999), a biography of Verrier Elwin (1902–64), the British environmentalist and writer who opposed both imperialist and nationalist lobbies during a protracted debate on India's tribal communities. A similar focus from the perspective of American race politics animates Becky Thompson's study of white self-critique in *A Promise and a Way of Life: White Antiracist Activism* (2001) and Emily Bernard's edited volume *Remember Me to Harlem* (2001), a collection of letters detailing the controversial, four-decade-long friendship between the black, single, sexually ambivalent Langston Hughes and the white, married, and homosexual Carl Van Vechten.[13] This book aligns itself strongly with the efforts of these writers, elaborating their emphasis on minor narratives of crosscultural collaboration between oppressors and oppressed. Its principal theoretical point of departure is taken from Ashis Nandy's early book, *The Intimate Enemy* (1983), one of the few works of postcolonial scholarship sympathetically to engage with "the numerically small but psychologically significant response of many who opted out of their colonising society for the cause of India."[14] Very rarely, Nandy concedes, did this enterprise register on the center stage of colonial encounter, its protestations scarcely observed on either side of the imperial divide. Yet in its commitment to "recognising the oppressed or marginalised selves of the First and Second world as civilisational allies in the battle against institutional suffering," it posited a radical, if fleeting, "newness" against the barren space of colonial division.[15]

For Nandy, such a project of ethical "inventiveness" is *eo ipso* "utopian." Those "wholly" opting out from the idiom of their own colonizing culture may be described, in his words, "as persons searching for a new utopia untouched by any Hobbesian dream."[16] Utopianism, I will argue after Nandy, was indeed the constitutive ingredient of the western anti-imperialism that briefly elaborated itself at the end of the nineteenth century, animating its action of departure from inherited communities and its yearning for an other-directed ethics and politics, and accounting also for its relative unintelligibility to the existing field of postcolonial studies. Let me explain. If the imperial project, and its recourse to the exclusionary structures of instrumental binary reason, demanded from its votaries strict observance of the ideological thresholds separating insiders from outsiders, us from them, similars from foreigners, masters from slaves, the precise energies of the individuals and subcultures that I examine accrued in the main from innovative border crossing, visible in small, defiant flights from the fetters of belonging toward the unknown destinations of radical alterity. Yet these utopic flights from imperial similitude did not only traverse the paths of cultural or civilisational difference, abandoning "West" for "non-West," renouncing modernity in favor of orientalist consolation, going native. Far from treating empire merely as a cultural clash between West and non-West, or as form of European territorial and capitalist expansionism, late Victorian radicalism discursively extended the semantic scope of imperialism to diagnose it as a peculiar habit of mind, discerning within its structure a complex analogical system relentlessly mapping hierarchies of race, culture, and civilization upon relationships between genders, species, classes, etc. In this schema, departure from the self-confirming orderliness of imperial habitation was at once an experience of profound psychic derangement: exile to the chaos of a world without taxonomy, variously in the company of sexual misfits, slaughterhouse animals, factory slaves, colonized subjects, unruly women—the wretched, as it were, of the earth. Yet it was precisely this perception of the imperial periphery as an undifferentiated, horizontal terrain that gave possibility to a new politics of unlikely conjunction and conjuncture according to which sexual dissidence, the struggle for animal rights, (proto-)posthumanist spiritualism and religious heterodoxy, pro-suffrage activism and socialism could each be regarded as varieties of anti-imperialism. In other words, once imperialism was troped as shorthand for all that was wrong and iniquitous in the world, its abandonment—and the project, thereby, of anti-imperialism—came to carry, we will see, the promise of ideal community, a utopian order of things.

While unique in its emphasis, the anti-imperial subculture of late Victorian radicalism with which this book is concerned, and the socialist revival of the 1880s that ushered it in, was certainly not without historical precedent. Drawing upon an intermittent but long tradition of metropolitan anti-imperialism in place by the beginning of the nineteenth century, socialism in the 1880s also obtained much of the distinctive cosmopolitanism of its outlook from the move for the internationalization of labor that had asserted itself in the late years of Chartism and reached its apotheosis with the formation of the First International, or International Working Men's Association, in 1864. As is acknowledged, a strong commitment to transnational solidarities marked the activities of the Chartist-inspired Fraternal Democrats and International Association, manifesting itself especially in sympathetic partisanship toward Polish militants engaged in the Cracow uprising and participants in the revolutions of 1848, and finding further expression, when these movements were suppressed, in the forging of novel alliances between British workers and revolutionary exiles and émigrés from Poland, France, Germany, and elsewhere.

Long after the demise of Chartism, this spirit of transnational collaboration continued its forward momentum through the slow socialist revival of the 1860s, articulating itself in gestures of solidarity from British labor toward the aspirations of the Italian Risorgimento, the Polish uprising of 1863, and the abolitionist North during the American Civil War. The subsequent network of alliances, between domestic and migrant workers, between socialism and struggles for national liberation, and (more guardedly) between white workers and the faceless mass of black American slaves was finally gathered and formalized within the structure of the First International. Inaugurated in London under the chairmanship of E. S. Beesley—and soon given its true direction under the guardianship of Karl Marx—this organization was, in the decade or so of its influence over British labor, clear without being entirely comprehensive in its reservations about the nationalist and parochial rivalries, as of the global inequities, endorsed by European imperialism. Testifying to the anticolonial credentials of the First International, a report in the *Beehive* on its inaugural meeting pays particular attention to Beesley's condemnation of Britain's colonial and foreign policies with regard to Ireland and other parts of the world: "England wrongfully held possession of Gibraltar from Spain, and her conduct in China, Japan, India and elsewhere was cowardly and unprincipled."[17]

By the time of the socialist revival of the 1880s, the political thinking of these congenial preceding traditions was available for appropriation, and the activists and revolutionaries of the new era made good use of this legacy in forging their own initiatives. At the same time, their take on the anti-imperial concessions of the British labor movement was almost always inflected with elements from other clashing traditions, often regarded very unfavorably by adherents of Marxist orthodoxy within the First International. So, for example, in the hands of late Victorian radicals the inherited culture of socialist transnationalism was combined with ideological materials from a deeper history of utopian thought and experimentation in England, to transform the measured principle of cosmopolitan solidarity into a battle cry for the uncompromising eschewal of all "given" community. Likewise, while drawing readily on socialist internationalism's permission to oppose domestic élites in the exercise of transcultural solidarities, the radicals of the 1860s found greater energy for insurrectionary action in the extreme anti-authoritarian commendations of dissenting anarchist factions within the First International, preferring to declare war on the very idea of government in their ardent pursuit of utopic sociality.[18] Thus, weaving together the disparate energies of Marxism, utopian experimentation, and continental anarchism, these individuals and movements facilitated the mutation of "internationalism" into a series of countercultural revolutionary practices for which I claim the name "politics of friendship." I will argue that this politics rendered metropolitan anticolonialism, albeit briefly, into an existentially urgent and ethically inventive enterprise.

There are two principal reasons for my use of the term "politics of friendship": first, this book builds its theoretical claims upon the narrative and historical scaffolding of multiple, secret, unacknowledged friendships and collaborations between anticolonial South Asians and marginalized anti-imperial "westerners" enmeshed within the various subcultures of late Victorian radicalism. Second, it privileges, after Derrida, the trope of friendship as the most comprehensive philosophical signifier for all those invisible affective gestures that refuse alignment along the secure axes of filiation to seek expression outside, if not against, possessive communities of belonging. Chapter 2 will amplify the theoretical ramifications of a "politics of friendship" with reference to E. M. Forster's famous defense of friendship in *Two Cheers for Democracy*: "If I had to choose between betraying my country and betraying my friend I hope I should have the guts to betray my country."[19] Forster's epigrammatic manifesto (in which the idea of the "friend" stands in as a metaphor for dissident crosscultural collaboration) is once again apposite and urgent in the maelstrom of the contemporary world, where a range of individuals find it increasingly difficult entirely to condone the international commitments and networks forged by their governments. In their recent book *Empire* (2001), Michael Hardt and Antonio Negri argue that the current era of powerful global and supernational alliances marks the emergence of a new "empire" that places more and more onerous ethical and political burdens on the "citizen": can one simultaneously condemn global terrorism and global "peacekeeping"? Sympathize simultaneously with the victims of both projects? Who is the friend or the enemy? For Hardt and Negri the time is ripe to refuse the ambivalent mantle of citizenship in order to foment a new politics of anti-imperialism, closely attentive to forms of transnational or affiliative solidarity between diffuse groups and individuals. Something of this project, and its descent from Forster's manifesto, is captured in Derrida's commentaries on "friendship," "hospitality," "cosmopolitanism," and "forgiveness," with which we will engage in some detail while keeping an eye upon earlier renditions of these themes from within the scene of late Victorian radicalism.

With chapter 3 will begin closer historical consideration of the sites and subcultures of fin-de-siècle anti-imperialism. Set against the backdrop of Victorian evolutionary biology, social anthropology, and sexology, this chapter on sexual dissidence examines the strange and emphatic conjunction of homosexuality and anti-imperial thought in the life and work of the socialist reformer Edward Carpenter. My aim is to assess the circuits along which the libidinal economy of late-nineteenth-century homosexuality came to traverse equally the incongruous circuits of crosscultural affinity and same-sex desire. What, in other words, were the ethico-political ingredients in Carpenter's late Victorian homosexual self-apprehension that required him to call, in an article written for the *Humane Review* in 1900, for the "ruin . . . *the sooner the better* of these fatuous Empires"?[20] Why could his homosexuality, more often than not, only speak its polemical name in and as a denunciation of western hegemony? Similar questions apply to the discourse of late-nineteenth-century British vegetarianism in its curious links with anti-imperialism. For many late Victorian vegetarian and animal-rights campaigners, such as Henry Salt, prevailing attitudes toward nonhuman life were tragically symptomatic of imperial reason, its tireless binarism, and its insistence upon rigid dichotomies between races, cultures, species, genders, sexualities. In this context, dietary reform and the language of animal rights were very often postulated as variations on the theme of anti-imperial politics. What, I ask in chapter 4, are the discursive and ethical continuities between the critic of the fox hunt and the critic of empire? Is it possible to read the politics of animal welfare as a form of revolutionary sociability whose anti-imperial energies derived, to borrow some words from Hardt and Negri, from an "anthropological exodus," fiercely resistant to systematic "boundaries between the human and the animal, the human and the machine"?[21]

Where conceptual links between sexual dissidence, animal rights, and anti-imperialism are readily accessible to view, chapter 5 will attempt to establish a more contentious continuity between fin-de-siècle spiritualism and coeval critiques of empire by giving close attention to the relationship between the Jewish French mystic Mirra Alfassa and the Indian nationalist, extremist, and mystic Sri Aurobindo. Drawn to eastern religion (like so many of her contemporaries) through her exploration of Theosophy, Alfassa entered into a lifelong spiritual collaboration with Sri Aurobindo with whom she founded a devotional ashram community in Pondicherry, South India. Together Mirra Alfassa and Sri Aurobindo developed a culturally collaborative "spiritualist" critique of both imperial culture and its anticolonial nationalist derivation. By positing a neglected variety of anticolonialism in its arguments on behalf of heterodox theism, chapter 5 also undertakes a direct critique of the secular rational calculations of European political thought. The effort to liberate alternative understandings of "the political" is augmented in the defense of aestheticism that engages chapter 6, expressed in two claims: first, and *contra* postcolonial orthodoxy, that late Victorian aestheticism consistently translated "literariness" into a critique of Empire, and second, that far from being, as alleged, a "mask of conquest," English literature more often than not fueled the energies of anticolonialism in South Asia. The discussion will take as its point of departure the story of Manmohan Ghose: a late Victorian, Oxford-educated Hindu, drawn through a series of ideological accidents into the welcoming space of Oscar Wilde's circle. Hailed briefly as a minor decadent poet, Ghose returned to India to disseminate a radical reading of "aestheticism" as a profound and effective rehearsal of anti-imperial "autonomy."

Typical in many ways of their milieu, Edward Carpenter, Henry Salt, Mirra Alfassa and Sri Aurobindo, and Manmohan Ghose and Oscar Wilde, like others who populated the subcultures that I examine in this book, gained their energies from the chaotic world of late-nineteenth-century anarcho-utopian politics. The concluding chapter returns to the scene of utopian socialism in the 1880s to trace how it was disqualified by the discourse of scientific socialism. Condemned by Engels as a hopeless "mishmash" and later by Lenin as an "infantile disorder" exemplifying an inadmissibly "immature" form of the political, the anti-imperial politics to which this book attends had all but disappeared from view by the beginning of the twentieth century. We are, I have been arguing, still hostage to this occlusion; and any chance that we might have of giving credence to and reviving the diffuse transnational politics that Hardt and Negri, among numerous others, posit as prophylactic against the all-consuming malaise of contemporary imperialism demands that we revisit and interrogate the charge of "immaturity" which led to the historical eviction of utopian socialism and its offshoots from the space of the political. In undertaking the task of such interrogation, however, it is not the business of my conclusion to rehabilitate fin-de-siècle radicalism as a respectable, "adult" form of politics. Rather, I hope to defend "immaturity" as the ethical and philosophical hallmark—the crucial ingredient—in that politics of friendship to which this book is ultimately committed.

2

MANIFESTO

Anticolonial Thought and the Politics of Friendship

PREAMBLE: CHARLIE'S ANGELS

A few kilometers from the outskirts of South Delhi, just before the city begins its smoggy cannibalization of the tiny hamlets of Sheikh Sarai and Yusuf Sarai, there rises on the road, briefly and unmemorably, a shambolic concrete settlement cast in the mold of those numerous ad hoc colonies on the eastern side of the river Yamuna. Andrewsganj, as it is known, is unmarked on the pink tourist map of Delhi published by the Official Survey of India, and indeed Andrewsganj is unremarkable in all but name. But this innocuous settlement commemorates, in high municipal style, the life and work of Charles Freer Andrews (1871–1940), an English Anglican priest who arrived in India in 1904 to take on the post of vice-principal at St. Stephen's College of Delhi University, and whose lifelong association with the country drew him deep within the contentious heart of anticolonial nationalist politics.[1] As the "ganj" or "storehouse" of Andrews's memory Andrewsganj is rather more sepulchral than cornucopian. Yet it bears witness, in its own way, to this colonial Englishman's political entitlement to a share in the landscape of postcolonial India. Other figures of western anti-imperialism are less well acknowledged in contemporary India, on account of the comparative untranslatability of their politics into the grand modalities of anticolonial nationalism. These figures will account for most of my study, laying claim to its concerns precisely for reason of their unassimilability within "major" forms of the political. But it is with Andrews that I wish to begin. For closeted behind his crucial public demonstrations on behalf of Indian nationalism, we find an equally significant if more covert affective refusal of colonial division: an insinuation of "friendship," as Susan Visvanathan points out, into "the question of Indian nationalism."[2] Let us consider, then, some episodes from the life of C. F. Andrews as a narrative preamble to our proposed theorization, in this and subsequent chapters, of "friendship" as the lost trope in anticolonial thought.

In 1914, having resigned his post at St. Stephen's and donated his admittedly meager possessions to the Indian National Congress, Andrews set sail for South Africa to lend support to a certain M. K. Gandhi in his campaign on behalf of Indian indentured laborers. Gandhi, the records tell us, was waiting for Andrews on the dock, unrecognizable in his new incarnation as coolie-ascetic: "head-shaven, dressed in a white dhoti and kurta of such coarse material as an indentured labourer might wear, looking as though in mourning."[3] Approaching Gandhi, Andrews, as he records in a letter to his friend Munshi Ram, "stooped at once instinctively and touched his feet."[4] The rich symbolism of this encounter invites further comment. Indeed, one might claim it as an iconic anticolonial frieze: the London-trained Indian barrister defying imperial polarities of class and station in an elaborate costume drama; the Anglican priest reversing the fundamental civilizational hierarchy of Empire in a single, defiant gesture of self-abnegation.

In 1919 Andrews touched another pair of Indian feet. Traveling at Gandhi's request through the Punjab in the wake of the Jallianwala Bagh tragedy to investigate the indignity and provocation caused by martial law in the region, he chanced upon a young Sikh victim of imperial policing, deranged after a public flogging on the unverified suspicion of having damaged telegraph wires in the vicinity of his village.[5] Facing the Sikh in the small room to which he had since confined himself—and now well tutored in habits of anti-imperial histrionics by Gandhi himself—Andrews immediately "stooped down and touched his feet, asking from him at the same time pardon for the great wrong my fellow-countrymen had committed."[6] Once again, the minor affective transactions of this closet drama import an incalculable excess into the impasse of colonial encounter, collapsing for a brief moment the mutually quarantined categories of colonizer and colonized. In time, we might note, the House of Lords cleared the name of General Dyer, justifying his action in Jallianwala Bagh as appropriate to the fulfillment of law and thereby reinscribing the battle lines of Empire. On the other side of the divide, however, the troublesome figure of C. F. Andrews continued to confound the manichean logic of colonization by preventing anticolonial nationalism from resolving itself into pure oppositionality.[7] This Gandhi recognized, with his clear genius for the politics of transgression and small gestures, urging a mass meeting in Lahore on 15 November 1919 to pay due attention to Andrews's *tapascharya*, his "invisible sacrifices" always "hidden from the eyes of men." "As long as there is even one Andrews among the British people," Gandhi said, "we must, for the sake of such a one, bear no hatred to them." Only such resistance to polarization would, in his reasoning, "ensure early success of our efforts, for . . . the British will have no occasion to visit their evil propensities on us."[8]

My final example of Andrews's anti-manichean practice concerns his poised intervention into the controversy caused by the publication of Katherine Mayo's *Mother India* in 1927 (this time no feet were touched). Dismissed by Gandhi as "a drain inspector's report," Mayo's best-selling and excoriating account of Indian sexual and social morality offered international readers a catalogue of horrors: eight-year old child brides, desperate women licking the blood of freshly sacrificed animals in the hope of begetting sons, and sexually abusive mothers, prone, as Mayo coyly puts it, to "practice upon" their children, "the girl to make her sleep well," the boy "to make him manly."[9] Predictably, Mayo's critique was received in much the same spirit as that in which it was composed: a growing nationalist counterpolemic extolled the unmatched wonders of Indian civilization while simultaneously imprecating the lax morals of the western world and its wife. The anonymous author of *Sister India* (1927) attributed Mayo's crosscultural incomprehension to sexual unfulfilment; an enraged Kanhaya Lal Gauba penned a rejoinder called *Uncle Sham: Being the Strange Tale of a Civilisation Run Amock* (1929); and in a similar vein, Dinshah Gadiali, a Parsi in New Jersey, undertook to expose the sexual subjection of American women in his *American Sex Problems* (1929). Some ten years after this controversy Charlie Andrews published a small book called *The True India* (1939). Characteristically understated and antipolemical, Andrews's quiet volume postulates itself as testimony: offering to nationalist Indians a foreigner's defense of "Indian morals,"[10] and in equal measure offering to Mayo's readers an

Englishman's profession of "deep reverence for Indian civilisation as a whole."[11] In both cases his position eludes capture within either opposing suburb of civilizational identity: he addresses the Indian as a sympathetic but irreducible outsider, and to the "westerner" his address is likewise intractably "alien." What should we discern in this protean manipulation of identity? In Andrews's disruption of the fixed and settled places of polemic? How might we better organize our catalogue of his disparate acts of dissent into a more coherent typology? The answer, I submit, attaches to the single word "friendship" that circulates as a refrain through the vast archive of works by and about C. F. Andrews, qualifying almost every public and private action in his unassuming career. Some select examples: in 1913 he offered urgent prayer "for one thing to be granted—an Indian bosom friend";[12] through his life he gathered an exorbitant list of such friends (S. K. Rudra, Zaha Ullah, Gandhi, Tagore, Munshi Ram . . .); and it was to friendship with S. K. Rudra that he attributed his evolving sympathy with "the new progressive life of India."[13] Upon his death, the poet Rabindranath Tagore wrote in a somewhat hyperbolic vein, of the day when "from one who was till then a complete stranger to me, there was poured out upon me this generous gift of friendship. It rose like a river from the clear spring of this Christian sadhu's devotion to God."[14] During his speech on the Quit India Resolution, at a meeting of the All India Congress Committee on 8 August 1942, Gandhi, quietly but insistently competitive with Tagore, offered this epitaph for Andrews: "It is true that he was a friend of Gurudev, but he looked upon Gurudev with awe. Not that Gurudev wanted it . . . But with me he became the closest friend."[15] And most obituaries attribute the following "last words" to Andrews: "God has given me in my life the greatest of all gifts, namely; the gift of loving friends. I would acknowledge again what I have acknowledged in my books; this supreme gift of friendship both in India and in other parts of the world."[16]

Does Andrews's insistent discourse of and on friendship simply betray an excessive emotionalism? Is it symptomatic, as Tagore constantly complained, of that immoderate longing or attachment in his nature that ultimately prevented him from transforming the contingent into the universal, feeling into manifesto, the personal into the political?[17] In another way, should we read Andrews's iterative account of friendship as a sign of modesty, an attempt to explain his ethico-political activities as "unofficial" or "extra-institutional," attributing their energies to an unpremeditated or spontaneous rush of passion?[18] The trope of friendship, let me suggest, certainly gives evidence for the (mis)guiding imperatives of desire and affect in Andrews's life and work. But closer examination of his writing reveals something extra: the shape of what we might call an "affective cosmopolitanism," the ethico-political practice of a desiring self inexorably drawn toward difference.

We find better material for these conjectures in Andrews's creative reading of the New Testament's apostolic foundations, especially in his keen emphasis on the centrality of "fellowship," "friendship," or *koinonia* in the Gospels, a creed that he takes consistently as exhorting believers to depart from the possessive claims of inherited or received identity and belonging. "When our Lord," he writes in *The Good Shepherd* (1940), "had chosen and ordained his first Apostles, He brought them so close to Himself that He called them no longer servants, but friends . . . 'Greater love,' He declares, 'hath no man than this that a man lay down his life for his friends.' "[19] For Andrews the sacrificial imperatives of friendship thus extolled in the Gospels demand a radical unfettering of the theistic, believing self such that its affective intensities are equally liberated toward strangers as to kin: "No external distinction of race or caste or creed, or even family must come before the one supreme fact of the deepest fellowship of all earnest souls in doing the will of God."[20] Such, for instance, is the lesson that Andrews gleans in South Africa, where a decision to resign his ministry in face of the racial exclusivity of imperial Christianity is inspired by an epiphanic insight into apostolic friendship. "It became clear to me," he writes of this experience, "that I must take up a firm stand, even against my own fellow-countrymen and fellow-Christians, since as a Christian it was necessary to bear witness for Christ's sake . . . Even when Christ's own mother and brethren sought to speak with Him, He said, 'Who is My mother or My brethren? Whosoever shall do the will of God, the same is My brother and My sister and My mother.' "[21] Invoked in this way to eschew ties of race, nation, class, and religion, Andrews's credo of friendship is equally instrumental in his principled departure from the more insidious accretions of gender and species. Calling for the ordination of women into the Anglican clergy in 1940, he invokes the rhetoric of the *imitatio Christi* to insist that "just as in Christ there is 'neither Jew nor Greek' so also in Him there is 'neither male nor female' . . . no subordination of one race to another, or one sex to another."[22] And in *The True India*, writing against speciesism in the fierce idiom of Gandhi's *Hind Swaraj*, he laments the "butchers' shambles" of the androcentric West.[23]

Deriving in large measure from his idiosyncratic rereading of Christianity, C. F. Andrews's creative variations on the thematic of friendship were also profoundly enabled and clarified, as I will be arguing in the following pages, by the politics peculiar to the utopian socialism to which he was formally exposed: during his Cambridge years (1890–1904) by Brooke Foss Westcott, bishop of Durham, Christian socialist, and first president of the Christian Social Union, and in his Indian years through contact with local theosophical circles.[24] Yet apart from its muted afterlife in the colonial periphery through the early decades of the twentieth century, in 1892 utopian politics had died in Europe. Writing in his monumental *Degeneration* that year, Max Nordau had observed the irreparable ill-health of fin-de-siècle utopianism, commenting at length on its lamentable enervation, exhaustion, and hysteria. That was an optimistic prognosis, for by the time that more discerning physician Friedrich Engels appeared on the scene with his *Socialism, from Utopia to Science* the patient was finished, leaving in its exit no discernible trace, no apparent legacy of the "eclectic . . . mishmash of . . . critical statements, economic theories, pictures of future society,"[25] with which it had been afflicted. Believers insist that the ghost of utopianism returned to Europe in May 1968 and has been haunting the ruins of "the political" ever since, manifesting itself among the credulous in the shape of two linked convictions: First, and incidentally, that an aspirational and inventive politics of alternatives poised at the limits of thought and being, epistemology and ontology, is both expedient and inevitable in regard to a terrain where, as in Foucault, power is everywhere, "immanent to the social field, distributed through the brains and bodies of citizens."[26] And second, far from resolving itself only in an aggrieved refusal of, or flight from, the impoverished scene of sociality, such politics is obliged creatively to renegotiate ideas of community, communication, *conatus*.

There is no dearth of models, we know, for the figuration of community. Yet when confined to the canonical generalization of established affective formations (of family, fraternity, genealogy, filiation), community lapses all too often into a dull, replicative economy, ill-equipped to the task of positing alternatives. It is in response to this impasse that Derrida, writing in the timbre of a C. F. Andrews, recognizes in the unscripted relation of "friendship" an improvisational politics appropriate to communicative, sociable utopianism, investing it with a vision of radical democracy: yet "to come," "indefinitely perfectible," "always insufficient and future."[27] Such is the vision to which we will attend in the remaining discussion, seeking some paradigms for the figures and groups under consideration. But first, to clarify the cartography of our argument: apprehended by Derrida as the means whereby we might redesignate "the political" as the place of an always deferred and therefore always open and hospitable community, "friendship" categorically defines community as a countermand against social exclusion.[28] Still, endeavouring as it does to achieve indefinite gathering, utopian community cannot predicate the cessation of exclusion either upon the fixed telos of dialectical transcendence nor, in reverse, upon the presuppositions of a priori foundationalism. Jean-Luc Nancy is suggestive here. Being-in-common, he maintains in *The Inoperative Community*, "does not mean a higher form of substance or subject taking charge of the limits of separate individualities." Nor does it obtain its genesis "from out of or as an effect of . . . a process that emerges from a ground [*fond*] or from a fund [*fonds*] of some kind . . . It is a groundless 'ground,' less in the sense that it opens up the gaping chasm of an abyss than that it is made up only of the network, the interweaving, and the sharing of singularities."[29] Neither a settled arrangement from above nor one from below, the axes of utopic community are horizontal and latitudinal, seeking cohesion in what Nancy identifies as a process of "compearance." As he writes: "compearance . . . does not set itself up, it does not establish itself, it does not emerge among already given subjects (objects). It consists in the appearance of the *between* as such: you *and* I (between us)—a formula in which the *and* does not imply juxtaposition, but exposition. What is exposed in compearance is the following, and we must learn to read it in all its possible combinations: 'you (are/and/is) (entirely other than) I' [toi (e(s)t) (tout autre que) moi]. Or again, more simply: *you shares me* [*toi partage moi*]."[30]

Two consequences relevant to our concerns follow from the recognition of "compearance" as the distinguishing signifier of utopic communality. First, as the marker of direct affective singularity "between . . . you *and* I," the ethics of compearance defiantly contravenes the embargo on relationality through which power, colonial or otherwise, orchestrates its divisions and exclusions. It exposes, we could say, the meditative and antirelational operatives at the heart of modern imperial and totalitarian governmentality recently foregrounded by Giorgio Agamben, among others. "The State," in his words, "is not founded on a social bond of which it would be the expression, but rather on the dissolution, the unbinding it prohibits."[31] Thus, insofar as power expresses itself as the violence of unbinding, compearing community foments its nonviolent resistance through an anarchist politics of immediate conjunction, conjuncture, coalition, and collaboration "between" the most unlikely of associates. Second, as "the appearance of the *between* as such" (viz. of the space of relationality/conjunction rather than of discrete relational/conjunctive subjects), compearance requires of its agents a qualifying ethico-existential capacity for the radical expropriation of identity in face of the other—a capacity, that is, for self-othering. Nancy is apposite again: "singular beings are themselves constituted by sharing, they are distributed and placed, or rather *spaced*, by the sharing that makes them *others*: other for one another, and other, infinitely other for the Subject of their fusion, which is engulfed in the sharing."[32]

Affective singularity, anarchist relationality, and other-directedness are, I propose, the constitutive elements of the utopic community that we are conjuring under the sign of friendship, and in the memory of C. F. Andrews, on behalf of the utopian socialism consigned to the wastebins of the political in 1892. What follows in the rest of this chapter is an attempt to yoke these elements together into a more coherent manifesto that obtains its philosophical framework from that ethics of the "beyond," simultaneously committed to a transformation of the present, which Drucilla Cornell sees at work in certain strains of contemporary postmodern thought.[33] Such thought, we will see, delivers guidelines for the program we are seeking in its departure from the cult of the hybrid subject toward a noncommunitarian understanding of community.

THE CRISIS OF HYBRIDITY

The theoretical motivations of postmodernism and its allies are often explained as a reaction against the sort of regulative essentialism typified in Kantian notions of ethical agency on the one hand and (predominantly) Marxist notions of political agency on the other. Kant and Marx are, in this sense, rendered inextricable.[34] The disciplined solidarities of revolutionary politics, it is argued, require an ethical agent tutored (through Kant) in habits of invulnerability to the anarchic domain of desire and inclination.[35] This renunciatory inheritance Marxism further augments, Bataille complains, through the sly existential transactions attaching to its humanism. Holding out to "man" the promise of sovereign value only in his capacity as a producer, it tempts him to relinquish, in exchange, all those diversions of leisure and affect fundamental, in one reading, to his humanness. In Bataille's words: "For a Marxist . . . the sovereign value is man . . . But it remains to be determined whether man, to whom communism refers as the producer, has not taken on this sovereign value on one primary condition, having renounced for himself everything that is sovereign . . . For the irreducible desire that man is, *passionately* and *capriciously*, communism has substituted those needs that can be brought into harmony with a life entirely devoted to producing."[36]

Faced with this ethico-political demand for an agent constitutively free from the heterogeneity of consciousness and the distractions of experience, postmodernism has perversely begged to differ. Principally, its departure from the dyad of Kant and Marx has relied on the wild conjuration of an empirical or hybrid subject of desire: too slippery to be constrained within the unitary and austere solidarities of sex, race, nation, class; too whimsical to fix, in advance, the meaning of political or ethical action "independently of any articulatory practice."[37] There are many routes through which the protestation of desire might be said to enter the enclave of postmodernism. Some say it arrived into French philosophy through Alexandre Kojeve's and Jean Hippolyte's careless reformulation of Hegel as a philosopher of subjective longing (for recognition). Others blame the early Georg Lukács and his belated imitators for misreading Marx as a theorist of need who condemns, in his account of alienation, the tragic supercession (in the inexorable logic of capital) of use-value by exchange-value, such that the concrete embodiments of human labor (the muscles, nerves, cells, needs of real sensual producers) are progressively erased within the abstract structure of the commodity form. Both routes spell trouble: Kojeve's neo-Hegelianism arguably reanimates a rapacious subject who can only claim satisfaction through the "negation" or destruction of the desired object. And Lukács's distorted Marxism, likewise, infamously ends with the recommendation that the desiring, vital subject overcome alienation by refusing to countenance any independent object outside or apart from itself.

Tutored either by Kojeve or by Lukács, desire (in one rendition of this narrative) arrives into postmodernism under the sign of nihilism.[38] And indeed, designed to negate the political as we know it, the hybrid subject of new left, queer, and postcolonial theories, among others, has performed admirably, leaving in its wake "splinters," "fragments," "instability," "disarray," and "ruin," progressively exploding, in the words of Chantal Mouffe, "the idea and the reality of a unique space of constitution of the political."[39] Negation, the philosophers tell us, may well be the necessary prerequisite to a "different and positive reconstruction of the social fabric."[40] However, on account of its radical unsocialization, the hybrid subject has, I submit, proved ill-equipped to undertake the task of "positive reconstruction." Why?

Freed from the renunciatory protocols of Kantian and Marxist thought, the hybrid subject of desire (much like Hegel's "master" in *The Phenomenology of Mind*) is encouraged to approach the world and social fabric simply as the source of her enjoyment.[41] And in the very excess of this demand for existential satisfaction, its project begins to dovetail imperceptibly with the solipsistic individualism of the Kantian or Marxist agent. Where the latter arrives into self-regard through ascetic self-enclosure, the hybrid subject reaches similar destination through an insatiable demand for self-fulfillment, consuming the very world in/for/from which it must fashion its ethical capacity. Such, Nancy observes, is the fate of Bataille's revolutionary subject of passion, condemned to self-defeating nihilism through "the violent and unbridled movement of a free subjectivity disposed toward the sovereign destruction of all *things* as toward its consumption in NOTHING."[42] To these dangers the contemporary politics of hybridity stands exposed whenever it takes its cue solely from "the body as a seat of desires."[43] Similar risks attend the tactical politics, of which Michel de Certeau writes, achieved in those moments when "the housewife confronts heterogeneous and mobile data—what she has in her refrigerator, the tastes, appetites, and moods of her guests, the best buys and their possible combinations with what she has on hand at home."[44] The relation of such an agent to what surrounds her is that of the pure consumer, and one equipped to consume at will through a figurative or theoretical affluence.[45] Always favored by "plenitude," "excess," "multivalence" and "mobility," the liberatory potential of such a subject may only resonate, as Michael Hardt and Antonio Negri, have recently observed, "with the situation of an elite population that enjoys certain rights, a certain level of wealth, and a certain position in a global hierarchy."[46] Polymorphous and perverse, the hybrid subject is cloned, we might say, from the genetic substance of corporate capital and the world market.

To summarize: in its first (nihilistic) movement against a priori, regulative essentialism, postmodernism substitutes the austere and "stripped down" subject of Kantian deontology with its antithesis, namely the affluent and privileged subject of postmodern desire. In so doing, it raises a spoiled child, attentive only to the insatiability and availability of its own desires, who (to quote Charles Taylor out of context), "being in face of a world which offers him no effective resistance tends to sink back into a stupor of self-coincidence. He approaches the stagnant pole where I = I."[47] Having traveled this far, let us accompany postmodernism on the next leg of its journey, in the company of Maurice Blanchot.

AN ANTI-COMMUNITARIAN COMMUNITARIANISM

One of the many problems with the project of hybrid subjectivity is that it paradoxically sets itself in binary opposition against the dyad of Kant and Marx, contesting radical self-sufficiency with radical excess or desire. But soon becoming "*mutatis mutandis* a copy of that by which it felt itself to be oppressed,"[48] it starts to replicate the crippling solipsism of its ethical antagonist. Perhaps no postmodern thinker addresses these dangers more eloquently than Maurice Blanchot. His *The Unavowable Community*, especially, advises us that "self-sufficiency" meets its greatest challenge not in the opposing pole of "excess" but rather in the more interruptive principle of subjective "insufficiency," which in turn cannot be accomplished in the absence of association with other beings. A being, says Blanchot, achieves its "awareness of . . . insufficiency . . . from the fact that it puts itself in question, which question needs the other or another to be enacted. *Left on its own, a being closes itself, falls asleep and calms down*."[49] With this shift from an "ethics of excess" toward an "ethics of insufficiency," postmodernism begins its significant negotiations with the idea of communication/community, arriving, in a frenzied anti-Kantian momentum, at a junction already crowded with the travel-weary thoughts of contemporary communitarians.[50]

For what has happened in the subtle turn of Blanchot's thinking is an imperceptible (and, as we will see, potentially hazardous) theft of tropes from Hegel's monumental effort, *contra* Kant, to lay down the ethico-political imperatives of intersubjective community. I do not wish to dwell on Hegel. But for our discussion to proceed, we need to acknowledge again that any meaningful critique of Kantian autonomy conducted through the vector of community, communication, *conatus* must pass through Hegel's endeavor to reconcile the claims of moral autonomy with the highest expressive unity within and between "men." The marks of this philosophical passage are proudly displayed by contemporary communitarians like Alasdair MacIntyre, Michael Sandel, and Michael Walzer, each of whom foregrounds, like Hegel, the "thick" or embedded nature of ethico-political agency. Our ethical capacity, as Sandel insists, accrues from "the particular people we are—as members of this family or community or nation or people, as bearers of this history, as sons and daughters of that revolution, as citizens of this republic."[51] And in this theorem we can begin to see the first fault lines of a Hegelian inheritance, fault lines which postmodernism must repair before it can make any meaningful claim on a politics of community. What is the problem exactly?

Lest we forget, the projected Hegelian community, outlined in the dialectic of the master and the slave, relies exclusively on the principle of reciprocal recognition, according to which I can only enter into intersubjective or communal alliance with another whom I recognize as myself. So too, my "interlocutor" cancels my alterity, seeing in me, as Taylor paraphrases, "another, but one that is not foreign, which is at one with himself."[52] This action is not without political idealism, exemplifying that profound desire for universal equality (the elimination of hierarchy, preference, exceptionalism) that we find in Rousseau on the one hand and in the best traditions of modern neoliberalism on the other.[53] Yet it would appear that Hegel, although in the name of egalitarianism, has merely replaced Kant's self-identical subject with a self-identical community, extending, in Blanchot's observation, its "relation to himself, perpetually repeated."[54] Communitarian or partialist thought, no less, absorbs Hegel's valorized relation of Same with Same, always privileging commitments to those who are either "proximate," "given," or in some inalienable way "our own" (of the same nation, family, community, republic, revolution, etc.). So it is that the most radical communities of difference, founded upon solidarities of class, gender, race, or ethnicity, lapse into a politics of similitude—privileging separation over relationality, demanding uniformity as the price for belonging. K. Anthony Appiah is to the point: "The politics of recognition requires that one's skin colour, one's sexual body, should be acknowledged politically in ways that make it hard for those who want to treat their skin and sexual body as personal dimensions of the self. And personal means not secret, but not too tightly scripted . . . Between the politics of recognition and the politics of compulsion, there is no bright line."[55]

Now a number of questions present themselves, both more and less obvious. Does loyalty to "my own" liberate me of ethical obligations to all those who are not of my own nation, family, republic, revolution, etc.? Where do I go when the burdens of my deviancy put me at risk precisely from those who are unquestionably "my own"? If, following the advice of the philosopher Marilyn Friedman, I defiantly choose or "elect" my affinities, will I escape the deadlock of self-identical community?[56] Will my voluntary affiliations, still desperately seeking similitude (of sexual, intellectual, political, ethical, aesthetic orientation) endlessly replicate the deadlock of self-sufficient unity?[57] How, in other words, can I quarrel with Kant in the language of Hegel while quarrelling with Hegel in such a way that I don't return to Kant? That is to say, can I oppose radical individualism with community while opposing communitarianism in such a way that I don't return to a position of radical individualism/autonomy? Thus we arrive at the heart of our problem.

Seeking, from the outset of its journey, an open (anti-essentialist, inconsequentialist, nonteleological) ethics and politics of possibility, postmodernism produces a negative and solipsistic subject of desire. Such a subject can only be taught, remedially, to call itself into question through the lessons of community, communication, sociability. Although indispensable, however, the very idea of community (found or elective) presupposes closure: a circular return, ad nauseam, to the tedious logic of the Same. Now what? The arrival, to put it simply, of utopianism; the reappearance of a long forgotten ghost from 1892. For if the very idea of community is, notwithstanding its necessity, from a postmodern perspective inevitably unworkable, inoperative, negative, then we can only speak, under erasure, of an impossible community: perpetually deferred, "indefinitely perfectible," yet-to-come. In what remains of this discussion I propose to describe this ingenious compromise as a project of anti-communitarian communitarianism. At the heart of such a project we might imagine, also, a reformulation of subject-hood that sees the theme of "individuality" gradually replaced by one of "singularity": the former always amenable to perpetuation, extension, or generalization; the latter marked by an irreducible difference which renders it inassimilable within any system of resemblance. Thus unlike "individualities," "singularities," as Agamben puts it, "cannot form a *societas* because they do not possess any identity to vindicate nor any bond of belonging for which to seek recognition. In the first instance the State can recognise any claim for identity . . . What the State cannot tolerate in any way, however, is that singularities form a community without affirming an identity, that humans co-belong without any representable condition of belonging."[58] "Friendship," I suggest, is one name for the co-belonging of nonidentical singularities.

POLITICS OF FRIENDSHIP

First, let me tell you a story. Late January 2002: it's mid-morning and the sun is already cruel over the Great Victorian Desert in South Australia. A woman gets out of her four-wheel drive and starts determinedly to walk toward the infamous Woomera mandatory detention center for "unprocessed" asylum seekers. Inside the center, desperate inmates (mainly Afghan, Iranian, and Iraqi) have turned their protest against the inhuman conditions of their confinement inward, sealing their bodies against the inducements of food and speech with rough stitches through their lips. The white Australian woman who has come to fast with them in silence carries a placard bearing, in uneven, homemade letters, the following consolation: "You are not alone." She wants to perform her consolation, to embody it, within view of the detainees, face to face, but a news camera on site catches the demise of her incipient project: an enraged security guard blocks her progress and pushes her back into her abandoned car. She breaks down, diminished by her failure. Yet something, however imperceptible, is achieved in that single moment of violent dismissal when the guard allegedly policing her interests as a legitimate Australian citizen turns on her as though she were the illegal *arrivant*, the housebreaker, the foreigner. What name may we give to this disarticulated mission? One woman forfeiting the not inconsiderable pleasures of consensus with her own community and elected government for the sake of an ephemeral communication with "aliens" widely perceived as a potential threat to the integrity of the Australian state. What might we call this minor (insignificant?) gesture of self-endangerment in the name of a peace, committed, as a Levinas might tell us, to a tentative proximity to the other, and signifying "the *surplus* of sociality over every solitude—the *surplus* of sociality and of love"?[59] Let us, with seeming arbitrariness, call it the politics of friendship.

Our first archive, the history of friendship in western political philosophy, complicates the project. Far from being secret and unacknowledged, as we might desire it to be, the contiguity between friendship and politics appears endemic to this system. "Western political speculation," as Horst Hutter reveals in his book *Politics as Friendship*, "finds its origin in a system of thought in which the idea of friendship is the major principle in terms of which political theory and practice are described, explained and analysed."[60] There is another, more serious problem to which Derrida, writing some two decades after Hutter, alerts us. The configuration of political thought which so possessively captures friendship as its founding metaphor "rarely announces itself without some sort of adherence to the State, to the family, without . . . a *schematic* of filiation: stock, genus or species, sex (*Geschlecht*), blood, birth, nature, nation—autochthonal or not, tellurian or not."[61]

We will explicate the precise implications of this Derridean impasse in a moment, but first let us give full weight to the verdict that the canonical forms of western politics achieve their taxonomy within a "schematic of filiation." In other words (with a little help from Edward Said), these forms—indeed, "the political" itself as we know it—gain their inspiration from the domestic space of the family, thereby perpetuating in public life the perennial romance of self-repetition, similarity, resemblance, the order of the same.[62] Within such a schematic, the actions of the woman at Woomera, with whom we began this discussion, do not, needless to say, deserve the name "politics." But do they deserve the name "friendship"? And here lies the rub.

In search of answers, let us briefly return with Hutter and Derrida to Aristotle: the thinker whom both critics credit (Hutter admiringly, Derrida regretfully) with the decisive announcement of politics as friendship in western thought, a metaphoric association elaborated and augmented in the thematic unity between the *Nichomachean Ethics*, which pays close attention to the ethical obligations of *philia*, and the *Politics*, which pays close attention to the political obligations of citizenship. The gap between these two texts (between, we might add, *philia* and citizenship, friendship and politics) is bridged by Aristotle's conception of friendship as a *homophilic* bond owing principally, if not exclusively, to fellow citizens. If the *Politics* upholds the *polis*, or State, as the natural and highest representation of human sociability, the *Nichomachean Ethics* privileges friendship as the best rehearsal of citizenship—the elaboration, always within the boundaries of the *polis*, of a being-in-common. "Friendship," Aristotle writes, "seems to be the bond that holds communities together, and lawgivers seem to attach more importance to it than justice.[63]

This nativist conception of friendship, developed in historical conditions of extreme vulnerability for the minuscule Greek city-state,[64] borrows heavily, if wishfully, from the sparse vocabulary of filiation: "a friend is another self" (294); "The basis of affection is equality and similarity" (272); "like is friend to like" (292); and so on. The actions of the woman at Woomera, it would appear, may not even deserve the name friendship unless we were able to identify another model of friendship capable of proceeding without recourse to "a horizon of recognition."[65] We need also another contingent and nomadic model of the political, independent from the burdensome nomenclature of naturalness, homogeneity, origin. Our demand is in a sense of philosophy itself, which after all bears influential etymological traces of *philia* in its own name and purpose. This is what we ask: if friendship already inhabits the heart of the political, might we not in some fugitive night of thought smuggle in its place a radical substitute, an infiltrator who might unwork the logic of political similitude? Give us an anti-communitarian community? And what, then, might such a friendship be?

For the moment, we need not stray beyond the confines of post-Socratic philosophy. For the Aristotelian model of *philia*, with which we are quarrelling, meets its most immediate challenge in the fragments of Epicurus and his followers, in which friendship is construed very differently, as *philoxenia*, or a love for guests, strangers, and foreigners. And in sharp contrast to Aristotle, this ethic of fidelity to strange friends is predicated upon a principled distaste for the racial exclusivity of the polis. The polis, as Philodemus insists, is an unfriendly place: "If a man were to indicate a systematic inquiry to find out what is most destructive of friendship and most productive of enmity, he would find it in the regime of the *polis*."[66] Or, to recall Agamben's gloss on Aristotle, the polis ratifies "exclusion" as the principle that "founds the city of men," locating at the core of politics a principle of *exceptio* according to which the promise of the good life for some requires consigning others to the concentration camp, the detention center, the various inhospitable borders of modern civility.[67]

Thus Aristotelian and Epicurean conceptions of friendship clearly demand competing types of loyalty, which in turn produce mutually contradictory effects. *Homophilic* loyalties are enlisted as a source of security (for the State, the community, the citizen or ethical subject). Conversely, and much to the puzzlement of contemporary commentators, *philoxenic* solidarities introduce the disruptive category of risk into the otherwise determined Epicurean espousal of the ethical benefits of cultivated *ataraxia*, or invulnerability, and *autarkia*, or self-sufficiency.[68] Any sort of friendship (local or global) is emotionally risky, as it might bedevil the tranquil Epicurean sage with anxieties of affective dependence. But friendships toward strangers or foreigners, in particular, carry exceptional risks, as their fulfillment may at any time "constitute a felony *contra patriam*."[69] An eloquent appraisal of such *philoxenic* risk is available in the updated Epicureanism which informs E. M. Forster's famous defense of friendship in *Two Cheers for Democracy*: "I hate the idea of causes, and if I had to choose between betraying my country and betraying my friend I hope I should have the guts to betray my country. Such a choice may scandalise the modern reader, and he may stretch out his patriotic hand to the telephone at once and ring the police . . . Probably one will not be asked to make such an agonising choice. Still, there lies at the back of every creed something terrible and hard for which the worshipper may one day be required to suffer, and there is even a terror and hardness in this creed of personal relationships, urbane and mild though it sounds. Love and loyalty to an individual can run counter to the claims of the State. When they do—down with the State, say I, which means the State would down me."[70]

There is, as Forster reminds us in the histrionic rhetoric of his Epicurean predecessors, something unquestionably political and risky in the choice of "friend over country." The obvious practical dangers of such a choice notwithstanding (felony, treason, un-American activities), *philoxenia* is not reducible to a form of masochistic moral adventurism or absolutism, to a sort of ethics-as-bungie-jumping-at-any-cost school of thought. The expenditure is rather more existentially profound, involving the potentially "agonizing" risk of self-exile which haunts any ethical capacity to become (to suffer oneself to become) foreign to "one's own" and, above all, to oneself. Derrida's notes on ethics-as-hospitality are apposite here: "the stranger, here the awaited guest, is not only someone to whom you say 'come,' but 'enter' . . . come in, 'come inside,' 'come within me,' not only toward me, but within me: occupy me, take place in me."[71]

To explicate fully the import of Derridean hospitality and Epicurean philoxenia, we need to recapitulate our argument. In its journey away from solipsism and nihilism, postmodernism (eventually) finds itself at a critical juncture: there, much like E. M. Forster, it must choose between two historically parallel (rather than successive) regimes of western political thought, deriving from the opposed poles of sameness (communitarianism, the polis, regimes of security) and difference (hospitality, exile, risk). Tempted initially by the simple calculations of the regime of sameness, it comes to recognize in the consolations of self-identical community yet another variation on the theme of self-identical subjectivity: the eternal recurrence, we might say, of solipsism. In its subsequent efforts to exceed this impasse it relies, as we have been proposing, on two factors: first, it requires a subject-agent open to forms of sociality capable, *contra* Kant, of exacerbating the condition of its insufficiency. Second, such a sociality would have to be articulated, *contra* Hegel, within a community that was never itself—that is to say, never self-identical or "fusional."[72] Both conditions are arguably realized within the twinned tropes of hospitality and "guest-friendship." The ethical agency of the host-friend relies precisely on her capacity to leave herself open, in Blanchot's terms, to the risk of radical insufficiency. Poised in a relation where an irreducible and asymmetrical other always calls her being into question, she is ever willing to risk becoming strange or guestlike in her own domain, whether this be home, nation, community, race, gender, sex, skin, or species. So too, the open house of hospitality or the open heart of friendship can never know guests-friends in advance, as one might a fellow citizen, sister, or comrade. Such sociality might take the political form of Judith Butler's coalition, "an emerging and unpredictable assemblage of positions."[73] Or it might arrive in the form of Donna Haraway's fabulist cyborg community, "permanently partial . . . monstrous and illegitimate."[74] Always unfinished, yet-to-come, like the deferred interracial friendship between Aziz and Fielding in *A Passage to India*: " 'Why can't we be friends now?' said the other, holding him affectionately. 'It's what I want. It's what you want.' But the horses didn't want it . . . the earth didn't want it . . . the temples, the tank, the jail, the palace, the birds, the carrion, the Guest House . . . they didn't want it, they said in their hundred voices, 'No, not yet,' and the sky said, 'No, not there.' "[75]

There is no moral as such to my story. Utopianism, some might say, is just a matter of taste: you either want it now or you prefer to wait for it for as long as it takes to bring newness into the world. But at this time in world politics, when our solidarities simply cannot be fixed in advance (America or Iraq; liberalism or the agonism of the particular; citizen or refugee), a utopian mentality shows the way forward to a genuine cosmopolitanism: always open to the risky arrival of those not quite, not yet, covered by the privileges which secure our identity and keep us safe. In Kant's canonical rendition—readily absorbed within the coercive universalizing logic of former and current colonialisms—cosmopolitanism, we might recall, was privileged as the stable political zone of "perpetual peace," a prescriptive "being-in-common" bearing the promise of immunity to the psychic contagion of cultural difference.[76] In its affective mutation, however (as a form of anti-communitarian communitarianism, as a variation on "guest-friendship," as *cosmophilus*), cosmopolitanism may well be the means to puncture those fantasies of security and invulnerability to which our political imagination remains hostage. It might, for instance, teach us that risk sometimes brings with it a profound affirmation of relationality and collectivity. "Let us say yes," Derrida writes in this spirit, "*to who or what turns up*, before any determination, before any anticipation, before any *identification*, whether or not it has to do with a foreigner, an immigrant, an invited guest, or an unexpected visitor, whether or not the new arrival is a citizen of another country, a human, animal, or divine creature, a living or dead thing, male or female."[77]

There are many stories to recall in conclusion: of the Buddha who must leave the consolations of filiality for the unknown and terrifying promise of impartial compassion; or of the epic hero Arjuna, who must wage a terrible war against his own kin, eschewing all the learned maxims of nativist ethics to arrive at an as-yet indefinable and unknowable capacity to pluralize the Self and apprehend it in/as all creatures, all things, *atmaupamyena sarvatra*. Let me end, instead, with an excerpt from a poem by Vikram Seth, called "A Morning Walk":

A web hung from the avocado tree;
The spider rested in the dew and sun
And looked about the grove contentedly
Awaiting visitors; and I was one:
Neither a Californian nor a fly,
And humming to myself in Bhairavi.
Foreigner, hence! he may have thought, but chose
Instead to squat immobile as I came
Further into his district. Did I pose
An unpredictability? The same
Was true of him—bloated, yellow, with some
Sepia blotches not like those at home.
Our spiders are much blacker and much thinner,
Patrol their webs with greater frequency

And seem perpetually anxious about dinner . . .
My very turn of phrase—Foreigner, hence!—
Betrayed the web of jocularity
I had spun around me here; nor could I sense
The pain I felt at home when I could see
The hunger, half-resigned, half desperate
Of those like me but for a freak of fate.[78]

3

SEX

The Story of Late Victorian Homosexual Exceptionalism

In his early prose poem *Towards Democracy* (1883), the late-nineteenth-century socialist, animal rights activist, prison reformer, and homosexual Edward Carpenter excoriates England for the dubious "blessings of empire."[1] Writing in passionate if somewhat purple register, he condemns unequivocally all acts of imperial exploitation: "These are her blessings of Empire! Ireland (dear Sister-isle, so near at hand, so fertile, once so prosperous), Rack rented, drained, her wealth by absentees in London wasted, her people with deep curses emigrating; India the same—her life blood sucked—but worse: / Perhaps in twenty years five hundred million sterling, from her famished myriads, / Taken to feed the luxury of Britain."[2] Generally traduced by the press when it first appeared, *Towards Democracy* was not exactly a runaway success. Yet quite undaunted by the meager sale of some seven hundred copies over seven years, Carpenter continued to make additions to the book until 1902, when a new edition was released, once again to lukewarm press notices. By this time, however, the book had already become something of a subcultural classic, circulating as a manifesto among the numerous dissident communities clustered at the margins of imperial culture, many of which would echo, in different contexts, the spirit of Carpenter's fierce and unpatriotic critique of empire and "western civilisation."

Evidence of his influence can be found, for instance, in the pages of *Justice*, the journal produced by the Social Democratic Foundation, to which Carpenter gave substantial financial and ideological support. Edited by H. M. Hyndman, William Morris, and J. Taylor, *Justice* maintained a systematic attack on British imperialism, asserting full parity between the cause of workers at home and that of colonized "races" abroad. And in an extraordinarily polemical article, "Shall We Fight for India?," published as early as 1885 (well before Indian nationalism developed a coherent agenda), Hyndman called categorically for the cessation of the Indian empire, writing, "I do say here, however, unavailingly, that for the sake of England and of India, I would far rather that we were driven right out of the country than that we should continue the miserable rule which has disgraced us and injured the people for the last eight and twenty years; and I can only hope that not only Socialists but all working Englishmen will look carefully into the facts."[3] Carpenter also helped to inform a similar set of disparate affiliations in the activities of the Humanitarian League. Begun in 1891, with his support, to improve the treatment of animals, the league substantially expanded its constituency and concerns, drawing workers' movements to the cause of animal welfare and simultaneously asserting continuity between the struggles for animal rights and against imperialism.

It is indisputable and intrinsically relevant to the concerns of this chapter that Edward Carpenter was preeminent in the marginal culture of late-nineteenth-century western anti-imperialism. And in part, the ensuing discussion will bear historical testimony to his influence. Rather more specifically, however, my project acquires shape at the curious and emphatic conjunction of homosexuality and anti-imperialism in Carpenter's work and thought. Everywhere in his extensive oeuvre he stubbornly extols the experience and condition of homosexuality as the cornucopian source of his ethical and political capacity, as the privileged rehearsal ground for his strange affinities with foreigners, outcastes, outsiders. Reading Carpenter with any degree of biographical fidelity, we are thus obliged to consider the proposition (as this chapter will do) that however incidentally and inscrutably, "western" homosexuality might be secreted somewhere within the culturally complicated genetic structure of anticolonial thought. But what if we reverse this schema and, following Carpenter's hyperbolic intent, ask the following: Can a case be made for anticolonialism (or a critique of western civilization) as an affective determinant of the homosexual condition?[4] Did the libidinal economy of late-nineteenth-century homosexuality traverse, equally, the incongruous circuits of crosscultural affinity and same-sex desire? If the figure of the homosexual, such as

Carpenter, is constitutively anticolonial, on what basis can we accommodate him within a history of sexuality? How might we give him a corporeal habitation and a sexual name? To bring these themes into sharper focus, my overarching query in this chapter is quite simply to ask: What were the ethico-political ingredients in his late Victorian homosexual self-apprehension that required Carpenter to call, in an article written for the *Humane Review* in 1900, for the "ruin . . . *the sooner the better* of these fatuous Empires"?[5] Why, in other words, could his homosexuality (more often than not) only speak its polemical name in and as a denunciation of western hegemony?

In the ensuing pages it will be my claim that Carpenter's antiwestern polemic, and his attending affinities with Europe's subject races, can only be explained in terms of a homosexual politics whose distinctiveness accrues less from dissident "sex acts" and more from a radical reconfiguration of association, alliance, relationality, community. That is to say, I seek to argue that Carpenter arrives at his anti-imperial sympathies (not to mention his accompanying sympathies with criminals, prostitutes, workers, women, and animals) only after he has made it homosexuality's business to think of itself, first and foremost, as a capacity for radical kinship. There are particular historical pressures, as we will see, that drove Carpenter to this position. After Darwin, the colluding discourses of evolutionary anthropology and psychology hermetically sealed the frontiers of "civilized" community, only admitting within this privileged circle certain types of human being and, concomitantly, certain congruent forms of human alliance. The homosexual, unsurprisingly, was among the first to be denied admission. To be more precise, the historical moment of his psycho-pathological definition and emergence was already the moment of his exclusion. He arrived, or came into being, at the outer margins of "civilized" or intelligible sociality, and in the company of a crowd of outcasts and outsiders whose numbers included Europe's subject races. Faced with these existential materials, any speaking back in the name of homosexuality carried with it an obligation to refute, creatively, the élite prerequisites for civilized, intelligible sociality, and in so doing to posit a more all-encompassing alternative. What follows is the story, in microcosm, of this endeavor, one whose housing within a "pure" homosexual thematic is subject to severe theoretical complications. We might begin our reflexive recuperation of Carpenter and his kind by exploring some of these theoretical complications and possibilities.

A SEXUAL POLITICS

Although Carpenter was honored substantially by contemporaries for his expansive solidarities, his legacy found ambivalent reception among succeeding generations of British homosexual activists. For many younger homosexuals, coming out in the shadow of his sagacity, Carpenter's political dilettantism appeared all too often as a form of homosexual evasiveness: a chaotic profusion of political aims that wilfully obscured the particular social pressures entailed by discrepant sexual orientation. Thus Lawrence Housman, the homosexual-rights campaigner and younger brother of the poet A. E. Housman, observed in Carpenter's ethical eclecticism a sort of guilty, and ultimately unconscionable, cloaking of homosexual designs. Carpenter, Housman insists in his contribution to Gilbert Beith's *Edward Carpenter: An Appreciation*, tragically underutilized his political platform: "his public utterances on behalf of certain underdogs—especially on behalf of homosexuals—his manner of speaking often struck me as too indirect and evasive for his pleading to really get home . . . his claim for right of way was too much hedged in by an appeal to extenuating circumstances."[6]

The burden of verdicts such as these was not in any way mitigated by Carpenter's strangely coy iterations of (homo)asexuality; his awkward insistence, for example, that he "had never to do with actual paedestry, so called": "My chief desire in love is bodily nearness or contact, as to sleep naked with a naked friend."[7] In context, E. M. Forster's posthumously published *Maurice* (1970), which unembarrassedly espouses same-sex sex, is available to reading as a riposte to Carpenter's (often prescriptive) eclipsing of sensuality. Conceived and completed in 1914, as Forster tells us, after a visit to Carpenter's ashram-household in Millthorpe, *Maurice* inaugurates a new and recognizable era of homosexual defiance in its Lawrentian tale of a sexually liberatory affair between the class-privileged Maurice and a common gamekeeper. Determined to controvert, through its unapologetic defense of "lust," the common superstition that "the sole excuse for any relationship between men is that it remain purely platonic,"[8] Forster's novel retains at the edges some portion of Carpenter's utopian inclusiveness. The difference is that this time round any extrasexual ethical imperative—for example, Maurice's heroic determination to "live outside class, without relations or money"[9]—constitutes a subclause to the compelling specificity of sex acts and the choices that attend them. In short, and (as we will see) *contra* Carpenter, *Maurice* puts the sex back into homosexuality and, in so doing, foregrounds the rights of sexuality as the originary postulate of a homosexual politics.

Forster's initiative, if we might call it that, has been comprehensively amplified within much recent gay and lesbian scholarship. Thus, for instance, Gayle Rubin's influential essay "Thinking Sex" is especially notable for its reprehension of "sex-negativity" in all its variants, right-wing or radically feminist. Impatient with the pretensions of sexual seriousness—the obligation always to fabricate a metaphysical alibi for sex—Rubin disinvests sex acts of moral significance so as to create a hospitable social space for sexual alterity. The claims of sexual pleasure, her argument implies, supply adequate justification for the facts of sexual deviancy. Or, to put this differently, sexual minorities must demand their rehabilitation within the social fabric, unapologetically, as sexed creatures. In such acts of uncompromising self-sexualization we might learn finally "to recognise the political dimension of erotic life."[10]

Rubin's position gains support in Leo Bersani's recent demand for a radical respecification of homosexual sex acts. Imprecating all homosexual politics that seems ashamed of homosexual desire, Bersani's *Homos* charges (homo)asexuality with the suicidal fulfilment of the invisibility that a hetero-ized sociality wishes upon its perverts. For as Bersani reminds us in salutary vein, the distinguishing stigmata of homosexual identity are vested in the corporeal peculiarities of homosexual practice: "preferences do exist . . . Gay men mainly go to bed with other men . . . and lesbians—*pace* Wittig—do 'associate, make love, live with women' . . . It is not possible to be gay-affirmative, or politically effective as gays, if gayness has no specificity. Being gay has certain consequences, which may lead us into making alliances with other oppressed groups. But . . . we want something that is unique among oppressed groups: the right to have the sex we want without being punished for it."[11] Same-sex sex, to paraphrase, is the ontological basis for homosexual exceptionalism and, as such, demands an aggressive showing and telling in a world where homophobia and AIDS conspire relentlessly against the hope of living fearlessly, homosexually.

In the face of the compelling case for sexual specificity proposed by pro-sex gay and lesbian scholars and activists, we are left with three ways to address the "problem" of Carpenter's sexual evasiveness. First, a condescending historicization might allow us to credit him, as Housman does, with provoking radical homosexual effects despite his sexual equivocation. In Housman's words, "there has come a change of enormous significance—a great and hopeful revolution. Carpenter, one of the quietist revolutionaries ever known, lived to see the beginning of it; a beginning which, without his help, might not have been discernible."[12] Second, following Monique Wittig and Eve Sedgwick—in an argument already more conducive to our ends—Carpenter's euphemizing of sexuality could be condoned as one way of facilitating the important shift from a "minoritizing" to a "universalizing" politics: namely, from one which enables the self-representation of a small and distinct minority to one that discloses homo/heterosexual definition as/at the epistemological core of everyday sociality.[13] As Sedgwick explains: after the announcement of that nineteenth-century schema (which we will examine in greater detail) in which a global homo/heterosexualisation was mapped upon the deterministic gender binarization of every human being, there was no longer any "space in . . . culture exempt from the potent incoherencies of homo/heterosexual definition."[14] Such definition henceforth came to vitiate "even the ostensibly least sexual aspects of personal existence."[15] So, we might argue, somewhat megalomaniacally, all politics is *eo ipso* a sexual politics, and Carpenter accordingly was talking sex even when he was talking anti-imperialism. We will concur in large part with the impulse behind this conclusion. But first let us at least entertain the prospect of rehabilitating Carpenter without evading the fact of his sexual evasiveness; consider, however tentatively, his sexual evasions as a condition of possibility for another occluded politics of homosexual exceptionalism. To bear any weight we will need to amplify this project within the historical field of nineteenth-century sexology and its effect upon the emergence of homosexual identity as we now know it. This we will do. First, though, let us elaborate our third "defense" of Carpenter's sexual evasions across the theoretical terrain liberated by the contentious first volume of Foucault's *The History of Sexuality*.

In a thesis which notoriously disqualifies sex itself from the aetiology of resistance, Foucault, it will be remembered, refuses to credit "power" as an agency of sexual repression, as a force invested only with the prerogatives of refusal. "We must," he writes, "abandon the hypothesis that modern industrial societies ushered in an era of increased sexual repression,"[16] for the most cursory review of the compact between modernity and sexuality reveals in the place of sexual prohibition the scandal of an authorized "discursive explosion" of sexualities. Looking to find a moralizing incentive in the prudish soul of Victorian governmentality, we are confronted with the reverse: "the multiplication of discourses concerning sex in the field of exercise of power itself: an institutional incitement to speak about it, and to do so more and more; a determination on the part of the agencies of power to hear it spoken about, and to cause *it* to speak through explicit articulation and endlessly accumulated detail."[17] How can we make sense of this anomaly? By apprehending sex, Foucault suggests, as the means of extending the cartographic purview of power, such that it becomes a thing not merely to judge but to administer and manage—a path of access into the covert enclaves of psychic and corporeal life, facilitating "the encroachment of a type of power on bodies and their pleasures."[18]

Within Foucault's schema the perverse "sex act," indeed sexuality itself, changes its colors of revolution for those of recreancy. Far from occupying an autonomous and libratory "exteriority" in relation to power, sex/perversion is now shown to be constituted and produced by the very apparatus that it seeks in vain to counter. Thus every "speaking" or "performance" of sex is susceptible to the risks of collaboration, to the charge of extending the prurient arm(s) of power: "Pleasure spread to the power that harried it; power anchored the pleasure it uncovered."[19]

All too often Foucault's account of the appropriative deployment of power in volume 1 of *The History of Sexuality* is read as a pessimistic invective against the possibility of resistance per se. Slavoj Žižek exemplifies this reading in a recent critique of Foucault's apparently myopic underestimation of the disruptive force of antagonism within any relation of authority. "He seems to draw the conclusion," Žižek complains, "that resistance is co-opted in advance, that it cannot seriously undermine the system—that is, he precludes the possibility that the system itself, on account of its inherent inconsistency, may give birth to a force whose excess it is no longer able to master and which thus detonates its unity, its capacity to reproduce itself."[20] Yet it is not so much that *The History of Sexuality* precludes the possibility of, as it were, detonating the system's capacity for reproduction as that it suspends from the scene of successful antagonism those deluded forms of resistance confined to a merely reproductive and replicative relationship with power. Thus in Foucauldian terms, we might implicate as collaborationist (or inadequately resistant) the anticolonial nation-state which fails to recognize its tragic duplication, ad nauseam, of the very imperial state from which it originally coveted its autonomy. Or for similar reasons, we might rehearse greater reticence with regard to the triumphalist claims of homosexual self-representation. For as Foucault writes, "nineteenth-century psychiatry, jurisprudence, and literature . . . made possible the formation of a 'reverse' discourse: homosexuality began to speak in its own behalf, to demand that its legitimacy or 'naturality' be acknowledged, often in the same vocabulary, using the same categories by which it was medically disqualified."[21]

Are there, in context and within Foucault's paradigm, any admissible forms of resistance that successfully short-circuit the tedious generativity of power under modernity? Its incarnation in and as an age of reproduction? Which, at the very least, trouble the doggedly filiative and homogenizing imperatives of modern power? Or, as Foucault himself asks in "What is Enlightenment?": "How can the growth of capabilities be disconnected from the intensification of power relations?"[22] His answer, in this essay, is to underwrite as resistance the bent for "inventiveness" secreted within a truly countermodern aesthetic imagination. Finding in Baudelaire an exemplary instance of such "inventiveness," Foucault hints tantalizingly at forms of resistance which may well elude the power of power to reproduce itself. In his words: "Modern man, for Baudelaire, is not the man who goes off to discover himself, his secrets and his hidden truth; he is the man who tries to invent himself. This modernity does not 'liberate man in his own being'; it compels him to face the task of producing himself."[23]

But how, we might ask with reference to the concerns of this discussion, does this romantic aestheticizing of resistance translate into the discursive field of sexuality? Stripped as he is of the insurrectionary force of sex/speech acts, how can the homosexual perform, like a Baudelaire or even a Sir Philip Sidney, such poetic inventiveness as might bring forth anew things that never were either in nature or in culture? To put this differently, which feature of homosexuality, if not sex, could form that "locus of intractability" which, in Judith Butler's terminology, might breach "the possibilities of imaginable and realisable . . . configurations within culture"?[24]

Some answers are given by Foucault himself in the course of a fractious interview conducted at his apartment in Paris in March 1982. Throughout the interview Foucault is at pains to demystify the revolutionary potential of homosexual sex on the grounds that "what most bothers those who are not gay about gayness is the gay life-style, not sex acts themselves."[25] Under the heading "life-style," and with characteristic semantic idiosyncrasy, Foucault lists all those forms of gay relationality, compelled as with Baudelaire, to produce themselves in the absence of established codes or guidelines. The unsettling power of homosexual resistance, its radical inventiveness, he suggests, may well accrue "from the prospect that gays will create as yet unforseen kinds of relationships that many people will not tolerate."[26] Thus unlike the perverse sex act, the creative intolerability of gay relationality eludes the reproductive intensity of power by manifesting itself as an anomalous and unprecedented homosexual effect upon the scene of everyday sociality. In these terms, gay relationality works against power through its reification of "new life-styles not resembling those that have been institutionalised."[27]

Foucault's predictions in the interview implicitly obtain from his account, in *The History of Sexuality*, of the frequently overlooked symbiotic relationship between sexuality and systems of alliance. Here he reminds us that in the main, sexuality safeguards and delimits imaginable circuits of sociality by imbuing systems of alliance with a "new tactic of power."[28] In any society relations of sex produce, sustain, and authorize, in their turn, "a *deployment of alliance*: a system of marriage, of fixation and development of kinship ties, of transmission of names and possessions."[29] Peculiar to modernity is the family cell, mediating "the interchange of alliance and sexuality"[30] through that set of intersecting filiative axes which link, crosswise, the husband-wife and parent-child relation in a sacramental tableau of normalization. The sex act is inextricably twinned to alliance, sociality, and community. Accordingly, a practice of effective homosexual exceptionalism needs to transform not only the modalities of sex but also, perhaps more importantly, the attending modalities of alliance and kinship.[31]

To summarize our argument so far: after Foucault, the sex-speech-act appears to be hopelessly implicated in the production of power, so much so that its performance—its showing and telling—becomes in effect an act of collaboration with power. This conclusion does not necessarily signal an apocalyptic death of sex, but it does signal the inadequacy of sex *qua* sex (or homosexuality-only-for-the-sake-of-homosexual-sex) as a viable or effective form of autonomy or resistance. Indeed, the claims of *The History of Sexuality* make it possible to conceive of sexual evasiveness as a judicious and purposive refusal to collude in the generative economy of power. But what then of resistance and the demand for its countermodern coupling with inventiveness that we have observed elsewhere in Foucault? Perhaps, and insofar as the normalization of sexuality achieves its authorizing effects in the normalization of alliance, we could recuperate as politics that variant of (homo)asexuality whose evasion of sex *qua* sex makes way or is the prelude for a radical reinvention and reimagining of community, kinship, and sociality, such that the figure of the homosexual comes to traverse, in Foucault's words, those "mobile and transitory points of resistance, producing cleavages in a society that shifts about, fracturing unities and effecting regroupings."[32] It was certainly a similar figuration of homosexuality that Edward Carpenter had in mind when he claimed—by way of explaining his anticolonialism—that the homosexual was uniquely equipped to show society "the wealth and variety of affectional possibilities which it has within itself."[33] But what might a queering of community, kinship, sociality, and association entail?[34] Before we turn to the scene of the late nineteenth century let us briefly consider an exemplary and inventive instance of queered relationality in the strange tableau of Michelangelo's last *Pietà*.

INTERLUDE: *PIETÀ*

There are countless references to Michelangelo in the literature of fin-de-siècle homosexual apologetics. He is praised as an apostle of "friendship-love" in Carpenter's *The Intermediate Sex* (1908), as a noble example of "sexual inversion" in Havelock Ellis's pathbreaking study *Sexual Inversion* (1897), and as a heroic votary of "Greek love" in John Addington Symonds's *The Life of Michelangelo* (1893).[35] Yet each of these writers, among others, is at pains to foreground the enigma of the sculptor's man-loving asexuality. While asserting Michelangelo's abnormal predilection for male beauty and attachments, Ellis finds "no reason to suppose that he formed any physically passionate relationships with men."[36] His assessment is endorsed by Symonds, who discerns in Buonarotti's "inverted" temperament a poignant physical frigidity. "Self-control," he writes, "seems to have been the main object of his conscious striving."[37] And indeed, while making due allowances for the defensive censoring intent of these late Victorian pro-homosexual commentators, Michelangelo's oeuvre is curiously reticent about sex, representing, as a recent critic observes, the sex act only in a single drawing, "as one of the seven deadly sins."[38] Such sexual reserve (or nausea) notwithstanding, the text of Michelangelo's homosexual desire is subtly elaborated in the misalliances which animate his pictorial and sculptural arrangements, perhaps nowhere more so than in the group that composes the threnodic tableau of his last "Florence *Pietà*."

Clustered around and supporting the body of Christ in various postures of psychic grief and physical effort, the Florence *Pietà* displays the linked figures of the Virgin, Mary Magdalene, and Nicodemus, named in St. John's Gospel as the disciple who came to his master in the dead of night and also prepared his body for burial: "And there came also Nicodemus, which at the first came to Jesus by night, and brought a mixture of myrrh and aloes, about an hundred pound weight. Then took they the body of Jesus, and wound it in linen clothes with the spices, as the manner of the Jews is to bury."[39] Intended by Michelangelo for his own tomb, the group passed through a number of hands and locations before it was installed behind the high altar of the Florence Duomo, to be moved in 1930 to one of the chapels of the north transept and more recently, along with other refugees from the Cathedral, to the Museo dell'Opera del Duomo. Thus the modern viewer's experience of the group is framed by its abrupt transformation, doubtless in sharp violation of Michelangelo's purpose, from sacral object to artefact, from the experience of worship to the secular business of appreciation. But this is not all. The amateur tourist, in hot pursuit of Michelangelo through a frantic summer of Italian cathedrals, expects to find in a *Pietà* the familiar representation of a "Virgin seated and holding the dead Christ in her arms, after He had been taken down from the Cross."[40] However, instead of the enclosed familial compact of a mother and son we are faced with a crowd, each member comforting the others as strangers might after a shared catastrophe, and in that comfort interrupting and reversing all "legitimate" circuits of affective intensity.

Nicodemus towers at the apex of the group, assuming the dominant upright posture of the Virgin in most recognizable *pietà*s, and the Magdalene takes over the Virgin's traditional place on the right of Christ. The diadem on her forehead confirms this appropriation through its image of the winged *amorino*, or symbol of love, shown opening its wings on the Virgin's breast in an earlier *Pietà* drawing. The twice displaced Virgin, in turn, mirrors the Magdalene on the left, and in her positioning completes the profound relational inversions of the group, its challenge to the institutional priorities of generationality and generativity. The women, mother and female companion, traditional bearers of the vertical axis of genealogy (of blood, birth, and sex), now traverse the horizontal axis of affiliation (of voluntary association) across the body of Christ. And vice versa, the vertical or filiative line descends intimately and dangerously along the upright male bodies of the friend-disciple Nicodemus and his friend-master Christ. What is achieved, if indirectly, in this reformulation of kinship, association, and relationality is a contingent remapping of gender and erotic performativity. The heavily cowled Nicodemus-Virgin figure, widely acknowledged as a self-portrait of Michelangelo, stands as mother to the freshly released body of Christ, the sculptor giving birth to marble children, one hand possessively pressed into the Virgin's back. The Virgin herself is sculpted into disturbing tactility with her son: her left hand passing beneath his left arm clutches at his breast, fingers barely missing his left nipple;

his left leg, now missing, was once draped over her lap; from one side their faces appear to dissolve into each other, the right side of her face obscured by the stony folds of his hair. And on the other side, the Magdalene's hands betray a similar restless promiscuity, one supporting Christ's right thigh, another placed across Nicodemus's right leg, behind the group.

How similar the complex significations of this group are to those of the Antigone story, recently retold by Judith Butler as dramatizing the fatal antagonism between normative heterosociality on the one hand and "unrecognizable" forms of kinship on the other.[41] Simultaneously daughter-sister to her father-brother Oedipus and sister-aunt to his sons, and bearing a name that can be construed as "anti-generation," Butler's Antigone introduces into the heart of Sophocles, through her infraction of the family cell, the sort of "kinship trouble" that Michelangelo arguably introduces into the soul of Christianity.[42] And in both cases we may discern in the transgression of socially intelligible lines of kinship an appeal for what Butler names the "liveability"[43] of misaligned desires.

We have painful evidence that Michelangelo understood too well the discrepant alliances of the Florence *Pietà* as a tragic embodiment of his own discrepant desires. Apparently when the work was nearly completed he approached it with a hammer, and in a frenzy set about pulverizing the marble of his creation. There was nothing random in this self-destroying violence. For each time the hammer fell it was with deliberation, severing the links between the various figures. The left arm of Christ, breaking at the shoulder, took with it the Virgin's inappropriately searching left hand; his left leg, slung over her lap, cracked into pieces. Another blow to the right arm of the Magdalene divided her connection from the body of Christ, even as his shattering right hand, amputated from wrist to knuckles, withdrew its tentative caress from her shoulder. Some have attributed Michelangelo's destruction of the group to a growing impatience with the flaws in the marble with which he was working, others to a loss of creative nerve. It suits our purpose to imagine otherwise, reading in his final substitution of life-giving chisel for life-taking hammer an elegy for the dream of an impossible community. To a considerably more sober English negotiation of such a dream at the beginning of the last century, let us now turn.

While it is useful in theoretical terms to situate Edward Carpenter's politics—with which we began this discussion—in a generalizable problematic of homo/heterosexual definition, its ideological and lexical peculiarities were framed by quite specific local developments within the allied Victorian disciplines of evolutionary biology, social anthropology, and sexology. To be more precise, we could explain the entire field of late-nineteenth-century homosexual polemics as a mediated reaction to the publication in 1871 of Charles Darwin's two-volume study *The Descent of Man, and Selection in Relation to Sex.*

Consisting of two vast subjects, man's putative "descent" from animal forms and the role of "sexual selection" in the process of evolution, Darwin's opus achieved enormous popularity in its time and became in due course the source book for at least a generation of evolutionary psychologists, race theorists, and ethnographers.[44] The success of the book can be attributed in part to its mitigation of some of the anxieties previously generated by Darwin's *The Origin of Species* (1859): specifically, the tracing of an evolutionary schema in which "Man," as Gillian Beer puts it, "is a determining absence,"[45] and one in which he is entirely susceptible, through the laws of natural selection, to the random and unpredictable vagaries of the environment. Replacing the disciplinary parameters of biology with those of anthropology, Darwin's *Descent* consoled his agitated readers through two concessions: first, by restoring Man to narrative centrality, and retelling the story of evolution from his perspective, and second, by foregrounding those unique features of human existence exempt, in some measure, from the leveling laws of natural selection.

While continuing to insist upon the biological determinants of human morphology, *Descent* concedes that man is made unique, and is distinguishable from his animal cousins, by virtue of his privileged access to morality, culture, and civilization. We do not know for certain, Darwin concedes, whether morality translates directly, through heredity, into an improved biological tenacity among individuals. But we do know that "civilization"—that product of human will, agency, and intention—increases the historical advantage and supersession of some cultures over others, thereby counteracting the random effects of natural selection. "With civilised nations," Darwin writes, "as far as an advanced standard of morality, and an increased number of fairly well-endowed men are concerned, natural selection apparently effects but little."[46] Needless to say, Darwin in his wisdom reserves the evolutionary magic of civilization for Europe alone: "the western nations of Europe . . . immeasurably surpass their former savage progenitors and stand at the summit of civilisation."[47]

But what, if any, are the characteristic features of "civilization" or evolutionary priority? Darwin's epochal answer, "sexual selection," announces the major theme of *Descent*, asserting, as Sulloway puts it, "that the ultimate test of biological success lies in reproduction, not in "the survival of the fittest." For if the fittest do not reproduce, Darwin well knew, they are generally of "no evolutionary importance to the species."[48] Other consequences follow. The tasks of successful reproduction demand an acute sexual dimorphism in nature, sharply distinguishing the secondary sexual characteristics of males and females as romantic (or aesthetic) inducement to the grisly business of productive mating. In Darwin's words: "the sexes often differ in . . . secondary sexual characteristics, which are not directly connected with the act of reproduction; for instance, in the male possessing certain organs of sense or location, of which the female is quite destitute, or in having them more highly developed, in order that he may readily find or reach her; or again, in the male having special organs of prehension so as to hold her securely."[49] But herein lies the rub. For once again, those crucial signs of sexual difference, which make men men and women women, only come into view among higher species and societies. So, for example, secondary sexual characteristics never appear among the poor mollusca, "for most of these animals . . . have their sexes united in the same animal."[50] Nor are they visible among the lower races. "The sexes of the American aborigines do not differ from each other,"[51] and in most "savage" societies, a distressing gender ambiguity erases the difference between the sexes: "the men are more highly ornamented than the women, and . . . the women . . . perform the greatest share of work."[52] Only in the "civilised" world do we witness the comprehensive implementation of the sex or gender divide, which in turn holds the key to successful (monogamous) reproduction.[53]

Darwin's peculiar arguments in *Descent* had numerous consequences, not least of all for the role of women, whose gender incarceration could now be explained as an altruism for the sake of the race; service to that immunizing reproductive economy which curtailed the dangers of natural selection.[54] But for our purposes, Darwin's assertion of a pernicious continuity between "civilization," "reproductive sex," and "sexual difference" also added up, as late Victorian sexology recognized, to an insistence upon the compulsory heteronormativity of (western) civilization. As the redoubtable Iwan Bloch would observe, after Darwin, "obvious is it that the whole of civilisation is the product of the physical and mental differentiation of the sexes, that civilisation has, in fact, to a certain extent a heterosexual character."[55]

The principles of sexual selection, as we will see below, were thus instrumental in producing the nonheterosexual or homosexual as a "civilizational" aberration. But in so doing, they also conferred upon this figure a potentially symmetrical relation to all those other savage, colonized peoples concurrently relegated to the jealous margins of western civility. Clearly not every nineteenth-century homosexual was alert to this symmetry, but for those who were, the critique of colonialism was at least available as an affective or political response to the constraints of their own condition. Let us pursue the development of these themes through a closer look at the scene of contemporary sexology.

THE AMPLIFICATION OF HETERONORMATIVITY

The true translation of Darwin's *Descent* into a manifesto for heteronormativity occurred within the nascent sexology movement, which first emerged as a recognized field of study in the 1870s and early 1880s.[56] In the main, writers in this tradition obtained from Darwin the belief that civilization was held in place by the enthusiastic practice of consensual and pleasurable reproductive sex, and at the same time by the immutable laws of sexual difference which made such sex possible. Thus, heralding the "discursive explosion" which Foucault points to in *The History of Sexuality*, sexology unleashed, in the name of medicine, a vast psycho-pathological literature in praise of the marvels of straight sex. So, for instance, the introduction to Krafft-Ebing's influential *Psychopathia Sexualis* extols "sexual life" as the "potent factor in individual and social existence," ascribing to it variously "the mightiest impulsion to the exercise of man's powers, to the acquisition of property, to the establishment of a domestic hearth, to the awakening of altruistic feelings."[57] Writing in a similar vein, August Forel passionately denounces the "sexually anaesthetic individual," while fulminating at large against the "jumble of hypocrisy, mysticism, prejudice, pecuniary interests, veneration for old traditional customs called good manners . . . which absolutely confuses all ideas of a healthy sexual morality."[58] The derivative Iwan Bloch likewise protests against the pretensions of "spiritual" affection, on the grounds that love—being quintessentially treelike—gains its fundamental nutrients from the dark soil of "sensory" love, remaining "irrevocably as ever dependent upon the physical."[59]

As signaled earlier, sexology's encomia to sex were consistently accompanied by a Darwinian insistence on the immutability of sex differences. These were singled out by Bloch, among others, as "the original cause of the human sexual life, the primeval preliminary of all human civilisation," and by Patrick Geddes and J. Arthur Thomson as the foundational principle of human evolution, labor, and sociality.[60] But as with Darwin, this subsidiary discourse of sexual dimorphism began subtly to police the frontiers of civilization, disqualifying as inadequately "differentiated" the contiguous figures of the nonwestern "savage" on the one hand and the western homosexual on the other. The discrete sexual allotments of the human species, as the liberal Havelock Ellis confirms in concurrence with the verdict of his generation, are simply more developed in Europe "than are usually to be found in savage societies."[61] The homosexual, or invert, as he argues elsewhere, is likewise tainted by a determining psychic hermaphroditism that sees, as in Darwin's mollusca, both sexes tragically "united in the same animal": "Each sex is latent in the other, and each, as it contains the character of both sexes . . . is latently hermaphrodite. A homosexual tendency may thus be regarded as simply the psychical manifestation of special characters of the recessive sex, susceptible of being evolved under changed circumstances, such as may occur near puberty and are associated with changed metabolism."[62]

It is important to note that the tenuous homology of the "savage" and the "homosexual," produced by the discourse of sexual difference, gave way to a symbiosis, as the functions and identifications of these two excluded figures began imperceptibly to collapse into each other. Summarily captured by the exclusionary prose of "degeneration," which cast an acute and unforgiving eye on those disruptive pathologies internal to civilization, the homosexual was progressively (though not by any means universally) diagnosed as a throwback to a former stage of "savagery," an outcast or at best an irrelevance to civilized society.[63] Thus, following on from his panegyric to heterosexual sex, August Forel dismisses homosexuality as a bad joke: "It seems absurd," he claims, "that the whole sexual appetite and amorous ideas of a man can be directed all his life to persons of his own sex . . . and it is obviously absurd to apply the term 'normal' to a sexual appetite absolutely devoid of its natural object, procreation."[64] Concurring with this verdict, Bloch directly invokes, though in muted form, the vocabulary of degeneration to reject homosexuality as a "primitive" and "markedly retrogressive step."[65] Referring tirelessly to that sublime hetero-ized schema according to which "it is unquestionable that evolution and the progress of civilisation have resulted in an extremely marked differentiation between the two sexes," he rubbishes all "varieties" that diverge from the "genuine man and the genuine woman" as "phantoms, monstrosities, vestiges of a primitive sexual condition."[66] For these reasons, he asserts categorically, inverts "cannot play any serious part in the future course of human evolution."[67] It is worth noting that the homosexual's expulsion from civilization, and identification as "foreign" matter in the clear substance of evolutionary progress, also made him or her particularly susceptible to charges of anti-national affiliation. So, as David Hilliard has argued, the heavy odor of homosexuality attaching to Anglo-Catholicism left its votaries open to the suspicion of being simultaneously "un-English and unmanly."[68] For similar reasons, by the turn of the century sexual perverts were increasingly figured as, in Lucy Bland's words, "traitorous lovers of all things German."[69] And in such ascriptions we can perhaps discern the source for E. M. Forster's curious notion, in *Two Cheers for Democracy*, of homosexual choice—for the claims of "friendship"—as a potentially traitorous act against the competing claims of "country."

Even as the homosexual was undergoing the discursive surgery that would transform him into a savage, primitive, foreigner, and traitor, a similar ideological-semantic operation was slowly and surely rendering the "savage" non-West into *the* zone of (homo)sexual perversion. These efforts took their cue, mistakenly, from the publication in 1885 of the first ten volumes of Sir Richard Burton's acclaimed and unexpurgated translation of the *Arabian Nights*, complete with a "Terminal Essay" which identified the non-West, specifically the "Orient," as a "sotadic zone" where homosexuality thrived without social constraint. Situated, in pseudo-geographical jargon, approximately between the latitudes 43° and 30° north, Burton's sotadic zone just includes "meridional France, the Iberian peninsula, Italy and Greece, with the coast-regions of Africa from Morocco to Egypt . . . embracing Asia Minor, Mesopotamia and Chaldea, Afganistan, Sind, the Punjab and Kashmir . . . enfolding China, Japan and Turkistan . . . the South Sea Islands and the New World."[70] Invoking throughout the essay the laws of sexual dimorphism, he subtly discloses in the apparent and acknowledged sexual indeterminacy of savage, nonwestern peoples the decisive somatic index of their homosexuality. The effeminate and smooth skins of Egypto-African priests, the distressing flat-chestedness of Turkish and Kashmiri women, the "kohl'd eyes and rouged cheeks" of Afghan boys, the cross-dressing proclivities of Lahori men, all catalogue the rich variety of "Le Vice," as Burton campily calls it.[71] And while at pains to establish the continuity between ancient Greek and Oriental varieties of homosexual love, Burton's study effectively displaces the sexual precedent of Hellenism upon the putative Orient, granting to an amorphously nonwestern world the cultural prerogative of same-sex desire.

Written in a contradictory idiom that simultaneously excoriates and exalts "sotadism," Burton's "Terminal Essay" is readily available to reading as a doubled defense of homosexual and nonwestern culture, and a critique of heteronormativity and western culture. Thus his lyrical testimony to the Sufi idealization of homosexual intent as the "beau ideal which united in man's soul the creature with the Creator" dovetails with his wide-eyed defense of Islamic cultural achievement at a time when "the dark clouds of ignorance and superstition hung so thick on the intellectual horizon of Europe as to exclude every ray of learning that darted from the East and when all that was polite or elegant in Literature was classed among the *Studia Arabam*."[72] In this regard the fictive and ever-widening latitudes of Burton's "sotadic zone" testify less to his scholarly acuity than to his wishful identification of the "East" as a world free from the theological and moral repressions of western Christendom.

Over time Burton's collected oeuvre would play an important part in rendering the Orient into a homosexual utopia for Europe's sexual refugees.[73] More immediately, however, the defensive rhetoric of the "Terminal Essay" helped fuel the energies of a moralizing chorus intent on accumulating (homo)sexual evidence for the savagery of Europe's subject races. It was thus Burton's dubious ethnography that allowed Bloch to condemn homosexuality as an Oriental national tradition,[74] Forel to diagnose it as an Eastern affliction,[75] and William James to assert as common knowledge "the fondness of the ancients and of modern Orientals for forms of unnatural vice."[76] This ubiquitous and mutually damning identification of homosexuality and the non-West would eventually lead Magnus Hirschfeld, the homosexual-rights activist exiled from Nazi Germany, to write bitterly about the insidious collusion between western heterosexism and racism: "Heterosexuals, who regard themselves as 'normal' because they are in a majority, and who (in the prime of life, at any rate) are apt to have an instinctive dislike for homosexuals and their ways . . . hypocritically incline to pretend that homosexual practices cannot have arisen spontaneously in their own happy land and among their own fortunately endowed 'race.' Hence the canting insinuation that homosexuality must have been introduced from without, from the foreign land or by the foreign people with whose name it is associated."[77]

To draw some conclusions, we could argue that the disciplinary mutations of Darwin's *Descent*—in particular his theory of "sexual selection"—forced a strange kinship upon the "homosexual" and the "savage." Both were exiled to the desert surrounding the heavily policed oasis of western heteronormative civilization, and in the ideological mirages to which this desert was prone, their features slowly began to merge into each other so that no one could any longer say for certain who was the "real" homosexual or who was the "true" savage. The two, we could claim after Bataille, found themselves inhabiting a "negative community," or "a community of those without a community," thrown into accidental coalition through the conjuncture of their shared expulsion from western civility. But the compact of savage and homosexual that we are examining here also lays claim to the more complex connotations of "negativity" in Bataille's thought, implying not only the nihilistic privation of positive value but also a means of troubling the

Hegelian dream of self-identical community, realized, as we observed in chapter 2, at the summit of the master-slave dialectic in the *Phenomenology of Mind.*

As it will be remembered, in that fleeting moment when Hegel's master and slave first face each other they are both suffused by the experience of desire as separation and negativity. For human desire, as Judith Butler notes in her gloss on Hyppolite's reading of Hegel, "articulates the subject's relationship to that which is *not* itself, that which is different, strange, novel, awaited, absent, lost." However, the necessary satisfaction of this desire in Hegel demands "the transformation of difference into identity: the discovery of the strange and novel as familiar, the arrival of the awaited, the reemergence of what has been absent or lost."[78] In other words, to achieve self-identical community the two characters in Hegel's drama must progressively negate the very negativity that constitutes their initial desire. Thus community or relationality within this paradigm is predicated upon a formative violence to difference. But could we imagine another kind of anti-communitarian community, where the participants refuse the reciprocal negation of negativity, defiantly preserving ontological difference as the basis, indeed as the signature, of their communication? In these terms, and following Jean-Luc Nancy's reading of Bataille, the "negative community" might be reconceptualized as one which comprehends "separation" as ethically exigent, such that the dialectic of Hegel's self-identical community is "*suspended* on the limit of its access to *self*"; that is, at the point of its resolution into an order of similitude, similarity, identity.[79]

In recent years several thinkers, Nancy and Agamben preeminent among them, have thus attempted to arrest Hegel's *Phenomenology* at the moment when it first articulates the experience of "negativity" in the dialectic of recognition. At that moment, they contend, Hegel becomes available to reading as "the first to take thought out of the realm of identity and subjectivity," thus intimating the possibility of radical community.[80] For inaugural negativity expresses a unique experience of insufficiency (also recommended, as we might recall from chapter 2, by Blanchot), which draws us sharply into "the very heart of *ethos*, humanity's proper dwelling place": that is, into the imperatives of being with others *qua* others.[81] Exemplifying the limits of bounded, reflexive, and enclosed subjectivity, negativity thus becomes a declaration, as in Nancy, of "the archi-impossibility of Narcissus that opens straight away onto the possibility of the political."[82] Conceived in these terms, as the constituting nonplace of being—the authenticating symptom of its "ungroundedness"—inaugural Hegelian negativity also possesses a compelling utopic dimension, urging the bounded subject to apprehend the nonplace of her own identity as an invitation to take place or to find place among various undenominated others—to collaborate, as Nancy puts it, in the "recognition of one put-out-of-itself by one put-out-of-itself."[83]

To bring these comments in line with our discussion, I am not proposing that we refuse, in the name of neo-Hegelian theory, the pleasures of mutual and enabling recognition to the western homosexual and the nonwestern savage. Nor am I suggesting that this recognition was never historically achieved. Rather my claim is simply that any compact between these two sets of outcasts, forged as it is not only against but outside community, manifests the radical "negativity" or principle of "ontological difference" to which Bataille refers, safeguarding and bringing something ineluctably foreign, strange, and unfamiliar into the very heart of sociality, association, and relationality. In this way the coalition achieves the "inventive" quality of resistance that Foucault theorizes as the decisive hallmark of a homosexual politics, and that Michelangelo performs while philosophising, like Nietzsche, with a hammer upon his last *Pietà*. It is time, finally, to return to Edward Carpenter and the scene of his anticolonial homosexuality.

A LITERATURE OF INVERSION

Fin-de-siècle homosexual politics, with which we are concerned here, aligned itself within a "negative community" in two ways: first, by liberating itself from the law of immutable sexual difference, authorized by Darwin's *Descent*, and second, by rejecting categorically the very principle of sex so enthusiastically extolled by sexology and its offshoots. We will examine the strategies for this project through a close reading of Edward Carpenter's writing. But first, it is useful to amplify the theoretical basis of the double resistance we are considering through a quick glance at Monique Wittig's critique of "the straight mind" and Michel Foucault's defense of cultivated "ascesis" or *askesis* in volume 2 of *The History of Sexuality*.

Wittig's *The Straight Mind*, we might recall, sees heterosexuality as an institution, indeed as the prevailing social contract founded on the ineluctable categories of sex. The "category of sex," she writes, "is the political category that founds society as heterosexual . . . For to live in society is to live in heterosexuality."[84] Framed in these terms, homosexual desire and identity are inescapably politicized in and as an existential obligation to break with the prevailing social contract by destroying the sociological reality of the sexes:[85] "If we as lesbians and gay men, continue to speak of ourselves, and to conceive of ourselves as women and as men, we are instrumental in maintaining heterosexuality."[86]

By imagining homosexuality as a third position outside the binary of sex, and thereby outside the social contract itself, Wittig secures a powerfully utopian provenance for the business of homosexual self-identification,[87] one that demands at its heart a radical reformulation of relationality. The act of withholding consent to the categories of sex, she insists, is always accompanied by the fomenting of "voluntary associations" with a range of other "fugitives."[88] For if, as Wittig suggests, the "straight mind" is susceptible to the wider inequities nourished by binary thinking—"Shouldn't we mention that the paradigm to which female, dark, bad, unrest belong has also been augmented by Slave, other, different?"—then the "bent mind" is, or ought to be, in some green, Blakean world, constitutively exempt from and innately critical of these susceptibilities. Furthermore, to borrow some words from Butler, it is precisely because the "totality" of Wittig's homosexual utopia "is permanently deferred, never fully what it is at any given juncture in time," that it also possesses the capacity for "open coalition . . . an open assemblage that permits of multiple convergences and divergences."[89]

Wittig's polemic finds a Foucauldian resonance in its emphasis upon homosexuality as a form of revolutionary "association." The links between the two theorists are further reinforced in Wittig's insistence that homosexuality is principally an ethico-epistemological resistance to binary thought and only incidentally a matter of sexual action and preference. As she notoriously observes: "it would be incorrect to say that lesbians associate, make love, live with women, for 'woman' has meaning only in heterosexual systems of thought . . . Lesbians are not women."[90] While Foucault does not entirely concern himself with the problematization of the sex and gender system, he implicitly joins with Wittig in a complementary endeavor—discussed earlier—to dissociate homosexual social potential from homosexual sex. Such dissociation, he suggests, was once authorized in Greek antiquity as part of the recommendation to work upon desire and pleasure through strategies of ethical self-fashioning, or *askesis*.[91] In its Foucauldian incarnation, Greek askesis is not reducible to a self-denying austerity or even to "asceticism" as it is commonly understood. Rather, it is seen to furnish an ethical (and eventually aesthetic) access to such forms of self-mastery—or distancing (of the self) from the (mis)identifying flux of desire—as might enable the homosexual to reconstitute himself not in sex alone but in the surprise of relationality. By mastering, ascetically, our impulse to find the secret truth of our being in our desires we might, Foucault implies, finally be free to query "what sorts of relations can be established, invented, multiplied, modulated through homosexuality . . . the problem is not to discover in oneself the truth of one's sex, but rather to use, from now on, one's sexuality to achieve a multiplicity of types of relation."[92]

These theoretical paradigms—for asceticism and against sexual difference—come together in the period under consideration in the trope of the "urning": a highly euphemistic designation for the homosexual, popularized by the maverick German activist Karl Heinrich Ulrichs (1825–95) within a series of extravagant writings penned under the pseudonym Numa Numantius. Based very loosely on passages in Plato's *Symposium,* Ulrich's urning owes its genealogy to a socratic discussion in which one Pausanias explains that there are two types of Eros and, correspondingly, two Aphrodites. The elder goddess, Urania, created by the god Uranos parthenogenetically, lacks two sexes in her genetic makeup and presides exclusively over spiritualized same-sex love. By contrast, the younger or "common" Aphrodite, coming to being in conventional reproductive manner through the joint labors of Zeus and Dione, supplies her heterosexual genius to your everyday sensual cross-sex lovers. So it is that the "urning" (that privileged votary of Aphrodite senior) "is not a man"[93] but rather the member of a "third-sex," one distinguished both by its capacity for exalted loving and deep sympathy with (other) dispossessed minorities. "Our position," Ulrichs writes, "in every instance is on the side of the victims . . . whether they be Poles, Hanoverians, Jews, Catholics . . . We battle against the arrogance of despotic majorities."[94]

It is in Ulrichs that we can identify the distant source for Edward Carpenter's homosexual critique of sexual difference and of sex. He elaborates this critique, in the deceptively muted prose of Victorian evolutionary psychology, across a range of texts of which his *Love's Coming of Age* (1896) and *The Intermediate Sex* (1908) are the most representative. In the main, his recoil from the categories of sex conceives of heteronormativity as a closed masculine economy in which femaleness (or effeminacy) is variously effaced, repressed, and banished from modes of production and signification. Thus *Love's Coming of Age* squarely blames the late Victorian cult of masculinity (sustained, Carpenter argues, through a dialectical relation to femininity) for a multitude of sins, including imperialism and race prejudice. The pure man, factory-produced by the public school system on a diet of sport and beef, is fashioned, Carpenter protests, to rule India and exploit South Africa,[95] his flaws exacerbated by the bad offices of the pure woman, herself "twisted . . . into a ridiculous mime of fashion and frivolity."[96] Modern civilization, in Carpenter's understanding, is diseased with sexual difference and can only be cured, on his strong recommendation, through the therapeutic intervention of "intermediate types" or homosexual physicians.

Drawing on and subverting the rhetoric of eugenics and evolutionism, Carpenter projects homosexuals as a possible species of the future who might improve upon the palpably inadequate temperaments produced by the prevailing categories of sex. As he argues in *The Intermediate Sex*, "We do *not* know, in fact, what possible evolutions are to come . . . It may be that, as at some past period of evolution the worker-bee was without doubt differentiated from the two ordinary bee-sexes, so at the present time certain new types of human kind may be emerging, which will have an important part to play in societies of the future —even though for the moment their appearance is attended by a good deal of confusion and misapprehension. It may be so; or it may not. We do not know." Here as elsewhere, Carpenter's tactical utopianism situates the homosexual beyond knowledge, and so beyond representation. But—as with Wittig—it is precisely by withholding from homosexuality what Butler calls "the normative telos of definitional closure"[97] that he reformulates the homosexual project as an "open coalition" capable of accommodating conjunctural solidarities and counteralliances between disparate and shifting groups. "Eros," he writes, in an expanded definition of homosexuality, "is a great leveller. Perhaps the true Democracy rests, more firmly than anywhere else, on a sentiment which easily passes the bounds of class and caste, and unites in the closest affection the most estranged ranks of societies."[98] Elsewhere, and as mentioned earlier, he singles out the homosexual for his affective versatility, a product of a doubled or hybrid nature which enables him to perform and to reveal to society "the wealth and variety of affectional possibilities which it has within itself."[99]

Inverting the judgments of evolutionary psychology, Carpenter thus reclaims the homosexual's gender ambiguity as proof of his exceptionality. And with similar consequences, he extends this privilege to the sexually undifferentiated "savage," also relegated, as we have seen, to the bottom of Darwin's phyletic ladder. In his *Intermediate Types among Primitive Folk* (1914), Carpenter writes enthusiastically in this vein of the prevalence and spiritual valorization of bisexuality in nonwestern culture, reserving the greatest awe for the "tendency to cultivate and honour hermaphroditism" within Hindu mythology: "Brahm, in the Hindu mythology, is often represented as two-sexed. . . . Siva, also, the most popular of the Hindu divinities, is originally bi-sexual.[100] Linking the homosexual and the "primitive" in a double encomium, Carpenter's study demonstrates the homosexual's sympathetic capacity to appreciate the proper significance of "primitive intermediacy," while at the same time praising "primitive" cultures for their perspicacious exaltation of sexual indeterminism. So it is that the "savage" and the "invert" are named as natural allies and collaborators in a shared battle against (western) categories of sex: bound to a common cause through uncommon gifts.

If Carpenter's homosexual exceptionalism relies in part on a determined eschewal of sexual difference, it also gains substantial energy from his insistence that the "intermediary," unlike the heterosexual, is uncontaminated by the base chemicals of sexual desire and practice. Issuing in all his writing a fierce invective against sex, he appeals continually for the pleasures of "non-satisfaction," the need "to transform grosser passions," the cultivation of "hardy temperance" between lovers, the deflection of "physical desire," the practice of asceticism.[101] Carpenter is not alone in this emphasis, as most nineteenth-century pro-homosexual literature is united in its determined espousal of "inversion" as a mastery over sex. So, for instance, John Addington Symonds valorizes, albeit hysterically, "Greek love" for its capacity to transform "into a glorious enthusiasm, a winged splendour," the "passion which grovels in the filth of sensual grossness."[102] In a similar vein, Magnus Hirschfeld insists that "just as same-sex acts infrequently point to contrary sexual feelings, its total lack does not rule them out; to the contrary, its apparent lack can be a sign of especially strong homosexual sensibility."[103] It is possible, of course, to read in the too-muchness of these protestations a defensive posture. Homosexual behavior was subjected to much greater scrutiny after the infamous Labouchere Amendment to the Criminal Law Amendment Act of 1885, which extended the scope of the law to cover all homosexual acts, committed in public or private. As is well known, these increased legal sanctions eventually culminated in the trials of Oscar Wilde in 1895, radically changing the experience and expression of homosexuality in fin-de-siècle England. The long terror consequent upon these trials certainly finds its way into the anxious apologetics that inform much contemporary homosexual literature. Anomaly's *The Invert* (1927) is a case in point, urging abstinence as part of the desperate struggle to "encourage every symptom of sexual normalisation" in the face of potential blackmail.[104]

Written directly after the Wilde case, Carpenter's *Love's Coming of Age* is likely to have been informed by similar fears. But it is not sexual circumspection that we find in Carpenter so much as aggressive sex-negativity. Isolating in the sexual overdevelopment of heterosexual society the pernicious first cause for "half-grown" natures, Carpenter finds two reasons to recommend his own form of askesis. The first, fashioned as opprobrium, identifies in sex the basic nutrient of tyranny and the will to mastery, manifest especially in the oppression of women and as imperialism. Whenever "sex . . . retains the first place," he writes, it produces "men so fatuous that it actually does not hurt them to see the streets crammed with prostitutes . . . men to whom it seems quite natural that our marriage and social institutions should lumber along the bodies of women, and our "imperial" enterprise over the bodies of barbarian races."[105] Second, he argues, the libidinal economy of hetero-sex lends itself to such egregious brutality because it stunts the free development of affectional possibilities, inhibiting sympathies with the oppressed of the earth, resolving all love into "a mere égoïsme à deux."[106] Discerning, in the manner of a Foucault, a hard contract between forms of sexuality and alliance, Carpenter rants at large against marriage, monogamy, and the family cell, finding in each "a life sentence" for "the . . . immense variety of love," the "differentiation . . . of needs of the human heart," the "understanding and tolerance of . . . other loves."[107] In such a world, and given the natural inhibitions upon his sexual expression, the intermediary (once again) has easy access to the asceticism, or askesis, that holds the key, as in Foucault, to a "multiplicity of types of relation": "it is possible that in this class of men we have the love sentiment in one of its most perfect forms—a form in which from the necessities of the situation the sensuous element . . . is exquisitely subordinated."[108] Carpenter's preferred term for this perfected love sentiment is "friendship," and he elaborates its themes in *Ioläus: An Anthology of Friendship* (1904), a compendium cataloguing a rich variety of extrafiliative associations between unlikely and unorthodox pairs, separated by culture, color, class, age, and race. Forced underground by the conventions of modern existence, friendship, Carpenter proposes, is on the verge of a renaissance, "destined . . . to arise again, and become a recognised factor of modern life, and even in a more extended and perfect form than at first."[109] Its fulfilment awaits the age of the intermediary, that species of the future, free from the logic of dimorphism and the imperious desires that it entails. We can discern a similar emphasis in John Addington Symonds, who directly attributes the homosexual capacity for friendship to an accompanying sexual abstinence. Drawing on Walt Whitman's distinction between the mutually antagonistic "amativeness" of sexual love and the "adhesiveness" of friendship, Symonds discerns in the latter form of kinship "a social and political virtue . . . destined to regenerate political life and to cement nations, an intense, jealous, throbbing, sensitive, expectant love of man for man."[110]

To summarize: standing on the outskirts of civilized sociality, the nineteenth-century homosexual understood his eviction, and negative community with the nonwestern savage, to be an effect of their shared failure to fulfil the psychosomatic rules of sexual dimorphism and so of the sexual practices that made alliance intelligible. His response, posed as a refutation of evolutionary psychology, was categorically to reject these foundational laws of western civility, on the grounds that they inhibited rather than promoted the free and ethical development of human community. The rigid categories of sex spawned affectively handicapped forms of hypermasculinity; the practices of hetero-sex, indeed sex itself, cloistered the relational possibilities of the human heart. In this dystopian world the "invert" alone was exceptional: a species of the future destined to correct the inequities of western heteronormativity through his capacity for radical kinship. Liberated from the dull monochrome of sexual dimorphism, this constitutively doubled and hybrid intermediary was endowed with variegated sympathies and desires. His asceticism likewise equipped him for the complex affiliative demands of friendship. Here, in a nutshell, we have the raw materials for Carpenter's critique of western civilization and congruent affinities with Europe's subject races. That he directly turned to the East we know from his odyssey to India and Ceylon in 1890, recorded (with vivid examples of imperial bigotry) in *From Adam's Peak to Elephanta* (1892); his lifelong friendship and correspondence with the Sri Lankan P. Arunachalam; his seeking of wisdom from a Hindu "Gnani" who taught him, among other things, secret techniques for "the subjection of desire."[111] We could easily end our narrative here, having given an account of Carpenter's part in expanding, however briefly, the ideological scope of "modern" homosexuality. But what of any part that modern homosexuality and the literature of inversion might have played in the history of anticolonial thought? To answer this question comprehensively we would have to undertake a monumental un-closeting of history, which is entirely beyond the scope of this discussion. However, we do have access to one very small and revealing story of cultural traffic. Let me retell it on our way to a conclusion.

In 1889 Carpenter wrote his polemical *Civilisation: Its Cause and Cure*. Diagnosing imperial Europe as perilously diseased with "civilisation," Carpenter's book continually asserts the superiority of "savage" and "barbarian" societies, prescribing a cure for the West in "a fresh influx of savagery."[112] The "present competitive society," he claims, "is more and more rapidly becoming a mere formula and husk within which the outlines of a new and *human* society are already discernible. Simultaneously and as if to match this growth, a move towards . . . savagery is for the first time taking place from within."[113] *Civilisation*, like many of Carpenter's writings, elicited a mixed welcome at home.

But by some coincidence, it fell into the hands of the young M. K. Gandhi during a four-month visit to London in 1909, where he had come unsuccessfully to campaign for the rights of South Africa's Indian minorities. On the voyage back to South Africa, bitterly disillusioned with his unfavorable reception in England, he produced *Hind Swaraj*, a scathing critique of western civilization thirty thousand words long and written over an unbroken ten-day stretch, sometimes with his right hand and sometimes with his left (demonstrating, we might note, the ambidexterity often associated in both western and eastern cultural psychology with bisexual temperaments). Condemning in no uncertain terms the British presence in India, this early work clearly announces the Gandhian demand for *swaraj*, or self-rule; the techniques of non-cooperation required to achieve it; and the ethics of *ahimsa*, or non-violent passive resistance, which must constitute the improved soul of nonwestern anticolonialism. To be regarded in due time as the key manifesto of the Gandhian revolution, *Hind Swaraj* acknowledges Carpenter, along with a few other like-minded writers, in its brief bibliography. He is also cited, *en passant*, in the text: "A great English writer," Gandhi announces in a chapter on "Civilisation," "has written a work called 'Civilisation: Its Cause and Cure.' Therein he has called it a disease."[114] Hardly evidence to give Carpenter pride of place at the formative origins of Indian anticolonialism. But evidence enough to note his welcomed presence at these origins.

How much, we may wonder, did Gandhi observe of Carpenter's own ethics of inversion? Did he even register Carpenter's fleeting defense of Greek homosexuality as an improvement upon heterosexual marriage?[115] Did he read *Love's Coming of Age* and *The Intermediate Sex*? We have no way of knowing. We can, however, claim—as Ashis Nandy has, so persuasively—that Gandhi's ethico-political practice was animated by his own peculiar brand of bisexual radicalism.[116] In a milieu where orthodox Indian nationalism was countering imperial allegations of "effeminacy" through a hysterical recuperation of a lost Indian "manhood," Gandhian *ahimsa* was predicated on a rigorous refusal of heteronormative masculinity, western or eastern.[117] In Gandhi's understanding, the *ahimsaic* agent is obliged to feminize the activity of resistance by emulating the admittedly stereotypical selflessness of motherhood, self-containment of widowhood, and so on. His own "queering," as it were, of gender positions is frequently expressed in his aspiration to transcend gender relations or, as he puts it, "mother" his companions and in so doing become "God's eunuch."[118] So too, and with reference to our discussion so far, his religious hermaphroditism does not signify the zone of a transgressive sexuality so much as project sexlessness—true *brahmacharya*—as the necessary effect of bringing femaleness to bear upon maleness. And his own aversion to sexuality is sharply crystallized in his insistence upon the inherently violent or *himsaic* nature of marriage and thus of the family cell, whose enclosed sexual economy requires and condones repetitive acts of violence upon the naturally non-consenting bodies of women. In his words, "Young men in India . . . are married early . . . nobody tells them to exercise restraint in married life . . . The poor girl wives are expected by their surroundings to bear children as fast as they can."[119]

The resonances between Gandhi's "sexual politics" and Edward Carpenter's homosexual exceptionalism are striking enough for us to ask whether the famous writer of *Hind Swaraj* found in *Civilisation: Its Cause and Cure* a sympathetic critique of (western) civilization or a sympathetic politics of inversion. But as we have been arguing, perhaps the two projects are indistinguishable after all. What we have in either case is grounds for sympathy, collaboration, and kinship across multiple registers between Gandhi and Carpenter: a friendship, of sorts, between an Indian anticolonial revolutionary and an English homosexual polemicist. Acknowledging these complex shared circuits, the animal-rights activist Henry Salt took care to write to Gandhi at the end of 1929, the year that Edward Carpenter died. "All good causes," Salt reported to the Mahatma, "have suffered a loss this year by the death of Edward Carpenter."[120]

CODA

But Edward Carpenter "died" well before 1929, his politics helped into a shallow grave by the eager ministrations of Sigmund Freud. Although inadvertently, Freud dismantled the complicated edifice of homosexual exceptionalism in roughly three ways. First, and to most effect, by defining homosexuality (or diffuse object choice) as an originary and universal condition he categorically denied the "third-sex" position which had placed the homosexual outside the fixed binary of heterosexual difference. In his words: "Psychoanalytic research is most decidedly opposed to any attempt at separating off homosexuals from the rest of mankind as a group of a special character. By studying sexual excitations other than those that are manifestly displayed it is found that all human-beings are capable of making a homosexual object-choice and have in fact made one in their unconscious . . . psychoanalysis considers that a choice of an object independently of its sex—freedom to range equally over male and female objects—as it is found in childhood, in primitive states of society and early periods of history, is the original basis from which, as a result of restriction in one direction or the other, both the normal and the inverted types develop."[121]

In other words, after psychoanalysis the homosexual could no longer lay any claim to ontological exceptionality and its relational effects. Nor for that matter would he be allowed to valorize his kind on the basis of their conscientious objections to sex, because of Freud's second move: through his relentless pathologizing of all sexual inhibition, Freud interrupted the discursive logic of the homosexual recoil from sex by diagnosing as illness such forms of (homo)asexuality as we have encountered in the likes of Carpenter and Symonds. Thus, while writing about homosexual sex with apparent lack of moral judgment—indeed with deliberate compassion—Freud renders Leonardo da Vinci's alleged homo-asexuality, for example, into a revealing symptom of ill-health. The artist's "cool repudiation of sexuality," his "chaste . . . even abstinent" lifestyle, his privileging of work over sex, "place him," Freud observes, "close to the type of neurotic that we describe as 'obsessional'; and we may compare his researches to the 'obsessive brooding' of neurotics, and his inhibitions to what are known as their 'abulias.' "[122] Elsewhere Freud explains neuroses as a pathology peculiar to the repression or denial of aberrant drives: "symptoms are formed in part at the cost of abnormal sexuality; neuroses are, so to say, the negative of perversions."[123]

Far from being the prelude to a melioristic social order, then, the refusal of sex (straight or gay) was henceforth reconstituted as the onset of psychological disease. This leads to our third point, which is Freud's resistance, underwriting these refabrications of the homosexual condition and *contra* Carpenter and others, to any adversarial relationship with "civilization" itself. While conceding the profound psychic costs entailed by the civilizing process, Freud deems it simply ungrateful to demand its abolition.[124] Anathematizing, for these reasons, utopianism and ascetic withdrawal as particularly delusional flights from the Real, he claims that "whoever . . . sets . . . upon this path . . . will as a rule attain nothing."[125] And so the homosexual and the savage, we might add, were denied recourse to that common ground for their negative community at the liminal outskirts of western heteronormative civility. In return for all these sacrifices, the homosexual after Freud was granted compensatory access to the rich consolations of normalization and relatively guiltless, if "immature," sex. No small gains these, and not to be underestimated. But let us also not forget that these Freudian gifts were in fact expensive psychic transactions, demanding invention as collateral for acceptance, liberating the homosexual body at the cost, we could say, of the homosexual soul.

4

MEAT

A Short Cultural History of Animal Welfare at the Fin-de-Siècle

PREAMBLE: HOMESICKNESS

It's lunchtime late in the century before last, and the young Indian man, whom we must imagine standing hungrily on Farringdon Street, is not charmed by London. At least not today, Monday, 22 October 1888, a grey day announcing the irrevocable onset of winter. His disenchantment with the imperial metropolis carries the contagion of failure: to borrow the language of his devout *vaishnav* family, it is almost his *dharma* as a colonial arrivant to love London unequivocally, enthusiastically. A month hence, recalling in his diary the initial affective and financial impediments to his legal studies in England, he will note defiantly, "The difficulties which I had to withstand have made London dearer to me than she would have been."[1] Three years later his memory will cleave even more vividly to the exilic fantasies of his misspent youth: "I thought to myself, 'If I go to England not only shall I become a barrister (of whom I used to think a great deal) but I shall be able to see England, the land of philosophers and poets, the very centre of civilisation.' "[2] In time, true to that perverse psychic distortion which makes us homesick for those places in which we were foreign, he will come to miss London bitterly: "So much attached was I to London and its environments, for who would not be? London with its teaching institutions, public galleries, museums, theatres, vast commerce, public parks . . . is a fit place for a student and a traveller, a trader and a 'faddist.' "[3]

For the moment, however, on Farringdon Street, his homesickness is rather more conventional: an acute state of corporeal diaggregation, a maladjustment of a body ill at ease among sofas, carpets, cornices, porticoes, vestibules, flower beds, pavements, morning suits, bread, porridge, and potatoes. Mostly bread, porridge, and potatoes. To put it plainly, he is distraught about food, its lack and its unrecognizability. No stranger to meat eating and its guilty pleasures (but more of that later), he has had his sojourn authorized by the elders of his *modh bania* family only under condition of a vow to abjure, as *brahmacharya* requires, the triple temptations of liquor, meat, and sex. Trouble sets in from the moment he boards the *Clyde* in Bombay on 4 September 1888, to find the steamer's kitchen ill prepared for Indian vegetarian contingencies, although profuse in provisions of "oatmeal porridge . . . bread, butter . . . meat and potatoes *ad libitum*."[4] An English passenger noticing the boy's tortured abstemiousness commends meat as a medicine: "It is all very well so far but you will have to revise your decision in the Bay of Biscay. And it is so cold in England that one cannot possibly live there without meat."[5]

Some weeks later, while boarding at temporary lodgings in Richmond on a staple diet "both for luncheon and dinner . . . [of] . . . spinach and bread and jam,"[6] a fellow lodger and friend will similarly protest in vain on behalf of nonvegetarian transgression: "Had you been my own brother, I would have sent you packing. What is the value of a vow made before an illiterate mother, and in ignorance of conditions here? It is no vow at all. It would not be regarded as a vow in law. It is pure superstition to stick to such a promise. And I tell you this persistence will not help you to gain anything here. You confess to having eaten and relished meat. You took it where it was absolutely unnecessary, and will not where it is quite essential. What a pity!"[7] On another occasion the friend will read out passages of Bentham's "Theory of Utility" to his vegetarian companion, presumably to make the case that the measure of "civilised" sociality consists in maximizing pleasure (in this case eating well) and minimizing pain (in this case starving wilfully). "By utility," as Bentham has it, "is meant that property in any object, whereby it tends to produce benefit, advantage, pleasure, good, or happiness (all this in the present case comes to the same thing) or (what comes again to the same thing) to prevent the happening of mischief, pain, evil, or unhappiness to the party whose interest is concerned."[8] Or perhaps, the friend chooses as the text of his sermon one of Bentham's many fulminations on the errors of asceticism: that inversion of manner "approving of actions in as far as they tend to diminish his happiness; disapproving of them in as far as they tend to augment it."[9] To the unconsenting object of this utilitarian instruction, however, every gesture of scrupulous self-denial affirms the family he has temporarily lost, distilling an intangible spiritual pleasure from the viscosity of physical discomfort. Yet the untranslatability of his vow into this alien culture, the seemingly impassable chasm between vegetarianism and filiality on the one hand, and meat eating and imperial civility on the other, compounds his sense of homesickness: "My mother's love . . . haunted me. At night the tears would stream down my cheeks, and memories of all sorts made sleep out of the question. It was impossible to share my misery with anyone. And even if I could have done so, what was the use? I knew of nothing that would soothe me. Everything was strange—the people, their ways . . . their dwellings. . . . Even the dishes I could eat were tasteless and insipid."[10]

Recently, though, the Anglo-Indian landlady of his new digs in West Kensington, and author célèbre of many plates of porridge, has mentioned the curious mushrooming of vegetarian restaurants in the city. And today he has come to Farringdon Street with a mission, determined to find the ominously named Porridge Bowl at 278 High Holborn. Instead he stumbles upon the Central at 16 Saint Bride Street, the sight of which, as he writes later, filled him "with the same joy that a child feels on getting a thing after its own heart."[11] He notices for sale under a glass window near the door a copy of Henry Salt's *Plea For Vegetarianism*. Buying the book for one shilling, he walks into the dining room. We do not know exactly what he ate that day, although his early notes describe in some detail a menu typical of vegetarian eating houses in London for the month of October 1888. There are three varieties of soup (green pea, scotch broth, florador and milk), four kinds of porridge in sugar or syrup (oatmeal, wheaten, maize, and anglo scotch), a choice of lentil cutlets with sprouts, turnips, or tomatoes, and four kinds of vegetarian mains (tomato and macaroni, yorkshire pudding with haricots, curried egg and rice, sprout and baked potatoes). Five puddings offer a grand finale: "college," tapioca and custard, blancmange and jam, maize and peaches, wheat and jelly. There is also a range of stewed fruit, cakes, and cheese.[12] Choosing, we have reason to believe, a six-penny dinner for three courses in the "first division" of the restaurant, over the gourmand "second division" (where "you select your dinner according to your appetite and purse"), he sits down with his book and begins to read hungrily.[13] Some time in the next three years at a vegetarian convention the author, Henry Salt, will meet this young man, who in an unreliable version of this encounter will say with the obstinate singsong of Kathiawar in his vowels, "My name is Gandhi. You have, of course, never heard of it."[14] In a more authentic testimony Salt claims to "remember the now famous Mr Gandhi, who co-operated with us much more willingly than he has since done with the Indian government."[15]

In his compelling and histrionic autobiography *My Experiments with Truth*, composed in Gujarati during a prison term at Yeravada between 1927 and 1929, Mohandas Karamchand Gandhi rates his encounter with Salt's oeuvre as a life-changing experience: "I read Salt's book from cover to cover and was very much impressed by it. From the date of reading this book, I may claim to have become a vegetarian by choice. I blessed the day on which I had taken the vow before my mother . . . vegetarianism . . . henceforward became my mission."[16] Over the remaining three-odd years of his legal studies in London, Gandhi increased his involvement with fin-de-siècle vegetarianism exponentially. He devoured, as he puts it, "all books available on vegetarianism,"[17] including, with particular favor, Howard Williams's *The Ethics of Diet* and Anna Kingsford's *The Perfect Way in Diet*. These urgent private dietetic studies Gandhi supplemented with organizational and evangelical activism. By 1890 Josiah Oldfield, an official of the West London Vegetarian Society, had invited Mohan (as he was known to his friends) to attend the International Vegetarian Congress held at Memorial Hall from 11 to 13 September of that year. By the end of 1891 Gandhi had earned a position on the executive committee of the London Vegetarian Society. In the meantime a generous invitation arose out of his evolving friendship with Oldfield, who offered to make his residence in Bayswater available for the remainder of Gandhi's stay in London.

Totally immersed now in the vegetarian cause, Gandhi contributed a series of nine articles, six on "Indian Vegetarians" and three on "Some Indian Festivals," also his first published works, to the *Vegetarian* between 2 February and 14 March. Acts of cultural translation, these otherwise unremarkable articles are notable for the clues they give us to the wide cultural sympathies of contemporary English vegetarians. The author sentimentalizes the land of his birth *ad nauseam*, testifying sans embarrassment to the endemic worship of cows, the unorthodox tooth-brushing habits of Indian shepherds, the delicious idolatry of his pantheistic faith. So too, although tentatively, he refuses the cultural priority of Europe in matters of physique, religion, and ethics, all the while criticizing the imperial government for a series of admittedly minor misdemeanors, from the deleterious importation into poor India of alcohol, "that enemy of mankind, that curse of civilisation,"[18] to the besetting sin of cultural insularity: "Almost all Englishmen who go to India keep up their own way of living. They not only insist on having the things they had in England, but will also have them cooked the same way . . . One would have thought that they would look into the habits of the people, if only out of curiosity, but they have done nothing of the kind."[19]

Condoned, presumably, for this muted invective by his vegetarian peers, Gandhi's growing confidence in 1891 found expression in an initiative to start a new vegetarian club in Bayswater. He also volunteered a paper on "The Foods of India" at the Waverly Restaurant and was appointed an official delegate of the London Vegetarian Society to the conference of the Vegetarian Federal Union at Portsmouth between 5 and 6 May, an event graced by a plenary paper on "The Return to Nature" by Gandhi's vegetarian hero, Henry Salt. Upon his long awaited but now painful departure for India, the *Vegetarian* featured an interview with this Indian collaborator, in which he gave voice to the relief of having survived England without abjuring his vow, that is, to the simple but substantial satisfaction of returning home more or less unconquered: "I am bound to say that, during my nearly three years' stay in England, I have left many things undone, and have done many things which perhaps I might better have left undone, yet I carry one great consolation with me that I shall go back without having taken meat and wine, and that I know from personal experience that there are so many vegetarians in England."[20]

Gandhi's many biographers are undecided about the true import of his early immersion in English vegetarian affairs. Some like Stephen Hay credit this encounter as a formative initiation into the crucial political skills of biculturalism. "As a bicultural person," Hay writes of his subject, "he would prove able to negotiate with, and on occasions mediate between, both British and Indian National Congress leaders during the decades that led to their peaceful separation . . . Many more years of exposure to both British and Indian ideas and ways were to come, but these London experiences were pivotal ones."[21] For Rajmohan Gandhi, somewhat differently, the concord with English vegetarianism delivers for Gandhi a "vital legitimacy" to "his Indian inner voice," confirming a heady coincidence between the opinions of the advanced "West" and the injunctions of his beloved but illiterate mother.[22] While lending credence to both perspectives in his ever slippery and shifting self-narrations, Gandhi seems consistently to honor the English vegetarians —and their role in his fashioning—as exemplars of hospitality, and it is this reading that I wish to privilege in this chapter.

In the unpublished, twenty-thousand-word manuscript of his "Guide to London," begun in 1893 upon his return to India as an aid to other young Indian students and travelers to the imperial metropolis, Gandhi warmly commends English vegetarian hospitality as a palliative to the alien environment: "the people of the London Vegetarian Society are always kind and hospitable towards Indians and a more genial man than the editor of *The Vegetarian* it would be difficult to find."[23] Indeed, there is ample evidence to confirm Gandhi's experience of the English vegetarians as keepers of uniquely open houses. Oldfield's opening of his home to the Indian foreigner was matched in spirit by a chain of boarding and private homes made available to Gandhi whenever he traveled to Brighton, the Isle of Wight, Ventor, and even Paris. Once, puzzling over a French menu in a restaurant in Brighton, he was approached by an "old lady" who helped him to decipher the card and invited him to dine at her house in London henceforth every Sunday.[24]

While cognizant of being the personal and particular recipient of these favors, Gandhi takes care to generalize vegetarian kindness as a temperamental or ideological receptivity to colonial strangers deterritorialized at the flawed heart of empire. And it is on this faith that he urges all Indian student travelers to knock on vegetarian doors: "Having landed in London, where to go seems to present some difficulty. The editor of *The Vegetarian*, a paper published in London Memorial Hall, Farringdon Street, has kindly consented to give necessary directions and find them the proper lodgings where they can have everything cheap and nice . . . It would, therefore, be a great gain for every

Indian going to England to let the editor know of his doing so."[25] Notwithstanding the comparative dearth of Indian students in London at the end of the nineteenth century, Gandhi brings back to India a palpably excessive invitation from his vegetarian allies.[26] A testimony, we might say, to vegetarian *xenophilia*: that susceptibility to outsiders, aliens, strangers, foreigners, ratified in the enduring Epicurean challenge to the Aristotelian-Hegelian circumscription of community, consolidated in its transmission as a flight from self-identical, self-confirming sociality. But what then of the aetiology of risk integral to this project? The structural demand that in this case, Indian-loving must be accompanied by a readiness for self-estrangement? A willingness, as in E. M. Forster, to "run counter to the claims of the State"?[27] It is worth referring here to a public letter of 24 April 1894 from Pretoria to Indians in England, circulated by Gandhi and subsequently reprinted in the *Vegetarian*. Writing now in the more commanding prose born of increased political agonism, Gandhi informs his Indian readers that collaboration with English vegetarians is a duty, on the grounds, among others, that "the vegetarian movement will aid India politically . . . inasmuch as the English vegetarians . . . more readily sympathise with the Indian aspirations (that is my personal experience)."[28] Here we have it in rudimentary form: secreted within the culture of English vegetarianism, a variety of hospitality or xenophilia whose logical fulfilment may at any time "constitute a felony *contra patriam*,"[29] defying the imperial state in order to honor the "aspirations" of dispossessed (and hungry) Indian visitors. Such "unconditional hospitality," Derrida suggests, rehearses in affective code, and on behalf of the master's household/host culture, a fantasy of surrender, inviting the guest to take the master-host's place, to repossess his territory. In Derrida's words, "It is *as if* . . . then, the stranger could save the master and liberate the power of his host; it's *as if* the master, *qua* master, were prisoner of his place and his power, of his ipseity, of his subjectivity (his subjectivity is hostage). So it is indeed the master, the one who invites, the inviting host, who becomes the hostage—and who really always has been. And the guest, the invited hostage, becomes the one who invites the one who invites, the master of the host. The guest becomes the host's host."[30]

Can we read the vegetarian hospitality encountered by Gandhi in London between 1888 and 1891 as such a fantasy of dispossession, a cloistered invitation to breach the oppressive fabric of imperial housekeeping? Or, to put it simply, as quintessentially anticolonial? That the English vegetarians were anticolonial, or that they manifested themselves as such to the young Gandhi, I will attempt to establish in the following pages. The question of what it was in their peculiar scripture (in the intellectual conjunctures which enabled the evolution of their ethic) that might have made them hospitable to Gandhi in Derrida's sense is rather more complex, inviting consideration of Donna Haraway's claim that rich anticolonial possibilities accrue from ethically informed reassessments of human–animal sociality. As she writes in *Simians, Cyborgs and Women*: "Perhaps . . . we can learn from our fusion with animals and machines how not to be Man, the embodiment of Western logos."[31] It is apropos of Haraway's suggestions that this discussion takes on the tasks of historical inquiry, asking why and how the reformulation of human–animal community at the end of the nineteenth century provided a conduit for mutinous thought, attracting to itself the distinct but contiguous energies of socialism, anarchism, radical evolutionism-Darwinism, and so, anticolonialism. Answering this question is in a sense the chief burden of the following discussion. We will concentrate below on the peculiar accidents whereby late-nineteenth-century animal welfare came into conflict with utilitarianism: that philosophy of governmentality whose force was experienced most directly by the working classes at home, and the colonized races abroad. It is in the working out of this conflict that fin-de-siècle animal liberation in general, and vegetarianism in particular, opened themselves to contemporary radical thought, and in so doing substantially increased the political scope of any subsequent critique of speciesism. Derrida's notion of "hospitality" and Haraway's of a fused "cyborg economy" or "primate order" frame this enquiry.

But before we move on to a fuller application of the Derridean tropes with which we are concerned here, let us record a notable historical detail. As he was preparing to leave London, grateful for the hospitality extended to him by his vegetarian friends, Mohan Gandhi decided to hold a party. Booking for a private gathering the notoriously vegetarian-unfriendly Holborn Restaurant, the young man persuaded the management to cater for a strict vegetarian meal, thus delighting his friends with this parting takeover, or "reterritorialization," of a mainstream eating establishment. He was less successful in his speech, well-meaning but nervous. Nonetheless spirits were high, and in the midst of the ongoing festivities, or so the *Vegetarian* of 13 June 1891 tells us, the president of the London Vegetarian Society, Mr. Arnold Hills, rose and took the floor, with the clear intention of honoring the young Gandhi: "then, in that eloquent and beautiful speech of which he is such a master, proposed the toast of the evening, 'Our host . . .' "[32]

THE COMPANY OF STRANGERS

Let us begin our enquiry into vegetarian anticolonialism by drafting a fuller picture of the groups and organizations that Gandhi is likely to have encountered during his first formative sojourn in England, most but not all of which were vegetarianist, and all of which were without qualification motivated by a comprehensive concern for animal welfare. "Ethically," as Gandhi writes in his autobiography, "they had arrived at the conclusion that man's supremacy over the lower animals meant not only that the former should not prey upon the latter, but that the higher should protect the lower, and that there should be mutual aid between the two as between man and man."[33]

Of these groups those calling themselves "vegetarian" sought their genealogy within a long-standing if distinctly minor western tradition of complaint against meat eating: a discourse well in circulation, as Keith Thomas points out, by the beginning of the eighteenth century.[34] Thus far overdetermined by considerations of health, however, English vegetarianism achieved its specifically ethical provenance in about the 1790s, first gaining popularity among the Swedenborgians and other dissenting sects as an essential accoutrement to a life of restraint and abstention, and then gradually finding expression in an uncompromising critique of kreophagy, or meat eating, as a type of murder. This second, extremist strain in English vegetarian thought owes its inspiration directly to the work of the British soldier John Oswald, whose *The Cry of Nature* (1791), an impassioned denunciation of meat eating as violence, was composed after a close study of Hinduism while the author served as an officer with a Highland regiment in India.[35] Deriving its arguments from "Eastern" sources, Oswald's work played a significant part in ensuring that India would be enduringly identified as a compassionate haven for the animal kingdom and the "West" condemned as a wasteland of anthropocentric brutality and carnage. It is notable in this regard that the most common synonyms for "vegetarian" during the late eighteenth century and the early nineteenth appear to have been "Pythagorean" (in honor of that notable ancient and occidental vegetarian) and "Brahmin."[36] This strain of "orientalist" vegetarianism was readily absorbed and amplified by the second generation of self-professedly iconoclastic romantic poets, reaching its apotheosis with the publication in 1813 of Shelley's *A Vindication of Natural Diet*, a text which merges its hysterical condemnations of kreophagy with the author's signature expostulations against the institutional and authoritarian evils of western life.[37]

Thus leavened in its originary moments by a civilizational contestation well in excess of its basic theme of dietetic reform, English vegetarianism by the time it entered the nineteenth century was primed, we might conjecture, for anticolonial polemic. Certainly vegetarianism, most scholars and historians of the subject agree, mixed in as it was in its transmission with the intellectual and political matter of positive romantic orientalism, millennialism, and indigenous traditions of dissent, was already the preserve of radical counterculture, already possessed of excessive revolutionary aspirations.

For our purposes, the disparate strains of indigenous vegetarianism summarized above first obtained an organizational character in 1847 with the formation of the Manchester Vegetarian Society, which gradually increased its regional base to gain eight hundred official members by 1856 and some five thousand by the end of the century.[38] Appealing in the first instance to minimizing human rapacity vis-à-vis the natural world and its creatures, organized vegetarianism had in no small measure recovered by the last decades of the nineteenth century the wide reformist canvas of its radical forebears.

There is pleasing testimony for the close association of fin-de-siècle vegetarianism and radicalism in a letter written by Oscar Wilde in 1888—the year Gandhi arrived in London—to Violet Fane, in response to her tentative proposal to contribute an essay on vegetarian matters to *The Woman's World*, a journal edited by Wilde between 1887 and 1889. Beginning with a mock paean to the ethereal pleasures of roast snipe and burgundy, Wilde concedes, albeit teasingly, the nonconformist undercurrent of contemporary vegetarianism: "vegetarianism in your hand, would make a capital article—its connection with philosophy is very curious—dating from the earliest Greek days, and taken by the Greeks from the East—and so is its connection with modern socialism, atheism, nihilism, anarchy and other political creeds. It is strange that the most violent republicans I know are all vegetarians: brussel sprouts seem to make people bloodthirsty, and those who live on lentils and artichokes are always calling for the gore of the aristocracy and for the severed head of kings. Your vegetarianism has given you a wise apathy—so at least you told me once—but in the political sphere a diet of green beans seems dangerous."[39]

It seems extremely unlikely in context, given his hungry consumption of vegetarian literature, that Gandhi would have remained unaware of this close identification of dissident politics with the vegetarian cause. We gain indirect confirmation that he recognized contemporary animal welfare as a window onto the scene of late Victorian heterodoxy in the intimate accounts of his life and opinion recorded by his secretary Pyarelal, for whom the significance of Gandhi's early vegetarian activities accrues precisely from their larger political ramifications. Pyarelal writes: "The leadership of the Vegetarian and Anti-Vivisection movements in England was drawn as much from the Thoreau Societies and Walt Whitman groups as from among the Socialists and Fabians. Vegetarianism was part of their humanitarianism and humanitarianism of their socialism. They were socialists because they were humanitarians and because they were humanitarian they were also drawn into the ferment of the vegetarian movement."[40]

This picture of composite politics painted by Pyarelal was realized almost exactly over the years of Gandhi's English adventure, which saw the emergence and consolidation of a range of animal welfare journals and magazines such as the *Vegetarian Messenger*, the *Vegetarian*, the *Animal's Friend*, and *Almonds and Raisins*. After being scattered across these disparate publications, vegetarian opinion finally achieved an "official" link with extra-vegetarian themes through the auspices of the Humanitarian League and its publications. Founded in 1891 (the year of Gandhi's most active involvement with vegetarian matters) and led by Henry Salt, the league sought a clear unity of contemporary radical causes, all the while postulating a necessary continuity between the exploitation of animals and that of human underdogs and scapegoats. "The suffering of animals at the hand of man," as John Kensworthy, a notable member of the league, comments in a representative and somewhat pontifical passage, "is the counterpart, the extension, of the suffering which man inflicts on man. The animals, in short, are equally involved with ourselves in our social conditions. Salvation for man means salvation for animals, but while man suffers, the animals must also suffer."[41] Such was also the burden of a letter which Salt wrote to Gandhi in 1931, affirming his sympathies with the anticolonial movement in India while reiterating the view that imperialism was one of the many perverse manifestations of kreophagy: "I feel as strongly as ever that food-reform, like Socialism, has an essential part to play in the liberation of man-kind. I cannot see how there be any real and full recognition of Kinship, as long as men continue either to *cheat*, or to *eat*, their fellow-beings!"[42] Well before this correspondence explicated Salt's personal allegiances, anti-imperial reserve appears as one in a family of linked humanitarian causes enthusiastically vouchsafed by the *Humane Review*, one of the league's two flagship journals, in its inaugural issue: "Among the subjects dealt with will be: first . . . the treatment of native races, the sweating system, the criminal law and prison system . . . and secondly, the various problems relating to the treatment of animals . . . which subjects will be regarded as part and parcel of the social question, and not as a separate or subordinate branch of it."[43] It is for this issue that Edward Carpenter penned his furious indictment of colonialism in his article "Empire: In India and Elsewhere," discussed more comprehensively in chapter 3.

Among the numerous causes thus harbored under the wide circumference of the league's umbrella, special favor was also extended to the small but vociferous anti-vivisection movement. Formed about 1870 in opposition to the belated growth of experimental or laboratory medicine in England during the last decades of the nineteenth century, the anti-vivisection movement gained momentum and notoriety through the activities of the idiosyncratic Frances Power Cobbe and her Victoria Street Society.[44] Cobbe aimed with little success to introduce effective legislation against experimental medicine. Her labor of love consisted mainly in reforming public opinion through a veritable avalanche of books, pamphlets, letters, petitions, and articles published under her domineering editorship of the journal *Zoophilist*. In circulation within England until 1956, a French edition called *Le Zoophile* was rapidly abandoned after an unsuccessful year in which French readers, much to Cobbe's extreme annoyance, complained about its dryness of tone and underlying atheism.[45] Not especially famed for its organizational harmony, anti-vivisection was often troubled by internecine battles between Cobbe and other leader-aspirants; among these was the accomplished and beautiful Anna Kingsford, whose *The Perfect Way in Diet* remained, we might recall, one of Gandhi's favourite vegetarian tracts. His contact with Kingsford's cause was greatly assisted through his evolving friendship with her collaborator and amanuensis, the mystic Edward Maitland, with whom he maintained regular correspondence until Maitland's death in 1897.[46]

Although much narrower in scope than the vegetarian movement with which it was eventually conjoined through the good offices of the Humanitarian League, the anti-vivisection movement retained through its links with Theosophy and contemporary spiritualism a profound and abiding interest in eastern religion and ethics. In this way it provided an important link with the orientalist vegetarianism of the late eighteenth century. For the same reason, however, it often tried the patience of its rationalist adversaries in the august establishments of nineteenth-century science and medicine, gaining a reputation for acute eccentricity to match, often with very good cause, the reputation for crankishness long enjoyed by contemporary vegetarians. As Harriet Ritvo observes, "By the early years of the twentieth century antivivisection had become a fringe movement, appealing to an assortment of feminists, labour activists, vegetarians, spiritualists, and others who did not fit easily into the established order of society."[47] Such then was the company that made up Gandhi's social circle in England toward the end of the century. How, we may now ask, did they manifest—if at all—their dietetic and affective anticolonialism to the callow youth in their midst?

ANTI-COLONIAL HOSPITALITY

On 29 January 1898 the *Vegetarian* published an interview with Dadabhai Naoroji, three times president of the Indian National Congress and the first Indian member of Parliament, presumably on the assumption that as an Indian he would extol unequivocally the virtues of a vegetarian diet. Early in the piece, however, Naoroji disabuses the interviewer—the bluff and genial Raymond Blaythwayt—of this misperception by declaring himself a committed carnivore. Undeterred by this confession, Blaythwayt presses on: "you are a very anti-British ruler and naturally enough pro-native . . . your views are sure to please my readers . . . you will meet with their approval in every sense of the word, unless, indeed, your avowal of non-vegetarianism doesn't rather horrify them."[48] If accustomed to anticolonial polemic, as Blaythwayt's comment reveals, the readers of magazines like the *Vegetarian* were more often than not primed for this strain in their dietary credo through consistent exposure to essays and opinions valorizing and promoting difference against the cultural monochrome of Empire.

Frequently purveying fawning interviews with notable Indians and Indophiles, and reports on their activities, animal welfare publications peppered their fare with informative articles on Indian customs and manners, among which were included, as we have seen, Gandhi's youthful perorations on Indian vegetarianism and Hindu festivals. English contributors, many of them entirely untraveled, were not far behind in offering encomia of "Eastern" ways. A typical article in *Almonds and Raisins* insists "that in gentleness to the dumb creation, Europe has much to learn from Asia"; and in a similar vein, Annie Besant describes India as a veritable nation of St. Francises to the *Animal's Friend*: "So in India you will find man after man in whom this same spirit of love and compassion is seen, and in the woods and the jungle and on the mountain these men may go wherever they will, and even the wild beasts will not touch them."[49]

Besant's unapologetic Indophilia here is matched, much like that of her other vegetarian compatriots, by an unusual culinary cosmopolitanism. In an interview with the *Vegetarian* in 1898, she publicizes her high opinion of Indian cuisine:

> "Do you mind telling me what is your favourite food?"
> "Dal and rice."
> "The former you bring over from India, don't you?"
> "I used to, but I don't now, so I only get the dal when I am in India; here I eat beans and lentils. I prefer the dal and rice, however, it is lighter and more nourishing."[50]

The paucity of authentic dal in London at the fin-de-siècle notwithstanding, vegetarian restaurants were rather more eclectic and imaginative in their menus (surely more likely to appeal to Indian or Indianist palates) than their nonvegetarian counterparts. We have some evidence for the relative monotony of nonvegetarian cuisine in Behramji Malabari's ethnography of the English, *The Indian Eye on English Life* (1893). While generally enthralled by English culture, Malabari finds indigenous English food sadly wanting: "In no respect does the average Englishman show himself so slow of imagination and wanting in taste as with respect to his daily food . . . As a rule the Englishman's dinner is plain and monotonous . . . The cook knows nothing of proportion in seasoning his food . . . The cookery is often worse than the materials, which may be seen any day hung up in the shops; carcasses of large animals and small . . . The sight is invariably unpleasant, and the smell is at times overpowering."[51] In defiance of this bleak picture, the numerous gormandizing recipes regularly printed in vegetarian publications appear to pride themselves precisely on generating variety in the preparation of food. Something of this effort is reflected in the oftentimes culturally diverse fare on offer at vegetarian restaurants. A review in the *Vegetarian Messenger* in January 1887 of the new Orange Grove eating house in St. Martins Lane, Charing Cross, lavishes praise upon the ecumenical board, which includes "Macaroni and Indian sauce," "Macaroni Napolitane," and the enticingly named "Home-Rule Potatoes." The same review is accompanied by an advertisement for tofu, or "Japanese bean-curd."[52]

During his time in London Gandhi would undoubtedly have seen, in pleasing testimony to the small but loyal demand for Indian cuisine, regular advertisements for pre-cooked and somewhat indistinguishable Indian preparations; the most widely featured was a curious notice for "Briggs Muscle-forming Indian Food," sold in tins "for 10d and 1 1/6," and accompanied by a picture of a ferocious, turbaned Indian with alarming pectoral development. This image and its message about the bodybuilding properties of Indian vegetarian food would have struck a deep chord with Gandhi, addressing if not allaying colonial anxieties about the myth of Hindu effeteness: that ubiquitous fable common to English imperialists and their Indian nationalist counterparts, attributing the conquest and enslavement of India to the physical enervation of the malnourished Hindu male body. It is worth pursuing this theme in some greater depth, for it holds in some ways the key to the direct political import of English vegetarianism for Mohan Gandhi.

Macaulay is relevant here, setting the tone for a pervasive imperial critique of Indian physical culture in one of his many damning verdicts on Indian civilization: "The physical organisation of the Bengali," he asservates, "is feeble even to effeminacy. He lives in a constant vapor bath. His pursuits are sedentary, his limbs delicate, his movements languid. During the many ages he has been trampled upon by men of bolder and more hardy breeds. Courage, independence, veracity, are qualities to which his constitution and his situation are equally unfavourable."[53] Quickly absorbing this stereotype into a negative self-image, Bengali intellectuals (the principal object of such imperial invective) had by the 1860s and 1870s, as John Rosselli observes, launched into a fervor of self-castigation, variously blaming environment, climate, and most of all the errors of national diet for their deficient masculinity. Thus they consolidated a schema in which vegetarianism emerged slowly but surely as the baneful signifier of colonial vulnerability. As Rosselli claims, "Diet was often invoked. Bengalis ate too much; or they ate too little . . . A rice diet, short of meat and other animal products was 'weak and innutritious.' "[54]

Of the many figures leading the charge for revivifying the national body politic none was more commanding than the charismatic Swami Vivekananda, who promoted "Beef, Biceps and Bhagvat Gita" as the reinforced tonic that would dispel the symptoms of colonial slavery. Needless to say, he was less than sympathetic to Hindu vegetarianism, as he reveals in a fiery letter of 24 April 1897 to Sarala Ghosal, editor of *Bharati*: "About Vegetarian diet I have to say this . . . So long as man shall have to live a Rajasika (active) life under circumstances like the present, there is no other way except through meat-eating. It is true that the Emperor Ashoka saved the lives of millions of animals by the threat of the sword, but is not the slavery of a thousand years more dreadful than that? Taking the life of a few goats as against the ability to protect the honour of one's own wife and daughter, and to save the morsels for one's children from robbing hands—which of these is the more sinful? . . . the forcing of vegetarianism upon those who have to earn their bread by labouring day and night, is one of the causes of the loss of our national freedom."[55]

Many of these ideas spread into the Gujarat of Gandhi's childhood, coming into sharp conflict with the strict vegetarianism of his predominantly *vaishnav* and *jain* milieu. As he tells us in his autobiography, an older friend particularly susceptible to this wave of "reform" eagerly alerted Gandhi to the pernicious links between vegetarianism and colonial subordination: "We are a weak people because we do not eat meat. The English are able to rule over us, because they are meat-eaters."[56] Simple logic, reinforced in doggerel composed by the Gujarati poet Narmad ("in vogue," as Gandhi tells us—with an unflagging eye for fashion—"amongst us school-boys"): "Behold the mighty Englishman / He rules the Indian small, / Because being a meat-eater / He is five cubits tall."[57] Converted under peer pressure to a medicinal regimen of meat (until the fateful vow to his mother in 1888), the young Gandhi readily identified vegetarianism with colonization and meat with anti-colonial freedom: "It was not a question of pleasing my palate . . . I wished to be strong and daring and wanted my countrymen also to be such, so that we might defeat the English and make India free."[58]

However much we might underestimate the role of Gandhi's English vegetarian companions in his political formation, there can be no doubt that they were instrumental in freeing him at the very least of his specifically dietetic colonial anxieties, and so too of defying the physiognomic basis of imperial argument. Tract upon tract in animal welfare literature contradicts the correlation between vegetarianism and colonial enfeeblement, simultaneously mocking the long association of beef and virility in English national culture.[59] *Almonds and Raisins* denounces "Britain's twin superstitions, beef and beer," and Anna Kingsford's erudite *The Perfect Way in Diet* assails as entirely false "the opinion that flesh-food contains the elements of physical force." The "most capable workers among animals," she maintains, "are precisely those which never taste flesh-meat: Their force and their endurance are invincible and surpass beyond comparison that of their beef-fed masters."[60] Almost always such protestations are buttressed by detailed testimonies about the unique strength-giving properties of a vegetarian diet. Henry Light's *Common-Sense Vegetarianism* is a case in point, ratifying its dietetic commendations with photographic accounts of boxing champions who practice vegetarianism "only when in training and desirous of attaining the highest form," and of unbeatable fruit-eating marathon runners completing 26 miles on hilly ground in a mere "2 hours 29 minutes 54¼ seconds."[61] Examples closer to Gandhi's home and heart appear in Ernest Crosby's encomia to meat-averse native races: rice-fed Hindu coolies in Calcutta capable of carrying a chest which four able-bodied Englishmen could scarcely lift; a bean-eating Egyptian *fellahin*, moving with agility despite the two trunks strapped to his back "in a way that would take away an Anglo-Saxon porter's breath to look at it."[62]

Notwithstanding the consolations made available through such case studies, it is only in its more naïve moments that the literature of animal welfare works its arguments into a field of rudimentary oppositions in which the series beef–Europe–imperial strength is replaced, defiantly, with the contrasting but hopelessly contingent series vegetarianism–native races–anti-colonial vigor. Far more interesting is the ideological tactic by means of which the discourse equating beef with imperial virility is hoist with its own petard, such that colonialism is rediagnosed precisely as the lamentable affliction of kreophagous virility. An occasion for elaborating a competing and "improved" masculinity, this tactic dovetails with the literature of homosexual apologetics, discussed in chapter 3, in its insistent attribution of all social evil to the straitjacketing of gender identity. "True manhood," as an article in the *Vegetarian* demurs, inheres in the capacity to master the cravings—in this case for sex and meat—of physical nature.[63] An earlier essay in the same journal on 18 February 1899 appeals for a restitution of "true" masculinity in the face of its "brute" counterpart. "Again and again," the author proclaims, "let us din it into the ears of a careless world that this is not a manly age, and that beefy-mindedness is not another word for manliness, but only a very excellent synonym for cruelty and every form of bestiality."[64]

What the cruelties attending beefy-mindedness might involve becomes the subject of a lampoon in the single mock-issue of *The Brutalitarian: A Journal of the Sane and Strong*, published in October 1904 by the Humanitarian League. Asserting the monstrous kinship of blood sport, flesh eating, vivisection, war, and imperialism, the issue showcases, in a column called "Words of the Wise," a fulmination from G. W. Steevens in praise of brute masculinity: "This (the new humanitarianism) is throttling patriotism and common sense and virility of individual character . . . Our forefathers burned, and marooned, and beheaded and shot, and fought cocks . . . So they bred hardihood. Brutes as you may call them, on these unhumanitarian principles they built the British Empire."[65] Q.E.D. For it is precisely upon the head of beefy masculinity that animal welfare lays the sin of imperialism, isolating in cruelty to animals the first cause of all consequent errors of European supremacy. As Salt opines in his *Killing for Sport*: "Under the fostering wing of Imperialism, brute force is developed more and more into a political science . . . The Englishman, both as soldier and colonist, is a typical sportsman; he seizes on his prey wherever he finds it with the hunter's privilege. He is lost in amazement when men speak of the rights of inferior races, just as the Englishman at home is lost in amazement when we speak of the rights of the lower orders. Here, as yonder, he is kindly, blatant, good-humoured, aggressive, selfish, and fundamentally *savage*."[66]

What Gandhi may have made of these ideas is beyond the scope of the present discussion. The animal welfare groups that he met did make available to him, as we have been claiming, an ultimately hospitable discourse, in Derrida's sense: hopeful in the main of surrendering the prerogatives of the (imperial) master's house, and excoriating *en passant* the figure(s) of beefy masculinity—that corpulent phantom haunting the scenes of colonial lack—as the pernicious link in a chain connecting cruelty toward other species with the exploitation of other races. In his mature political life Gandhi continued to invoke the concerns and metaphors of vegetarianism and anti-vivisection, famously describing the partition of India as a vivisection of the subcontinent, the final and cruelest cut of imperial rationality. In addition, fin-de-siècle animal welfare demonstrates a deeper discursive claim upon that association of unharmfulness and anticolonialism, compassion and anti-imperialism, fundamental to the rudimentary grammar of Gandhian *ahimsa*. But in Gandhi's characteristically idiosyncratic idiom, this trope meaning "non-violence" is also (and bafflingly) elaborated as a rhetoric of revolutionary obstinacy, a refusal of government, a character signifying the courage of contradiction. Itemized variously in his oeuvre as "passive resistance," "boycott," "non-cooperation," and "civil-disobedience," it is invoked again toward the end of his eventful life as a synonym for "anarchy," bearing the promise of his last, unfulfilled dream of India as an ungoverned society. So in the essay "Enlightened Anarchy: A Political Ideal," published in 1939, Gandhi argues that India can only achieve a condition of true *ahimsa* if it agrees to an experiment in statelessness, for the reason that the very structures of governance are hopelessly contaminated by violence, or *himsa*: "Political power, in my opinion cannot be our ultimate aim . . . In an ideal State there will be no political institution and therefore no political power. That is why Thoreau has said in his classic statement that that government is the best which governs the least."[67] Writing on the subject a year before the advent of Indian independence in "Congress Ministries and *Ahimsa*," Gandhi reiterates the conviction that Indian freedom can only be substantial as a freedom from all "rule": "I am convinced that so long as the army or police continues to be used for conducting the administration, we shall remain subservient to the British or some other foreign power, irrespective of whether the power is in the hands of the Congress or others . . . We might remember though that a Stateless society does not exist anywhere in the world. If such a society is possible it can be established first only in India."[68]

What possible connection can there be between this idiosyncratic rendition of ahimsa and the more straightforward embargo on human violence toward the "lower animals" rehearsed in the inchoate thoughts of the early Gandhi? It is my contention that Gandhian ahimsa obtains at least some of its semantic density from the self-definition of late Victorian zoophilia precisely as a resistance to what we have learned, after Foucault, to call "governmentality"—a resistance poised on the estimate that if modern power was a pathological form of nonrelationality, achieving its most pernicious dimension in the sequestering logic of imperialism, then its refutation had to proceed from the rehearsal of unmediated or immediate and extreme forms of relation between beings with "vastly different phenomenologies and ontologies," that is, across genders, races, classes, and paradigmatically across the species barrier. This unacknowledged strain in late Victorian animal welfare would prove crucial, I submit, to the affectivity and anticonstitutionalism of Gandhian ahimsa and, congruently, to his anti-imperialism. It is to the elaboration of this strain as an explanatory context for the seemingly ragged genealogy of ahimsa that I will now turn my attention. To pursue these themes with any seriousness, however, we must change our looking glass, substituting our interest in late Victorian denunciations of those who were palpably cruel to animals for a perspective on their conflicts with their contemporaries who were kind to animals. For what Gandhi encountered at the scene of animal welfare between 1888 and 1891 was not only a movement newly committed to the well-being of animals but also one split into a civil dispute between two pro-animal lobbies. One, which I call the "fin-de-siècle animal welfare" group, consisted of the cranks and eccentrics with whom Gandhi kept company, and while interested in legal reform it was principally concerned with achieving an improved affective relationship between the human and the animal worlds, between mice and men. The other, which I call the "early animal welfare" group, was much more respectable, mainstream, and closely linked to the Royal Society for Prevention of Cruelty to Animals (RSPCA); it did its work through the channels of legislative parliamentary reform. Coincidentally, the theoretical executors of the utilitarian position were also the architects of colonial government in India.

It is the quarrel between these two factions, as I will argue in the following sections, that comprehensively distilled the anticolonial essence of Gandhi's friends, bringing their politics more in line with the socialist-anarchism of his own later years. There is an interesting anecdote worth retelling, en route to this theoretical exegesis, that offers direct narrative evidence of at least a minor traffic in anarchist ideas between Gandhi and fin-de-siècle animal welfare. In 1929 Henry Salt was engaged in helping a friend to write a fuller version of his own "Life" of Henry David Thoreau, sage of "civil disobedience," and a man who Salt believed had "a constitutional *No* in him . . . part of his mission to question, to deny, to contradict."[69] Curious about Gandhi's relation to Thoreau's thought, he composed the following letter on 18 September 1929, his first to the Mahatma: "You will hardly remember me; but I had the honour of seeing you mention my book, 'A Plea for Vegetarianism,' in a translation of your Autobiography, and I once saw you, I think, at the office of the Humanitarian League in London. On the strength of this, I am taking the liberty of writing to you. Some forty years ago I published a Life of Thoreau . . . and an American friend of mine is now collecting material for a new and fuller Life . . . In the last letter which I received from this friend . . . he asked me whether I thought that *you* had been a reader of Thoreau, and had at all been influenced by him, as on many subjects your views and Thoreau's seem rather akin . . . That is the cause of this letter."[70]

The sixty-year-old leader of Indian nonviolent civil disobedience and noncooperation replied to Salt on 22 October 1929: "I was agreeably surprised to receive your letter. Yes, indeed your book which was the first English book I came across on vegetarianism was of immense help to me in steadying my faith in vegetarianism. My first introduction to Thoreau's writings was, I think in 1907, or later, when I was in the thick of passive resistance struggle. A friend sent me Thoreau's essay on civil disobedience. It left a deep impression upon me . . . That essay seemed to be so convincing and truthful that I felt the need of knowing more of Thoreau, and I came across your Life of him, his 'Walden' and other short essays, all of which I read with great pleasure and equal profit."[71]

UTILITARIANISM, ANIMAL RIGHTS, AND COLONIALISM

To argue the case for the socialist-anarchist anticolonialism of Gandhi's friends, we need to examine the peculiar political and ideological pressures that shaped their emergence at the fringes of late Victorian culture. Significant in this regard is the way they defined themselves against an earlier and dominant tradition of animal welfare well in place by the beginning of the nineteenth century. The years 1800, 1802, 1809, and 1810 each witnessed efforts to introduce into the English Parliament legislation for the prevention of cruelty to animals. These efforts finally bore fruit in 1822, when a historic bill, introduced in the Commons by Sir Richard Martin, member for Galway, succeeded in extending protection to "Horses, Mares, Geldings, Mules, Donkeys, Cows, Heifers, Bull Calves, Oxen, Sheep, and other Livestock." Henceforth anyone having charge of these creatures and caught wantonly beating, abusing, or ill-treating them was liable for a fine of between ten shillings and five pounds, or imprisonment for up to two months.[72] These stirrings of Parliamentary reform to improve the condition of animals in the early decades of the nineteenth century also inspired efforts to create an effective vigilante organization committed to animal protection and legislation that furthered it. Attempts were made to form such a society in Liverpool in 1809 and again in London in 1822, until in 1824 a group including Richard Martin met in a tavern in London to launch the Society for Prevention of Cruelty to Animals (SPCA), officially committed to bringing about in the sphere of "morals" the changes that Martin had introduced within the law. The SPCA was always better established and more respectable than the Manchester Vegetarian Society (and its various affiliates), which it preceded by over two decades. Favored from its inception by the patronage of the rich and famous, in 1840 it secured permission from Princess Victoria to prefix the much-coveted "Royal" to its name.[73]

Few early reformers directly called themselves "utilitarian," but the Victorian milieu of organized and official benevolence to which they laid claim was, to borrow some words from F. R. Leavis, "in a general sense utilitarian."[74] It was utilitarianism, as Keith Thomas has argued, that implicitly animated the "mode of thought which . . . as Cowper put it . . . wished 'all that are capable of pleasure pleased,' and although its main implications were for the human species, whether slaves, children, the criminal or the insane, the relevance to animals was inescapable."[75] Indeed, so comprehensively did utilitarian philosophy capture in its inception the ethical foundations of animal welfare that even today philosophers of contemporary animal liberation like Peter Singer continue to insist that utilitarianism alone comprehends and enables the appeal to the maximizing of pleasures and the equal consideration of interests that gives the animal world any chance for justice in the face of anthropocentric dominion. As Singer avers, "we very swiftly arrive at an *initially* utilitarian position once we apply the universal aspect of ethics to simple, pre-ethical decision making . . . The utilitarian position is a minimal one, a first base which we reach by universalising self-interested decision making. We cannot, if we are to think ethically, refuse to take this step."[76]

It is not incidental, in this regard, that the first serious mention of rights for animals comes directly from the pen of Jeremy Bentham, popularizer of the adage that civility and rationality proceed only and always from consideration of the greatest happiness of the greatest number. In a footnote to a larger discussion about ethics toward the end of his monumental *An Introduction to the Principles of Morals and Legislation*, Bentham records the words that would arguably change the status of animals in the eyes of the law, thus confirming his position, Singer writes, as "perhaps the first to denounce 'man's dominion' as tyranny."[77] Here is the substance of Bentham's footnote: "The day *may* come when the rest of animal creation may acquire those rights which never could have been witholden from them but by the hand of tyranny . . . The French have already discovered that the blackness of the skin is no reason why a human being should be abandoned without redress to the caprice of a tormentor. It may come one day to be recognised, that the number of legs, the villosity of the skin, or the termination of the *os sacrum*, are reasons equally insufficient for abandoning a sensitive being to the same fate . . . the question is not, Can they *reason*? Nor, Can they *talk*? But, Can they *suffer*?"[78]

It is widely acknowledged that Bentham's footnote strikes a significant blow to western anthropocentrism, and it does so in a grand gesture of philosophical iconoclasm so typical of his style. In making the question of animal rationality irrelevant to the right of animals to protection from human cruelty, he directly refutes a position defended by Kant in a series of lectures on ethics in 1780, the same year that Bentham completed the manuscript of his *Introduction*. Justifying the subordination of animals on grounds of their deficient rationality, Kant, it may be remembered, acquits "man" of any ethical obligation toward brute creation: "So far as animals are concerned, we have no direct duties. Animals are not self-conscious, and are there merely as a means to an end. That end is man."[79] Thus crossing swords with Kant, Bentham's claim about the unimpeachable validity of animal suffering, based on their status as sensate beings, also posits a direct and plain dismissal of Descartes's earlier decree that animals are incapable of pain or sensation, since they are mere machines or automata.

Many early animal reformers claimed direct inspiration from Jeremy Bentham. Lord Erksine, for example, putative author in 1809 and 1810 of the abortive bills for preventing cruelty to animals, diligently paraphrased Bentham's contentious defense of animal sensation in the course of a heated Parliamentary debate. "Almost every sense," he asserted to the unsympathetic Commons on 15 May 1809, "bestowed on man is bestowed on them; seeing, hearing, feeling . . . the sense of pleasure and pain."[80] Not everyone was as much impressed by the indiscriminate democratization apparently endorsed by the utilitarian discourse of rights. The self-fashioned "platonist" Thomas Taylor, for one, wrote an impassioned critique of the political costs likely to attend the profligate expenditure of privileges upon inferior beings. "We may therefore," he protests in his tract *A Vindication of the Rights of Brutes* (1792), "reasonably hope, that this amazing rage for liberty will continually increase; that mankind will shortly abolish all government as an intolerable yoke; and that they will as universally join in vindicating the rights of brutes, as in asserting the prerogatives of man."[81]

But in Taylor's critique we are, I submit, in face of a supreme misunderstanding. In Benthamite hands the language of rights, far from conspiring to an overthrow of government, is principally if not exclusively concerned with amplifying government activity to a vertiginous degree. If available to reading as a subsidiary history of nineteenth-century benevolence, the story of utilitarian-inspired animal rights also contains in microcosm the secret history of modern governmentality. This is the crux on which the ensuing discussion turns, and to understand it better we must return once more to Bentham's famous and influential defense of animal rights. Here, in the text framing his footnote, we find arguments for increasing both the scope and scale of the law, that *summum bonum* of utilitarian theology. What, then, is the burden of Bentham's argument?

The question of our relation to other humans and to other animals, Bentham opines, is properly speaking the subject of private ethics, or "the art of directing men's actions to the production of the greatest quantity of happiness, on the part of those whose interest is in view."[82] But maximizing happiness requires policing individual desires to such a degree that morals, to quote Halevy on Bentham, "assume a commanding governmental nature."[83] From the perspective of utility, Bentham insists, "private ethics and the art of legislation go hand in hand. The end they have or ought to have is of the same nature."[84] However, if ethics and legislation, so defined, are of the same epistemic family, what is to prevent their active collaboration, making "legislation," again in Halevy's words, "a special branch of morals"?[85] Nothing—since for Bentham the ethical subject is intrinsically the consenting object of legislation, and conscience, concomitantly, is that critical rupture in the fabric of the otherwise integral self through which the law can enter, without breaking, to work with and upon the innermost recesses of the empathetic individual. It is this process, whereby utilitarianism transforms the "man of feeling" into the ideal citizen, that Foucault has in mind in his famous exculpation of Bentham as the genius behind "what might be called in general the disciplinary society": the bid, in other words, to achieve an automatic functioning of power that transforms the moral subject into the author of her own subjection and lends to the exercise of modern government the opaque features of "governmentality."[86] Where once, Foucault argues, the offending individual experienced power as a singular force exerted ritually, violently, as a constraint from the outside, the utilitarian intervention achieved the opposite: reducing the costs of government and capitalizing on the unmanageable increase of human population through an inspired dispersal of power within "the cumulative multiplicity of man."[87] We will return to Foucault later: understanding the precise techniques by which utilitarian governmentality is held in place is a prerequisite to identifying the principles upon which its undoing might proceed. For the moment, however, I simply wish to argue that the distinctly utilitarian inspiration for early animal welfare—in Parliament and through the activities of the RSPCA—makes itself visible in a sustaining will to governmentality, one authorized to enforce the habits of conscientious obedience upon all those with underdeveloped or untutored natures: women, children, the working poor, the inferior races.

A closer examination of early animal reform, most historians of the movement agree, reveals a constitutive class bias and a relentless subjection of the working classes to increased scrutiny from the law, as the subtly widening sphere of amerciable transgressions made the task of policing the poor gradually overwhelm the ostensible commitment to protect animals.[88] These features are deployed as arguments against animal protection as early as 1800 by William Windham, parliamentarian and conservative champion of "old" English ways. In response to William Pultney's proposed bill, in that year to prevent bull baiting, Windham contends that the sentiments of animal welfare are doubly tainted: by a deplorable, myopic prejudice against the sports of the poor (while the equally bloodthirsty sports of the rich are disregarded), and by a mean spirit of legislative intrusiveness: "This petty, meddling, legislative spirit," he maintains, "cannot be productive of good: it serves only to multiply the laws, which are already too numerous, and to furnish mankind with additional means of vexing and harassing one another."[89]

That early animal welfare offers a pretext for meddling governance is amply revealed in Pultney's arguments on behalf of his defeated bill, condemning bull baiting not only because "the practice was cruel and inhuman" but chiefly because of its multiple "inconveniences" to gentlemen. The sport, he argued, "drew together idle and disorderly persons; it drew also from their occupations many who ought to be earning subsistence for themselves and families; it created many disorderly and mischievous proceedings."[90] Pultney's sentiments are endorsed and reiterated by most subsequent would-be legislators for animal protection in the early decades of the nineteenth century. William Wilberforce finds in the embargo on blood sport a means of checking the lamentable profligacy of the working classes; the Hon. Mr. Smith similarly approves legislation against cruelty to animals as an opportunity to "raise" the working poor "in the scale of behaviour . . . to cultivate their manners and to instruct them in the principles of morality"; Lord Redesdale complains that the main evil in bull baits is their "great terror and annoyance to the neighbourhood"; and the redoubtable Lord Erskine sees in legislation to improve the condition of post-horses a welcome chance to discipline the insubordination of their drivers.[91]

These legislative efforts to civilize and invigilate the working poor through the welfare of their animals were corroborated by the activities of the RSPCA. In its inaugural meeting of 1824, for instance, the chairman noted in acutely utilitarian jargon that the object of the fledgling organization was not only "to prevent the exercise of cruelty towards animals, but to spread among the lower orders of the people . . . a degree of moral feeling which would compel them to think and act like those of a superior class."[92] But of course, as we know from Bentham, such self-governing moral acumen needs careful supervision and training, or, in the language of the RSPCA, "eternal vigilance" from the superior classes.[93] Such was the motivating watchfulness that S. S. Monro, RSPCA secretary for Tunbridge Wells, demanded as late as 1890 in a pamphlet called *Hints to Workers in the Cause of Humanity*. Urging all users of the notorious London cabs to observe, from the state of mouth and fetlocks, that "hired animals were not overworn," Monro also exhorted respectable householders vigilantly to "notice the condition of animals used in bringing coals or any household or other goods to our houses."[94] To achieve more professional supervision over the "butchers, drovers, carmen, grooms, coachmen, farm servants, railway servants, domestic servants," under suspicion in Monro's pamphlet, the RSPCA by 1838 employed permanent and paid inspectors authorized to impose the law and deliver wrongdoers into the arms of overtaxed local magistrates. An illustration of 1833 shows a voluntary RSPCA inspector engaged in such service, directing (with the approving collaboration of a well-dressed and overfed owner of a pedigree dog) a duly disreputable-looking bird seller to deliver his (now happy) captives into the unfriendly London sky.[95]

In every way, and as Windham had predicted in 1800, early animal welfare substantially increased the intrusion of the law into the lives of the poor to render them capable of self-regulative obedience. Notably, it is precisely in praise of this increased government interference that John Stuart Mill underwrites, in his *Principles of Political Economy* (1848), the achievements of early animal welfare, a tradition provoked in no small part, as we have seen, by the labors of his famous predecessor: "The reasons for legal intervention in favour of children, apply no less strongly in the case of these unfortunate slaves and victims of the most brutal part of mankind, the lower animals. It is by the grossest misunderstanding of the principles of liberty, that the infliction of exemplary punishment on ruffianism practised towards these defenceless creatures has been treated as a meddling by government with things beyond its province; an interference with domestic life. The domestic life of domestic tyrants is one of the things which it is most imperative on the law to interfere with."[96]

Claimed as a means to justify the regulation of the working classes, indirectly, through the rhetoric of animal welfare, Mill's defense of government interference also points the way, directly, to the colonial imperatives of utilitarian philosophy. His advocacy of untrammelled legal intervention is framed by utilitarianism's abiding "romance" with governmentality, one articulated within the defining paradigms of what Asa Briggs has so fittingly defined as an "age of improvement": the confident period between 1783 and 1867 guided by Macaulay's conviction that "the history of our country during the last hundred years is eminently the history of physical, moral, and of intellectual improvement."[97] In this milieu, so preoccupied with enumerating indices for progress, utilitarianism offered yet another benchmark, taking the view that nothing marked the distinction between savagery and civilization more acutely than the difference (and distance) between natural or nongovernmental society on the one hand and political or governmental society on the other. To put it simply, where savage men in a state of nature lacked habits of obedience, and therefore a right to democracy, civilized or political men were constitutively obedient and congruently deserving of democratic privilege. As Bentham maintains, "governments, accordingly, in proportion as the habit of obedience is more perfect, recede from, in proportion as it is less perfect, approach to a state of nature."[98] Receiving this gift of government from within a discourse of "improvement," political men, we might add, were also entitled if not obliged to spread the gospel of governmentality as a civilizing mission. So it is that Mill rewrites colonialism as the forcible attempt to civilize or governmentalize the East—the ends, as always, justifying the means. For "those backward states of society in which the race itself may be concerned as in its nonage," Mill observes, "the early difficulties in the way of spontaneous progress are so great, that there is seldom any choice of means for overcoming them; and a ruler full of the spirit of improvement is warranted in the use of any expedients that will attain an end, perhaps otherwise unattainable. Despotism is a legitimate system of government in dealing with barbarians, provided that the end be their improvement, and the means justified by actually achieving that end. Liberty, as a principle, has no application to any state of things anterior to the time when mankind have become capable of being improved . . . Until then, there is nothing for them but implicit obedience."[99]

The younger Mill's justification of colonialism as the principled rectification of inadequately governmental societies directly echoes similar arguments proffered by his father, James Mill, in the infamous *The History of British India.* This detailed invective against Indian customs and manners, composed, as the author confesses, without the strength of a single visit to the country, paints a picture of unmitigated barbarism. Mill withholds the prerogatives of civilization from India on both familiar Hegelian grounds (the lack of "history" or "historicism" in the East) and familiar utilitarian grounds (the absent traditions of law, government, and obedience, in Indian culture). "So bad a government as theirs," he argues voluminously, begs the intervention of "a great man, full of the spirit of improvement . . . to induce a people, jealous and impatient of all restraint, to forgo their boundless liberty, and submit to the curb of authority."[100] The lasting and popular appeal of these utilitarian maxims is confirmed in Kipling's "Servants of the Queen," a story from *The Jungle Books* in which a chieftain from Afghanistan, accustomed to a world where "we only obey our wills," is informed that imperialism is the price for unregulated sociality: " 'And for that reason,' said the native officer, twirling his moustache, 'your Amir whom you do not obey must come here and take orders from our Viceroy.' "[101]

Eric Stokes, in the company of a few other scholars, has convincingly demonstrated the intimate philosophical contribution of utilitarianism to the formulation of colonial government in India. And as is well known, several notable utilitarians were directly involved in the business of Indian administration. In 1819 James Mill entered the executive government of the East India Company as an assistant examiner, to be duly promoted to the chief executive office in 1838. His son, J. S. Mill, followed suit as the company's chief conductor of correspondence with India in the matter of native states between 1823 and 1858. Both father and son, Stokes argues, saw their service as a means to achieve "practical realisation of the utilitarian theories," thus fulfilling Bentham's abiding interest in the reform of Indian legislation. Bentham's papers reveal plans to frame a constitutional code for India, and his influence guided a generation of utilitarian Indian administrators, intent on realizing "the simple authoritarian logic of the Utilitarian mind" through an administrative and judicial machinery that "continued to supply the daily framework of State action to the end of British rule and beyond."[102] This was the machinery that Gandhi encountered during his political struggles in imperial India, struggles whose emphasis on a vocabulary of conscientious law breaking ("disobedience," "resistance," "boycott," "non-cooperation") can now be read in context as a direct rebuttal of specifically utilitarian governmentality: the vast bureaucracy of British officials that Pyarelal excoriates in Gandhian terms for "its domineering habits and tradition of unquestioning obedience."[103]

To gather this discussion into the larger themes of our argument, what bearing does this utilitarian compact with colonialism have upon the history of fin-de-siècle animal welfare? To reiterate: it is our claim that through a series of accidents the history of late-nineteenth-century animal welfare gets caught up in the utilitarian project of producing a disciplinary society, one whose force is felt at home by the indigenous working classes (incidentally through the evolution of legislative animal reform), and abroad by the colonized races. This enmeshment of animal welfare and governmentality or disciplinarity is, I propose, challenged in two ways by the fin-de-siècle dissidents whom Gandhi meets in London between 1888 and 1891. The first, easier to apprehend, consists in their efforts to detach the project of animal welfare from the surrounding utilitarian agenda by making it perversely and directly coextensive with the liberation of the domestic working classes and the foreign colonized races—in other words, transforming animal welfare into an associated form of socialism and anticolonialism. Less obviously but possibly more profoundly, fin-de-siècle animal liberationists undo the symbolic logic of class- and race-oppressive (or colonial) governmentality by recasting, as we mentioned at the very outset of our discussion, human-animal relations as an enlightened model of anarchic, disobedient, and paradigmatically nongovernmental sociality, which in time Gandhi would call ahimsa. These procedures are inextricable and interdependent.

UNDOING GOVERNMENTALITY: CYBORGS AND SOCIALISTS

To proceed with the reading of fin-de-siècle animal welfare hinted at above we need to draw upon Foucault's analysis of the precise techniques of utilitarian disciplinarity, most palpable, he claims, in the model of Bentham's Panopticon or ideal prison. This model, Foucault asserts, is designed to keep inmates in a condition of constant, exposed visibility (subjected to "eternal vigilance") and eventually the perpetual, impassive and impersonal gaze from the central watchtower translates itself into the guilty and unforgiving eye of self-regulatory conscience. But the law of visibility enshrined in the structure of the Panopticon also relies heavily upon, and complements, its harsh architecture of separation. The technique of "disciplinary partitioning" constructed through the isolating cell walls makes each inmate singularly visible to the supervisor and in so doing simultaneously "prevent[s] him from coming into contact with his companions."[104] What is the logic of panoptical separation? How is the project of power *qua* disciplinarity served, its catechisms of obedience rehearsed, through these concrete cell dividers controlling the relations of men?

Within the Benthamite model, Foucault explains, it is understood that the inmate can only interiorize the disciplinary eye of power comprehensively if he is compelled into a state of extreme, pathological individuation: quarantined from collectivities, from their affective distractions and their tendency to foment (in collaboration, through conversation) the logic of counterdiscourse, countermanding the singularity of any law. As Foucault writes, "discipline . . . must . . . master all the forces that are formed from the very constitution of an organised multiplicity; it must neutralise the effects of counter-power that spring from them and which form a resistance to the power that wishes to dominate it: agitations, revolts, spontaneous organisations, coalitions—anything that may establish horizontal conjunctions. Hence the fact that the disciplines use procedures of partitioning and verticality, that they introduce, between the different elements at the same level, as solid separations as possible, that they define compact hierarchical networks, in short, that they oppose to the intrinsic, adverse force of multiplicity, the technique of the continuous, individuating pyramid."[105]

The inextricability of disciplinarity and the logic of separation made physically manifest in the Panopticon recurs at a discursive level throughout Bentham's writings. The work of the early Bentham, especially, conveys the clear sense that unmediated relationality, the horizontal arrangement of the "face-to-face" relation, or what he calls "conversation," is constitutively antithetical to the vertical axis of power along which are arranged the motions of obedience, the disciplinary rotations of governmentality. Formulating this schema in terms of the distinction between "natural" and "political" society in his *A Fragment on Government*, Bentham notes the following: "When a number of persons (whom we may style *subjects*) are supposed to be in the habit of paying obedience to a person, or an assemblage of persons . . . (whom we may call governor or governors) such persons altogether (subjects and governors) are said to be in a state of *political* society . . . When a number of persons are supposed to be in the habit of *conversing* with each other, at the same time that they are not in any such habit as mentioned above, they are said to be in a state of *natural* society."[106] That is to say, the condition of horizontal, direct, or immediate relationality—relationality sans obedience—equals a state of prepolitical, nongovernmental, and anarchic sociality. Governmentality becomes shorthand for the improved culture of mediated relationality: the superintending third term in a pyramidal structure continually interrupting the even groundwork of dialogic communication, compelling conversants to address each other henceforth only through the intercessory language of law. So it is that of the many nightmares that beset modernity, one in particular looms large, translating, to borrow some words from John Durham Peters, the "spectre of the mesmerised mass in the clutches of the leader" into "the fear of the lonely crowd, atomised and mutually oblivious."[107] In other words, the privileges of govermentality require the sacrifice of direct conversational pleasure. Vice versa, the unmediated "face-to-face" relation must eschew (or undo) the civilizing conveniences of disciplinarity.

It is relevant to our argument that Bentham's allergy to immediate relationality is accompanied by a corresponding nausea for untrammeled "feeling," "sentiment," "emotion"—the glue, that is, of affective affiliation. "Among principles adverse to utility," he writes in the *Introduction*, "that which at this day seems to have the most influence . . . is what may be called the principle of sympathy."[108] Elsewhere in the text he condemns the "caprice" of sympathy or sentiment as intolerably "anarchical."[109] In a well-known passage, J. S. Mill similarly testifies in his *Autobiography* to utilitarianism's informing suspicion of feeling: "the cultivation of feeling (except the feelings of public and private duty) was not much in esteem among us, and had very little place in the thoughts of most of us, myself in particular . . . we did not expect the regeneration of mankind from any direct action on . . . sentiments."[110]

Although addressed primarily to the problematic of human sociality, utilitarianism's credo on behalf of separation and against the claims of sentiment also spread by contagion in the nineteenth century, showing its symptoms within all available circuits of interaction: between human and divine and also between human and animal. Accordingly, most spokesmen of early animal reform render feeling or excessive sympathy between the species at best irrelevant and at worst detrimental to the cause of animal liberation. They are also determined that an equal consideration of animal interests does not in any circumstances imply an equivalence between human and animal interests.[111] Typically, Bentham is assiduously unsentimental in his defense of animal rights and insistent upon the hierarchy and unbridgeable gap separating human sensibility, whose capacities and claims are always privileged, and animal sensibility: "If the being eaten were all, there is very good reason why we should be suffered to eat such of them as we like to eat: we are the better for it and they are never the worse. They have none of those long-protracted anticipations of future misery which we have. The death they suffer in our hands commonly is, and always may be, a speedier, and by that means a less painful one than that which would await them in the inevitable course of nature. If the being killed were all, there is very good reason why we should be suffered to kill such as molest us; we should be worse for their living, and they are never the worse for being dead."[112]

Carrying these Benthamite principles into Parliament, William Wilberforce defends animal welfare as a distinguishing feature of human rationality, destined to prevent "man" from turning into the "brutes" vulnerable to his cruelty. As we are informed in the report of the Parliamentary debate against bull baiting in 1802, "He was certain . . . he would no longer defend a practice which degraded human nature to a level with the brutes."[113] This insuperable barrier between benevolence and affinity, legislation and affect, takes an interesting turn in John Kipling's study *Beast and Man in India (1891)*. Citing as examples of Indian prepolitical anarchy both the cruelty of Indians to their animals and the unpalatable consubstantiality of Indian animals and humans, Kipling's book catalogues the grotesque admixture of human and animal in Hindu iconography, the unwholesome proximity of *mahouts* with their elephants, the bizarre bed sharing of tigers and their tamers.[114]

But of course it is precisely this mode of affective consubstantiality that fin-de-siècle animal welfare invokes—as a means of transforming the very heart of human cruelty, but also as a symbolic means of dismantling the overriding principles of disciplinary partitioning. As mentioned earlier, in terms strikingly close to the concerns of our discussion, Donna Haraway poses throughout her corpus the struggle of colonial and anticolonial energies as a contestation between two types of identity: the one accruing from a culture of self-contained, self-reflexive humanism, the other from the permeable boundaries and mixed spaces of a "cyborg economy" or "primate order." Colonialism, she maintains, expresses a cloistered subjectivity: "individuation, separation, the birth of the self, the tragedy of autonomy . . . alienation, that is, war tempered by imaginary respite in the bosom of the other." And anticolonialism, by contrast, may well find its radical feet upon the uneven territory of self-dissolving coalition, affinity, and relationality, namely in the anarchic, "interdigitations of human, machine, non-human, animal or alien, and their mutants in relation to the intimacies of bodily exchange and mental communication."[115] Our historical subjects seem to anticipate Haraway's cyborg economy, entering into symbolic conflict with utilitarian governmentality in two ways that we will elaborate below: first, through a defiant discourse of zoophilia, or love for animals, and second, through the argument that the practice of such interspecies love itself paves the way to an enlightened, affective socialism, susceptible in its turn, and with some help from Charles Darwin, to the themes of anarchist anticolonialism.

The ideological fissures in nineteenth-century animal welfare, with which we are concerned here, first manifest themselves in the antipathy of fin-de-siècle radicals toward the anthropocentric condescension that they see at work in the efforts of early reformers, specifically their assiduous policing of the boundaries of humanity. The clearest statement of this critique appears in Salt's *Cruelties of Civilisation* as a contrast between two competing varieties of humanitarianism, the one redundant and obsolete, the other purveying the ethical materials for a utopian future. "Old-fashioned 'philanthropy,' on the one hand, or 'kindness to animals' on the other," Salt writes, "is now perceptibly on the wane"—giving way, we might interpolate, to a more comprehensive regard for sentience. The crucial difference is this: "This older humanitarianism was a form of benevolence which regarded the objects of its compassion, whether the 'lower orders' or the 'lower animals' with a charitable and merciful eye, but from a rather superior standpoint of unapproachable respectability . . . The new humanitarianism, on the contrary, clearly sees that the function of the beneficent 'superior person' is henceforth out of date, and the barbarous practices which still disgrace our civilisation can be successfully combated on no other ground than that of the broad, democratic sentiment of universal sympathy."[116]

Salt's distinctions prove to be ubiquitous, structuring the representative literature and endorsed by most major journals. "Sentiment," as the *Humanitarian* declares in the inaugural volume of its new series, "however fools may decry it, is the mainspring of progress, and the man who is devoid of sentiment—that is of feeling—is a dullard and a dunce."[117] A characteristic issue of the *Animal's Friend* likewise emphasizes the view that animal welfare begins with the cultivation of reciprocal friendship between humans and animals. "Those poor dumb beasts and birds," an impassioned contributor writes, "would most of them fain to be our friends if we would allow it . . . and if we are too hard-hearted and selfish to be *their* friends and protectors, then it would seem there is something nobler in them than in us."[118] In most of these writings, true to the spirit of earlier romanticism, sentiment is clearly assumed to be a critical faculty crucial to the ethico-political transformation of the prevailing social order. Searching for authorities to support this view, most writers find a sympathetic ally in Schopenhauer, whose *On the Basis of Morality* is enthusiastically received for its "unequivocal inclusion of the non-human races within the scope of ethics," its equally unequivocal annexation of feeling or compassion as "the sole source of disinterested action and the only moral incentive," and last but not least, its ratification of feeling as a salve for "the barbarism of the West."[119] Such is the spirit in which the parodic single issue of the *Brutalitarian*, cited earlier, posits "sentimentality" as a countermanding force against the perils of "manliness and patriotism": "It is full time . . . that some trumpet-tongued protest were raised against the prevalent sentimentality, and that there should be an attempt to organize and consolidate the forces . . . We think our party has hitherto made two great mistakes in its attitudes towards the sickly sentimentalists of the Humanitarian League and other bodies attempting to undermine the vigour of the national character. In the first place we have underrated the ability of these faddists to do mischief . . . Secondly, we have made the mistake of quibbling over words, of trying to pose as the true 'humanitarians' . . . instead of avowing and glorying in the fact of our anti-humanitarian principles . . . and standing loyally shoulder to shoulder—Imperialist with sportsman, sportsman with vivisectionist."[120]

While more or less unanimous in the affective thrust of their radicalism, most representatives of the group are at pains to variegate the many applications of "love," and the means for its cultivation. Henry Salt, for instance, discloses an affective askesis in the art of poetry, finding in its renunciation of epistemic certainties (in favor of the inchoate language of the heart) techniques for dissolving the disciplinary partitions that mar human rationality. His critique of contemporary education is revealing in its appeal for the restitution of the "soft" disciplines, and its equation of the "humanities" with "humane-ness": "the weightiest charge against University education is one which least often finds expression—that a learning which would strengthen the intellect only, and does not feed the heart, is in the main but barren and unprofitable, a culture of the *literae inhumaniores*."[121] Salt's favored champion (along with Schopenhauer) against anthropocentric rationality is, predictably, Shelley, described by him ad nauseam as the exemplary man of feeling, one whose largeness of heart is eo ipso a capacity for transgression, unmindful of the sequestering categories of race, class, gender, and of course species. Affect, in other words, is privileged as the defining property of Shelley's poetic war against separation. "There is nothing more delightful in Shelley," Salt observes, "than the utter absence of the 'superior person' . . . both as regards his human and non-human fellow beings. Whenever he speaks of animals, it is with an instinctive, child-like, and perfectly natural sense of kinship and brotherhood."[122]

Much like Salt, Frances Power Cobbe also places poets at the vanguard of the sentimental revolution, honoring them especially as beacons for animal welfare in her curious anthology of animal verse, *The Friend of Man; and His Friends—the Poets.* Celebrating those poets capable of conjuring the irreducible particularity of animal–human sociality, Cobbe defends affect as the ability to register the conjunctural singularity of all relationship. She poses her arguments against the maximizing and universalizing protocols of utilitarian ethics, which she describes as the "coldest of philosophies," and defends zoophilia as an aggressively minoritizing perspective, ineluctably partisan, defiantly immediate.[123] Where, she argues, the undiscriminating eye of benevolence or philanthropy makes no distinction between one dog and another, treating all as grist to the mill (or, indeed, the Bentham) of utility, the committed zoophile is incapable of "polydoggery," that "thing against which all feeling revolts."[124] Relentlessly particularizing the animals of her acquaintance in *False Beasts and True*, Cobbe lovingly details the unique criminality of one as against the signatory intensity of another, elsewhere valorizing the "divine law of love" as a force against the utilitarian calculus of pleasure and pain: "we might reasonably have hoped that in our day we should have certainly ceased to hear much of 'Rights' and 'Duties'; and certainly that these dry as dust definitions would not have been set up as a barrier against the extension of duty to the lower animals."[125]

If eccentric to say the least in her passionate zoophilia, Cobbe's intensities are entirely overshadowed by those of her fellow anti-vivisectionist rival and ally, the occultist Anna Kingsford. What appears in the prose of others as protestations on behalf of "sympathy" or "feeling" becomes in Kingsford's practice a form of acute psychic excess, elaborating itself in visionary dreams of agonizing self-identification with tortured animals. A gothic dream about a house leaking blood from secret animal experimentation onto the suburban street below provokes in the dreamer feelings of "despair," "anguish," and claustrophobia, while in another dream, recorded as "The Laboratory Underground," animals reveal themselves to Kingsford in human form, insisting on the unacknowledged kinship of species: "Then they brought a rabbit and thrust its eyes through with hot irons. And the rabbit seemed to me, as I gazed, like the tiniest infant, with a human face, and hands which stretched appealingly towards me, and lips which tried to cry for help in human accents." From this dream she wakes, "sobbing vehemently."[126]

A strong advocate of the theory of spontaneous hydrophobia, Kingsford often defends the view that dogs become rabid in reactive fear of vivisection and human persecution.[127] Thus, commending dog-love as a natural vaccine against rabies, Kingsford's career also chronicles an incremental and corresponding mistrust of the human race which finds expression once again in her vivid dream life, through anarchic fantasies of violence against leading vivisectionists: "Yesterday" she records, "November 11, at 11 at night, I knew that my will had smitten another vivisector! . . . for months I have been compassing the death of Paul Bert, and have but just succeeded . . . *I* have killed Paul Bert as I killed Claude Bernard; as I will kill Louis Pasteur, and after him the whole tribe of vivisectors."[128]

To summarize, the trope of "love" in fin-de-siècle animal welfare symbolically resists the credo of separation and the embargo on "sentiment" underscoring utilitarian governmentality. Additionally, it prepares the route to contemporary utopian socialism, through an internal logic that makes "love" a synonym for ascetic "sacrifice" and the simplification of life—the dissolution, in other words, of the disparity between rich and poor, the owning and the laboring classes.[129] "Love is sacrifice," thunders Henry Light in his *Common-Sense Vegetarianism*, "the perfected article finally breaks the bonds that would restrict its exercise to but one person, one family, one country, one race, or even one person. Love is noble, not selfish."[130] In strong agreement with this position, Cobbe hails for its demonstration of exemplary sacrifice the story from the end of the *Mahabharata*, in which Yudhishtra refuses to enter heaven without the dog (really his divine father in canine disguise), who has mysteriously attached itself to his company upon the wasteland after Kurukshetra: "Nothing in any literature . . . affords any parallel to the wonderful moral conception of a Duty of Fidelity owed—not by a Dog to a Man, but—*by Man to his Dog*; a duty calling on him for the sacrifice of beatitude itself. We may smile in our smug Utilitarianism at such an idea as this, but the poet of the Mahabharata was one of those Seers of whom I have spoken."[131]

It is the imperatives of zoophilia as sacrifice or affective self-denial that inform condemnations of the sports and fashions of the rich as "indulgent," "luxurious," "greedy," and "superfluous." The Humanitarian League is again representative, excoriating in its New Charter of 1896 the indolence and vanities of upper-class cruelty: "It is a settled opinion among our idle and wealthy classes, that the taking of animal life is an enjoyable and reputable pastime . . . the Prince of Wales and the German Emperor sitting—*sitting*, mark, behind their screens, with an elaborate equipment of guns and array of attendants, and shooting down the poor little half-tamed birds by scores, are, from any sane point of view, ridiculous . . . And now their lust for slaughter carries them over the world; the man—and sometimes the woman too—who goes abroad must bring back as trophy the skin, the tusk, or claw of something he or she has killed."[132] Where once cruelty to animals bespoke the brutality and profligacy of the laboring poor, it now becomes a signifier of conspicuous consumption: an indelible trail of blood connects the milliner's workshop, the glover's boutique, the aristocrat's hunting fields, the colonizer's touristic pursuit of exotic big game. In this regard, the league clarifies its class sympathies quite clearly through several contentious campaigns, especially those against the respectable traditions of the Royal Buckhounds and the Eton Beagles.[133] Throughout such campaigns Salt is at pains to emphasize the contrasting class hypocrisy of early reformers: "It is not as widely known as it ought to be that since the prohibition of bull and bear baiting, more than half a century ago, there has been particularly no further mitigation of those so-called sports which in this country absorb a great part of the thoughts and energies of the wealthier classes."[134]

Such condemnations of recreational class-indulgence are matched by the contiguous discourse of vegetarianism which takes as its target the culinary excesses of kreophagy. In this vast literature, perhaps the most coherent and influential case for vegetarianism as the key to the simplification of life comes from Count Leo Tolstoy. His *The First Step*, written in the first instance as a preface to the Russian translation of Howard Williams's *The Ethics of Diet*, condemns meat eating on two counts: as self-indulgent gluttony, in which "killing . . . is called forth only by greediness and the desire for tasty food," and as giving rise to an industry that relies, for the satisfaction of a few palates, upon the exploitation and dehumanization of a whole underclass of slaughterers, butchers, drovers, and cooks. As Tolstoy writes: "A moral man, living a life of comfort, a man even of the middle class (I will not speak of the upper classes, who daily consume to satisfy their caprices the results of hundreds of working days), cannot live quietly, knowing that all he is using is produced by the labour and crushed lives of working people."[135] Painting a vivid picture of the army of servants and workers required to bring a nonvegetarian meal to an affluent table, Tolstoy's lament for the labor involved in meat production finds many sympathizers among contemporary radicals. Kingsford, one of the few vegetarians in the anti-vivisectionist lobby, is especially eloquent in her anticipation of Tolstoy's objections. "Is it morally lawful" she asks, in *The Perfect Way in Diet*, "for cultivated and refined persons to impose upon a whole class of the population a disgusting, brutalising and unwholesome occupation . . . ? . . . Butchers are the pariahs of the Western world."[136]

Henry Salt too is characteristically devout, and his crusade for the cult of vegetarian abstemiousness becomes the subject of an affectionate satire in E. Nesbit's *New Treasure Seekers*. An episode in the story shows the reluctant Bastable children being packed off for a disastrous holiday to the austere household of a man, clearly an amalgam of Salt and Edward Carpenter, called Eustace Sandal. Committed along with his sister to the bare and bald principles of "Plain living and High thinking," he is described as "a vegetarian and a Primitive Social Something, an all-wooler, and things like that . . . as good as he can stick, only most awfully dull." Suffering from acute food anxieties—for what can be expected from a household where milk and bread are the food of choice rather than of punishment?—the children receive plenty, "but all of a milky, bunny, fruity, vegetable sort."[137]

Although alarmingly acute in her teasing exposé of the puritanical condiments in vegetarian food culture, there is one regard in which Nesbit confuses the ethos of early animal reform and the RSPCA with that of contemporary humanitarianism and vegetarianism. Portrayed as a man determined to improve the working classes, the hapless Mr. Sandal suffers an accident, bringing welcome relief to the Bastables' tedious holiday, when climbing up a scaffolding to lecture an already teetotaling worker about the perils of alcohol: "he fetched down half a dozen planks and the workman, and if a dust-cart hadn't happened to be passing just under so that they fell into it their lives would not have been spared."[138] Unlike Sandal, however, Salt et al. are not in the least preoccupied with converting or "improving" the working poor. If anything, their espousal of vegetarianism takes its cue from a movement distinguished, at least since the formation of the Manchester Vegetarian Society in 1847, by a strong working-class constituency well reflected among the readers and contributors of journals such as the *Vegetarian Messenger* and subsequently the *Vegetarian*. The *Vegetarian Messenger* in particular abounds in testimonies from working-class vegetarians insisting upon the productive symbiosis, on ethical and dietetic grounds, between meat abstinence and a life of manual labor. In one issue in 1856 a man from the "heavy-edge tool trade" attributes his legendary strength and focus to a staple diet of scotch oatmeal.[139] "Vegetarianism and Manual Labour," a pamphlet published later in the century by the Vegetarian Society, likewise testifies to the vegetarian achievements of the preceding decades: "we may well maintain that our system is adapted to hard manual labour . . . when we find puddlers, shinglers, moulders, forgemen, blacksmiths, engineers and platers living well, and doing their work well upon a vegetarian diet."[140]

The class affiliations that mark vegetarianism are less evident among the anti-vivisection movement. Often criticized for its predominantly middle-class constitution and discourse, this lobby nonetheless enters the odd field of animal welfare socialism, if inadvertently, through two routes. First, it takes for its target the overweening middle-class composition of the scientific and medical establishment, and the battle is applauded and endorsed by the *Animal's Friend* specifically in class terms: "We do not propose to merely save dumb animals from vulgar cruelty inflicted by ignorant carters and drovers and quietly consent to their torture at the hands of persons who call themselves 'men of science.'"[141] Second, anti-vivisection enters the discursive field of late-nineteenth-century socialism—specifically, its rhetoric of love as sacrifice—through a complex formulation of scientific knowledge as the epistemic greed of the educated classes, thereby redefining abstinence as a willingness, on affective grounds, to sacrifice the dubious benefits of experimental medicine. This is the reasoning that informs Kingsford's condemnation of contemporary science as a voracious "desire to know." In her words: "There are certain means of acquiring knowledge of which man cannot make use without forfeiting his place in the Divine Order."[142] Articulated widely and across a range of forums, anti-vivisectionist exhortations against the experimental indulgences of medical science are often addressed to women medical students. In 1888, for example, the *Zoophilist* launches a concerted campaign against the participation of students at Girton and Newnham in vivisectional demonstrations conducted at Cambridge by Professor Michael Forster. Drawing on the familiar antinomies of sacrificial love and selfish rationality, the journal urges women to greater self-consciousness about the perils that might attend the selfish, hungry pursuit of their education: "It is a consciously self-regardful and *only* a self-regardful sacrifice in which the student takes part. It follows that her natural feelings of pity and pain . . . are subdued for the sake of purely intellectual instruction . . . Love and tenderness, are made to give way to that thirst for knowledge which, at its best and purest, is an inferior part of our being."[143]

So, to recall our paradigms, fin-de-siècle animal welfare posits a counter-discourse against the procedures by which the doctrine of "separation" brings the force of governmentality, by degrees, specifically to bear upon the working classes. Its appeal to direct interspecies "love" or sympathy defies the mediating logic of disciplinarity. Moreover, in its sacrificial modality—that is, as a form of "abstinence," "self-restraint," "simplification"—the language of zoophilia paves the way for socialist class critique, exposing upper-class blood sport and fashion, kreophagy, and experimental science as selfish ruling-class luxuries. But there is one other minor footnote to this story: this war against disciplinary partitioning and its ideological consequences also gains immeasurably from the claims of Darwinian evolutionism. Darwin's hypotheses, especially his insistence upon the interconnectedness of sentient life, enables the fin-de-siècle politics of love that we have been discussing to transform itself into a "creed of kinship." This credo, as I will suggest briefly below, is instrumental in translating the ethics of human–animal sociality, once again by degrees, into a subtle form of anarchist anticolonialism.

CHARLES DARWIN AND ANTICOLONIAL ANARCHISM

On 27 December 1831 Charles Darwin sailed out aboard the *Beagle* on a voyage he would describe in time to come as "by far the most important event" in his "life and . . . whole career."[144] This opportunity, we might note in passing, was entirely framed by colonial imperatives. The cartographic investigations of the *Beagle* along the South American coast were intended to furnish the admiralty with information to assist in future military and commercial operations, and also, in the words of Janet Browne and Michael Neve, to "enable Britain to establish a stronger foothold in these areas, so recently released from their commitment to trade only with Spain and Portugal."[145] Ever susceptible to such designs and aspirations, Darwin's own commitment to British expansionism is revealed in a glowing encomium to Empire recorded toward the end of the *Journal of Researches*, which is devoted to his amateur naturalist and anthropological musings. "It is impossible," he writes, "for an Englishman to behold these distant colonies, without a high pride and satisfaction. To hoist the British flag, seems to draw with it as a certain consequence, wealth, prosperity, civilisation."[146]

In large part, Darwin's patriotic fervor and singular failure of sympathy with the "native" races he encounters is fashioned by a distinctly utilitarian view: that because these races lack recognizable forms of government, mediation, and obedience they also lack civilization, progress, and improvement. As he observes of the tribes in Tierra del Fuego: "The perfect equality among the individuals composing these tribes, must for a long time retard their civilisation. As we see those animals, whose instinct compels them to live in society and obey a chief, are most capable of improvement, so is it with the races of mankind. Whether we look at it as a cause or a consequence, the more civilised always have the most artificial governments."[147] Yet, and inadvertently, the evolutionary train of thought to which Darwin succumbs during the voyage of the *Beagle* comes eventually to contravene the principles of governmentality —certainly as they have been identified in the preceding discussion.

Darwin's accidental and indirect countermand to governmentality appears to have been provoked by a little bird, the American ostrich or "Rhea," replaced in southern parts of the continent by a different but closely allied species. The peculiar geographical distribution of the Rhea sets Darwin firmly on the course of contemporary evolutionary speculation, particularly in its challenge to earlier naturalist assumptions about the immutability of species. From the beginning of the nineteenth century most evolutionary thinkers were agreed that far from being fixed within bounded taxonomic categories species became mutable through principles of lineal descent, changing constitution in the slow transition from vanishing to extant forms. To this advance in nineteenth-century evolutionism Darwin acknowledges his debt in *The Origin of Species*: "Some few naturalists . . . have believed that species undergo modification, and that the existing forms of life are the descendants by true generation of pre-existing forms."[148] But Darwin's *Origin* poses an even more radical challenge to earlier theorists of the immutability of species. Dispensing with the current notion of separate lineages, according to which mutation only occurs vertically in a linear series linking one species in the dead past to one in the living present, Darwin proffers two modifications. First, he claims, species also branch horizontally in time, so that any given species might leave a variety of seemingly disparate descendants all intimately related to each other through shared ancestors. Second, dramatically extending the first observation, Darwin asserts the single origin of all extant species: "Several classes of facts . . . seem to me to proclaim . . . plainly, that the innumerable species, genera and families, with which this world is peopled, are all descended . . . from common parents."[149] It is this notion of a shared community of descent which fuels Darwin's contention that all sentient life is therefore knitted together in an "inextricable web of affinities."[150] As he writes, with rising excitement, in a notebook entry of 1837: "If we choose to let conjecture run wild, then animals, our fellow brethren in pain, diseases, death, suffering and famine—our slaves in the most laborious works, our companions in our amusements—they may partake [of] our origins in one common ancestor—we may be all netted together."[151]

It is not hard to imagine why Darwin's hypotheses would be of revolutionary significance to late Victorian advocates of unmediated human–animal relationality. In particular, and with reference to our larger discussion, his characterization of sentient life as an inextricable web is eagerly absorbed within fin-de-siècle animal welfare as a theorem for radical cosmopolitanism, authorizing intimacy with apparent strangers and facilitating, for our purposes, the anticolonial hospitality of which Mohan Gandhi becomes a direct beneficiary. Thus, refusing to concede propinquity or "similarity" as a prerequisite for community, Salt's *The Creed of Kinship* invokes Darwin to transform zoophilia, and its claims on behalf of interspecies relationality, into a rehearsal ground for xenophilia, and its unpartisan favor toward foreign guest-friends. Condemning imperial patriotism and nationalism in these terms, he evokes the subtle pleasures of imaginative identification with strangers and outsiders: "in a happier age than any the world has seen it will be possible, and indeed necessary, that each individual, while not less conscious than now of the claims of neighbourhood, shall also be moved by a wider regard for the well-being of others—of those who are at present looked upon as 'outsiders'—and by a determination that they shall not be sacrificed to any interests or supposed interests of his own."[152]

Salt's sentiments are ubiquitous in the literature of fin-de-siècle animal welfare, and no writer of note fails to see in Darwinian evolutionism a means of recasting the political as a demand for the claims of strangeness over propinquity, alterity over similarity, or, as Howard Moore puts it in *The Universal Kinship*, as a struggle between "altruistic" and "provincial" ethics.[153] And in each case, Darwin is invoked to confer a new status upon animal welfare, corroborating the view that human–animal sociality holds the key, as in Haraway, to a more generally egalitarian world. The "culture of sympathy," as a writer for the *Vegetarian* avers, is subject to "the law of exercise," and a tutored identity with the animal world tends accordingly "to strengthen our sympathies in all direction."[154] But while Darwin's metaphor of a "web of affinities" finds tacit political expression in these ways, it is his attending theory of ecological cooperation that achieves, once again despite his intentions, direct revolutionary articulation.

Even as nature, represented variously in *Origin* as a branched "tree" or "coral," confirms the kinship of sentient life, it also, Darwin argues, demonstrates in the apparently harsh economy of its selective procedures the necessity of cooperative coadaptation between successful species, augmenting the subtle relation of life forms with a demand for their interactive sociality. Changes in one organism directly produce contingent effects in all other organisms with which it interacts in the prevailing ecosystem, thus creating complex genetic material. Thus the evolving structure of woodpeckers, for example, will depend in large part on successful relations established between previous generations of woodpecker and coeval tree, bird, and insect forms. In Darwin's words, "As natural selection acts by competition, it adapts and improves the inhabitants of each country only in relation to their co-inhabitants."[155]

In due course, Darwin's view of nature as "a tangled bank" demonstrating the complex interdependence of palpably different organisms falls into the hands of the anarchist Peter Kropotkin, settled in England from 1886 and a close ally of Salt's circle.[156] Reformulating anarchism as the law of immediate and cooperative sociality or "mutual aid," Kropotkin gains from Darwin a case for the irrefutable amity at work in the animal world. As he observes apropos of evolutionary thought in his *Mutual Aid*, "we maintain that under *any* circumstances sociability is the greatest advantage in the struggle for life. Those species which willingly or unwillingly abandon it are doomed to decay; while those animals which know best how to combine, have the greatest chances of survival."[157] Such animal sociability, however, is entirely natural, operating without the intrusive mediations of governmentality and the law, providing a model for cooperative human association. Indeed, Kropotkin writes, the jealous, vertically organized State has historically resisted the horizontal circuits of voluntary association, curtailing the affective intensities between people: "It was taught in the Universities and from the pulpit that the institutions in which men formerly used to embody their needs of mutual support could not be tolerated in a properly organised State; that the State alone could represent the bonds between its subjects . . . The absorption of all social functions by the State necessarily favoured the development of an unbridled, narrow-minded individualism. In proportion as the obligations towards the State grew in numbers the citizens were evidently relieved from their obligations towards each other. In the guild . . . two 'brothers' were bound to watch in turns a brother who had fallen ill; it would be sufficient now to give one's neighbour the address of the next paupers' hospital."[158]

Kropotkin is not by any means the only conduit for anarchism into late Victorian England.[159] But his intervention at this scene is crucial for the concerns of the present discussion, explicating through a specifically Darwinian model of human–animal sociality the terms of conflict and contestation between the discourse of immediate love, relationality, and affect, extolled by fin-de-siècle animal welfare, and the discourse on behalf of separation and against the claims of feeling that underpins the grim protocols of Benthamite or utilitarian governmentality. A crucial node in the complex historical processes which gave to fin-de-siècle animal welfare a distinctly anarchist provenance, Kropotkin's ideas are amplified and echoed throughout the literature associated with this movement. Leo Tolstoy's influential writings on vegetarianism are typically shaped by a profound mistrust of ruling institutions; Elisée Reclus, friend of Kropotkin, early theorist of "mutual aid," and author with Ernest Crosby of *The Meat Fetish*, consistently combines vegetarian apologia with a demand for the end of all government; and Edward Carpenter, the homosexual activist, vegetarian, and anti-vivisectionist encountered in chapter 3, seamlessly connects his own belief in a Darwinian creed of kinship with entreaties for nongovernmental sociality.[160] These are also the imperatives operating behind Henry Salt's lifelong appeal in the name of zoophilic kinship for an end of government at home and abroad, that is, in its class and imperial manifestations. "Oppression and tyranny," he claims in *Animal Rights*, "are invariably founded on a lack of imaginative sympathy; the tyrant or tormentor can have no true kinship with the victim of his 'justice.'"[161]

A complex ideological mixture of affective socialism and post-Darwinian evolutionary anarchism sustains the anticolonial hospitality, in the Derridean sense, that fin-de-siècle animal welfare offers to Gandhi between 1888 and 1891. But what is visible in the first instance as hospitality becomes over time a form of ideological parity, as Gandhi, much in the manner of his early companions, distils in the affective language of ahimsa the prose of anarchist refusal, demanding that the British quit India and that independent India in turn quit governmentality. Is this a case of influence? Most certainly. In very large part the business of my argument has been to claim that mature Gandhian politics owes at least part of its inheritance to the inchoate murmurings of a few radicals on the margins of late Victorian culture. But, equally, in a gesture—let's call it "postcolonial"—that Salt would doubtless condone, it has also been my purpose to offer a Gandhian reading of fin-de-siècle animal welfare, to assert under the comprehensive sign of ahimsa the integrity and organicity of its various and seemingly disparate obsessions: zoophilia, anticolonialism, affect, the simplification of life, class critique, socialism, cosmopolitanism, kinship, and anarchism. Let us end, in honor of anticolonial collaboration, with a somewhat clumsy poem that Salt wrote about Gandhi toward the end of his own life. It is called "India in 1930":

> An India governed, under alien law,
> By royal proclamation,
> By force, by pomp of arms, that fain would awe
> Her newly-awakened nation;
> While he who sways the heart of Hindustan,
> To more than Kingship risen,
> Is one old, powerless, unresisting man,
> Whose palace is—a prison![162]

5

GOD

Mysticism and Radicalism at the End of the Nineteenth Century

At the end of the nineteenth century numerous European men and women, some more gifted than others, arrived in India in the hope of finding a guru and a spiritual vocation. Indeed, we could safely argue that by the last decades of the nineteenth century India had become the principal reference point for a vast array of non-Christian spiritualities and spiritualists. It was also, of course, the principal reference point for empire. Yet emerging as they did against the backdrop of fin-de-siècle radicalism in Europe, which offered a heady blend of mysticism, socialism, suffrage, vegetarianism, (homo)sexual politics, and anti-imperialism, many western seekers assumed an easy continuity between their spiritual attachment to India on the one hand and their disidentification from the spoils and circuits of imperialism on the other. Despite their strong sympathies for the claims of anticolonial nationalism then taking form in India, however, critics and historians in our own time (in India and elsewhere) tend to view the spiritual proclivities of a Sister Nivedita or Edward Carpenter with suspicion, as a disqualifying mark against the maturity or seriousness of their politics. The objections of two groups of postcolonial critics and historians are representative. Members of the first, drawing upon a nationalist idiom, tend to base their reservations upon a narrowly orientalist typology. The second group, with whose objections this chapter is principally concerned, invokes a broader liberal or Marxist thematic to announce the dramatic incompatibility of spiritualist endeavor and (progressive) ethical and political capacity.

So, for instance, Parama Roy discredits the anticolonial efforts of

Margaret Noble, or Sister Nivedita (1867–1911), the Irish disciple and collaborator of the nationalist-mystic Swami Vivekananda, on the grounds that her nostalgic spiritualism appealed exclusively to recessive strains within Indian nationalism, favoring orthodoxy and revivalism over rationalism and reformism.[1] Likewise, and in an uncharacteristically Adornian reading of mysticism,[2] Ashis Nandy discerns a contaminating authoritarianism in the spiritual style exercised by the French Mother of the Sri Aurobindo Ashram in Pondicherry, accusing her of reinforcing rather than mitigating colonial hierarchies: "The Ashram itself became, under her powerful presence . . . highly status conscious, politically conservative and a means of oppressing the people around. After Aurobindo's death, for a while it even opposed the decolonisation of Pondicherry."[3] And in an otherwise sensitive account of western women in British South Asia, Kumari Jayawardene consistently views spiritualism as a distraction from, or constraint upon, the ethico-political agency of her historical protagonists. Privileging those "foreign" women whose critique of western imperialism was accompanied by an unambiguous rejection of "orthodox Asian reformers, religious gurus, and leaders whose nationalism lacked a Socialist vision of the future,"[4] Jayawardene extols the exemplary secular focus of the Marxist feminist Evelyn Roy (1892–1970), whose summary dismissal of western soul searchers is resonant in the context of the present discussion: "The tired intellectuals of Europe may look to the East in search of a new Messiah . . . But to all honest revolutionaries who understand . . . great movements as the Russian and Indian revolutions, all talk about 'spiritual welfare' . . . is . . . the babble of children or the fevered eloquence of intellectual degeneration in search of new illusions."[5]

Evelyn Roy's paradigmatic insistence on the gap between "honest revolution" and "spiritual welfare" (the one adult, rational, scientific, the other immature, incoherent, utopian) is symptomatic of those narrow (and narrowing) theoretical adjustments through which the "political" itself has come to be viewed exclusively as a sign of the philosophical and ethical exhaustion of religion. Our conception of the "political" or "ethical" is in many ways hopelessly circumscribed by the secular, rational calculations which underscore the movement of modern European thought—from Europe "out" into the (post)colonial world.[6] It is such calculations that this chapter aims to critique: not only through a

Gandhian appeal, in the manner of *Hind Swaraj*, to a culturally or civilizationally different understanding of politics and ethics, but rather through a renewed attentiveness to moments of departure and flight within western philosophy and culture itself. It is precisely in such moments that we might find some clues about the complex constitution of the dissent exemplified in the lives and careers of heterodox late-nineteenth-century western pilgrims and radicals.

Aiming to enter into dialogue with nonsecular conceptions of the social and political, we will take issue with what Dipesh Chakrabarty has identified as the two central ontological assumptions of European political thought. These are, in his words, "that the human exists in a frame of a single and secular historical time that envelops other kinds of time," and "that the human is ontologically singular, that gods and spirits are in the end 'social facts,' that the social somehow exists prior to them."[7] We will argue that these assumptions in turn, and the modern, liberal conception of justice through which they are sustained, owe their inheritance to a specifically Kantian understanding of moral agency and knowledge, one predicated upon a subject who is constitutively transcendental, self-sufficient, unified, and as such invulnerable to both desire (or that which is "empirical" in human nature) and prayer (or that which is or craves the "metaphysical" in human nature). Read from the perspective of recent radical theory (queer, postcolonial, etc.), it is possible to identify the "empirical" and the "metaphysical" as varieties of "hybridity," and so to disclose Kantian ethics itself as a powerful discourse *against* hybridity.

Over the last few decades, two broad streams of anti- and post-Kantian philosophers have attempted to reclaim hybridity as the basis for a more humane and humanizing ethics. The first, more popular, stream, represented by Michael Sandel and others, takes exception to the austerity of Kantian subjectivity and endeavors to recuperate *as ethics* the pluralism and affective irregularities of human experience. The second, quieter, stream, secreted within Derrida's corpus, nags relentlessly at the contradictions inherent in Kant's extradition of religion from the realm of ethics and justice. It does so to posit a certain type of metaphysical experience (Derrida calls this "fiduciary" faith) as a profound and utopian address to the other. Drawing on the efforts of both Sandel and Derrida, this chapter seeks out a project that radically departs from Kant by proposing an empirical-metaphysical politics of hybridity. The outline of this project can be found in William James's oeuvre and at the scene of fin-de-siècle radicalism—the context for James's work, and also for the European mystics and occultists who arrived in India in the age of empire. Thus, presenting James's work as meditation upon, for instance, the links between spiritualism and the plurality of the self divulged by the Society for Psychical Research, or as a response to Edward Carpenter's attempt to bring sexual difference and spiritualism into the very heart of socialism, I hope to foreground a forgotten variety of hybridity whose refusal of secular rationality and transcendental subjectivity is quintessentially political and anticolonial. Let us begin our exploration with a closer look at the story of one exemplary mystical arrivant in India in the early years of the twentieth century.

GOING EAST, OR, HOW TO READ LATE-NINETEENTH-CENTURY SPIRITUALISM

Toward the end of 1912 a thirty-four-year-old French-Egyptian-Jewish mystic called Mirra Alfassa (1878–1973) began diligently to write a spiritual diary every day in the house at 9 rue du Val-de-Grace in Paris that she shared with her second husband, Paul Richard, a minor politician and amateur occultist. In the same year, the Cambridge-educated classicist, nationalist, extremist, and mystic Aurobindo Ghose also began to record his puzzling spiritual experiments from within the solitude of his new habitation in the lawless French *comptoir* of Pondicherry, where he had arrived surreptitiously on 4 April 1910, seeking amnesty from the punitive jurisdiction of the imperial British administration. Under suspicion for a range of real and imputed terrorist actions in West Bengal, Ghose was for long regarded by imperial authorities as "the most dangerous man in India" and would remain under close British surveillance during his permanent retreat in Pondicherry.[8]

But for the accidental simultaneity of their stylistically very different spiritual log books, there is little apparent similarity of circumstance to link Sri Aurobindo, Anglicized Bengali revolutionary, and Mirra Alfassa, Paris bohemian and sometime confidante of Auguste Rodin and Henri Matisse. Yet, a combination of chance and will would eventually draw the two together into lifelong spiritual collaboration on eastern soil. In March 1914 Alfassa accompanied her husband to Pondicherry on a trip, ostensibly for electoral purposes, that would result in a momentous meeting between her and Sri Aurobindo, memorable, she later recalled, for its shock of mutual recognition: "I came here . . . But something in me wanted to meet Sri Aurobindo all alone the first time. Richard went to him in the morning and I had an appointment for the afternoon. He was living in the old Guest House. I climbed up the staircase and he was standing there, waiting for me at the top of the stairs . . . EXACTLY my vision! Dressed in the same way, in the same position, in profile, his head held high. He turned his head toward me . . . and I saw in his eyes that it was He."[9] In his turn, at a séance attended by the Richards during their visit, Sri Aurobindo received, as automatic writing, confirmation from his occult interlocutors of the intimate compact between him and Mirra: "I was going to say what you have said—She is a great soul always with you."[10] Turning this otherworldly kinship into practical partnership, Sri Aurobindo and the Richards quickly agreed to combine resources in producing a bilingual review to be called *Arya* in its English edition and *Revue de la Grande Synthèse* in the French. Early issues of *Arya* would feature Sri Aurobindo's first detailed writings on, and cultural defense of, Indian spiritual history and philosophy, defiantly composed against the backdrop of the imperial civilizing mission. Most of these were translated into the French by Alfassa.

Notwithstanding the force of this creative inaugural encounter with Sri Aurobindo, the Richards left Pondicherry in February 1915, their return to the West recorded by Mirra in her diary, while journeying back on board the *Kamo Maro*, as a dark night of the soul: "Solitude, a harsh, intense solitude, and always this strong impression of having been flung headlong into a hell of darkness. Never at any moment of my life, in any circumstances, have I felt myself living in surroundings so entirely opposite to all that I am conscious of as true, so contrary to all that is the essence of my life."[11] After a separation of over five years—most of them spent in Japan, where Paul Richard had gained a commission to advance the export of French products in Asia—Mirra Alfassa returned finally to Pondicherry in April 1920, where she became in due course the Mother of the devotional Ashram community and Sri Aurobindo's spiritual collaborator.

One of various European women and men who arrived in colonial India at the turn of the century to fulfill the secret imperatives of a spiritual vocation or destiny, the Mother, like her counterparts, strongly identified with the cause of Indian independence and the contingent reformation of Indian social and political life. The inexplicable spiritual-affective pull toward India that she notes in her earliest writings inevitably gained a distinct anticolonial complexion in the company of Sri Aurobindo, who kept close watch, albeit in occult register, upon the progress of the nationalist agitation throughout his retreat, constantly recording his spiritual assessments of various revolutionary leaders and their seemingly "moderate" negotiations with imperial authorities. As late as 1941, frustrated by his sense of the mishandling by Congress officials of the "Cripps Proposals," which offered dominion status to India in exchange for the promise of unequivocal commitment to the allied war effort, Sri Aurobindo would intervene directly, dispatching an emissary to Delhi to convey strong arguments for accepting the proposals, which he believed might forestall the partition of India. While Congress chose not to act on these recommendations it did not forget Sri Aurobindo, regularly inviting him to resume his position at the helm of the agitation. In 1920, when Gandhi launched his epochal noncooperation movement, Sri Aurobindo received two invitations to shape the future of revolutionary policy, one from B. S. Moonje, current chairman of the Reception Committee of the National Congress, who urged him to preside over the Congress session of 1920.[12] In the course of the movement Gandhi himself sent his youngest son Devdas to Pondicherry in an unsuccessful effort to draw the radical yogi back into direct action.[13]

Well aware of Sri Aurobindo's continuing transactions with the nationalist cause, the administration kept close vigil over his visitors and associates, and the Richards soon found themselves listed as pro-revolutionary suspects by the British imperial police. An official dispatch on Paul Richard is tellingly alarmist: "He is reported to hold dangerous opinions and started a society called 'Union de la jeunesse Hindoue' for the political, religious and literary education of young men in Pondicherry. He is constantly in the company of extremists there and himself claims a five years' friendship with Arbinda Ghose."[14] In response to nagging pressure from the British administration, the French government of Pondicherry finally ordered the expulsion of the Richards in January 1915. Nonetheless, even in the period of their tenure in Japan, while continuing the work of spiritual experimentation, Mirra in particular assiduously cultivated the company of those Japanese renowned for their opposition to European imperialism. The Richards' insistent dabbling in anticolonial matters while abroad did not escape official attention, and an Indian government document from this time disapprovingly describes a close associate of theirs, the Asian historian Shumei Okawa, as "the leading spirit of the pan-Asiatic movement in Japan . . . a person of considerable influence, who is deeply interested in Indian affairs and is bitterly opposed to British rule in India."[15] Through Okawa the Richards also came into direct contact with Rasbehari Bose, self-exiled in Japan from 1915 after a failed assassination attempt on Viceroy Hardinge, and founder of the local Indian Independence League.[16]

Many years later, when independence finally came to India, the French Mother of Sri Aurobindo Ashram would raise a flag in Pondicherry—on French imperial territory—over the terrace of Sri Aurobindo's room, while a gathering, which included some of the extremists who had first accompanied Sri Aurobindo to Pondicherry, sang Bankim's *Bande Mataram* in praise of the liberation of India. At the end of the ceremony, a disciple recounts, Mirra Alfassa "called out 'Jai Hind!' [victory to India] with such a look and gesture that we still remember the moment."[17] How might we best account for this complex braiding together of "sacred" and "secular" in the life and actions of a figure like Mirra Alfassa? Which are the circumstantial and philosophical ingredients that allowed for the admissibility of faith within her political endeavor? Speaking historically, the hybrid admixture of theism and ethics, belief and social justice, to which the Mother of Sri Aurobindo Ashram laid claim is firmly anchored in the style of the spiritualist revolution that spread, in subcultural form, across Europe and America from the second half of the nineteenth century onward. To comprehend this movement we must pay close, more sympathetic attention to what Logie Barrow describes as the "zig-zag connections" between late Victorian heterodoxy on the one hand and late Victorian radicalism on the other.[18] How were these connections forged and realized? What historical circumstances secured the inextricability of late-nineteenth-century spiritualism and contemporary forms of dissent?

By the end of the nineteenth century, scholars of the field tell us, if the potent combination of evolutionary biology, geology, and biblical criticism had provoked a reaction against the claims of (Christian) religious orthodoxy and a turn toward empiricism and secularism—toward the prerogatives, in other words, of Experience, Feeling, and Life—it had also paved the way for the clamorous arrival of a range of religious heterodoxies among those either unwilling or unable to inhabit a wholly disenchanted world.[19] Arriving into belief under the unlikely sign of science, most new religious heterodoxies found themselves in conjunctural alliance with the radical politics also thriving under the glare of contemporary empiricism, some forms of which we have reviewed. For those whose heterodoxy manifested itself expressly *against* mainstream Christianity, Theosophy and its contiguous offshoots offered a spiritual alternative in eastern religions, one that demanded a corresponding disavowal of the claims of "modern" western civilization. It was this tendency that brought the movement and its largely middle-class adherents into intimate commerce with parallel, secular, avant-garde critiques of western civilization, exemplified in the linked projects of dress and sexual reform, and homosexual exceptionalism; dietary politics, anti-vivisectionism, and vegetarianism; and aestheticism, or the repudiation of bourgeoisie materialism and philistinism in the form of class or colonial avarice.[20]

Comparable coalitions and cross-alliances, again anticolonial in texture, also marked the experience of the heterodox but not avowedly "anti-Christian" working classes, for whom, in the wake of orthodox religion, utopian socialism came increasingly to supply mitigatory spiritual content. As early as 1857, the utopian millenarianist Robert Owen saw no inconsistency in directing his Millennial Congress address to a composite audience of "socialists, spiritualists and secularists."[21] Some decades later, in the famous defense of her conversion to Theosophy, Annie Besant refuted all allegations of a disparity between socialism and theosophical pantheism.[22] And introducing in 1897 a new series of articles to the *Labour Prophet*, the journal of the Labour Church movement, Robert Blantchford explicitly claimed socialism as a variety of religious belief: "We have the right to refuse the name of socialist to those who have not grasped the economic truth. But an economic theory alone, or any number of economic theories will not make a religion . . . you must widen your definition of socialism. You must draw out all the ethical and spiritual implications of these efforts and desires for a juster social order . . . A new conception of life is taking shape, to which it is affectation, if not folly, to refuse the name of Religion."[23]

Profoundly syncretic in inspiration, utopian socialism of the 1880s gained its anticolonial energies from the peculiar conditions of its emergence, and specifically the reaction to the multiple failures of Gladstone's Liberal government, held responsible for a depression and rising unemployment at home, and an aggressive foreign policy involving military interventions in South Africa, Afghanistan, and Egypt, not to mention a reign of police terror against the nationalist movement in Ireland. A growing awareness of the interconnectedness between disparate domestic and foreign causes, combined with a skepticism toward what William Morris described as the sham of the parliamentary game, provided an ideal breeding ground for an earlier "subjective moment in politics," elaborated through a dizzying variety of interest groups and sects. Espousing the prerogatives of the body and the demands of affectivity and personal transformation within the realm of the political—through diet, dress, health, and sexual reform—the new radicalism was notable principally for its heterogeneity and coalitional style. Despite their differences, Christian Socialists, anarchists, New Lifers, suffragists, vegetarians, prison and land reformers attended each others' meetings, contributed to each others' journals, and organized joint demonstrations. Catering to this profoundly mixed clientele of the faithful, by the end of the century socialism had overtaken Theosophy not only in its willful combination of religion and politics but also, as H. M. Hyndman, putative leader of the Social Democratic Federation, noted with some irritation, as the favored "depository of old cranks, humanitarians, vegetarians, anti-vivisectionists . . . anti-vaccinationists, arty-crafties."[24]

Either as a middle- or working-class phenomenon, the paths of fin-de-siècle spiritualism, even in its wider European and American manifestations, passed almost invariably through the ideological suburbs of either Theosophy or socialism, picking up en route intractable habits of incredulity vis-à-vis the self-aggrandizing claims of the modern imperial West, both at home and abroad in the colonized world. The spiritualism to which Mirra Alfassa laid claim in late-nineteenth-century France certainly manifested the "zig-zag connections" to which it was so prone across the channel.[25] Her formative turn toward India and concomitant aversion to the "modern" West was shaped, though indirectly, by the influences of French Theosophy. Alfassa's first occult guide, Max Théon, a man well versed in Sanskrit and Hindu spiritualism, had collaborated with H. P. Blavatsky in Egypt, and she counted among her closest friends in Paris the Theosophist and orientalist adventurer Madame Alexandra David-Neel. True to her era, Mirra's spiritualist idiom is also heavily inflected by the rhetoric of contemporary anarcho-socialism, always demanding freedom from possession (material and affective) as the first principle of spiritual development, and extolling the spiritualist as an egoless "worker" or "servant" among "brethren."[26] As early as 1907 the publications and manifesto of the spiritualist group in Paris to which she belonged had attracted the attention of an exiled Russian revolutionary seeking, for his own cause, "a synthetical teaching which does not limit itself to theory, but encourages action."[27] Years later, visiting the Richards during their time in Japan, the Theosophist J. H. Cousins was similarly struck by the force of their enduring socialist convictions: "I recall . . . a conversation in the drawing room of Paul and Mirra Richard, at whose home in the suburbs of Tokyo I was a frequent visitor. Politics were then at the top of the conversational bill among people who trusted one another . . . I heard more socialism talked than I had done since my early twenties, when I was a devotee of Robert Blantchford with his spicy weekly paper, 'The Clarion.' "[28] At the age of ninety, toward the end of her life, ever faithful to the radicalism from which she had distilled the substance of her spiritualism, the Mother greeted the events of May 1968, as they broke out across her former city of Paris, with unguarded enthusiasm. "It doesn't look like a strike at all," she noted in conversations with a disciple later published as *Mother's Agenda*, "it looks like a revolution. I know that. I don't know if I have ever told you, but there has been—there has always been—an identification of this body's consciousness with . . . revolutionary movements . . . in Russia, in Italy, in Spain and elsewhere—always, everywhere."[29]

We can thus safely attribute the startling coincidence of mystical and revolutionary impulses in Alfassa's practice to the ideological cartography of the fin-de-siècle spiritualism in which she found herself implicated. In that set of historical conjunctures the path to heterodox theism, as with the alternative movements of our own time, often passed through the sidestreets of political radicalism. And it did so at least in part because the epistemological and ontological fiber of late Victorian heterodoxy made faith amenable to the realm of the ethical and the political. It is to the terms of such amenability that we must now turn, searching for the discursive components in the materialist and empiricist philosophies underscoring Alfassa's context that supplied her with an occult disposition capable of seeing theism as instrumental to the ethico-political transformation of subjectivity. Always accompanying her manifest support to a range of radical causes, the Mother's records and writings detail the progress of an agonizing spiritual labor, informed by a conviction that the risky rehearsal of faith facilitates such pluralization of the self as is crucial to the credo of noncoercive relationality with difference. In her idiom, belief is the only means effectively to countermand that ontological assumption of human singularity (or of unified subjectivity) upon which the manichean divisions of race, class, gender, and species are predicated. So, for instance, one of the first entries in her spiritual diary incants her profound aspiration for the dissolution of personality, "the day when I can no longer say 'I,'" while another laments "the gross illusion of 'me' and 'mine,' the intolerable burden of this obscure and cumbersome self."[30] Such pleas for the erasure of personal limits or personality preface Alfassa's fierce resistance to the illusion of separation between "ourselves and others," her desire always to "find the category of affinities which binds us to others."[31] This, we might note, is also the staple of Sri Aurobindo's askesis, recorded as a series of bizarre experiments in "thought sharing" with crows, butterflies, plants, squirrels, and alien human beings, each predicated on the will to overcome "our egoistic appropriation of whatever comes to us in our subjective experience."[32]

To make proper sense of the collaborative transformation of subjectivity to which the Mother and Sri Aurobindo devoted themselves from 1914, when they first met, and to which many of their contemporaries were also committed, we must now turn to that Kantian understanding of what it means to be an ethical political agent. It is to this conception that fin-de-siècle spiritualism posed its most profound philosophical and political challenge.

IMMANUEL KANT AND THE DISCOURSE AGAINST HYBRIDITY

Committed in all his philosophical work to an elaboration of the project of autonomy, Kant conceives of morality as the radical freedom of the ethical agent-subject. While the *Critique of Pure Reason* (1781) explains epistemology as the rational agent's progressive liberation from the external physical and natural world, the subsequent *Fundamental Principles of the Metaphysic of Morals* (1785) and *The Critique of Practical Reason* (1788) together elaborate a similar formula for the problem of moral cognition. In these later texts reason intervenes to liberate the moral agent from the empirical contaminants of her own nature. For to be moral subjects in the Kantian sense, we must rigorously stand aloof from the contingencies of our humanness and maintain strict independence from the domain of "luck" which circumscribes our desires and inclinations at any given moment. To be such a transcendental and unified ethical agent is thus to be constitutively free from the heterogeneity of consciousness, from the distractions of experience.[33]

This long cherished view of creative human autonomy elaborated through the three critiques—and, lest we forget, informed by a quiet but felt objection to prevailing political and religious orthodoxies[34]—finds its apotheosis in Kant's still later work, *Religion within the Limits of Reason Alone* (1793). A statement of and for absolute human moral freedom, Kant's *Religion* is pivotal to the questions being rehearsed in this discussion, insofar as it can be said to inaugurate the birth of modern secular ethics by comprehensively denying the moral subject access to all external influences: human, physical, and divine. A subject who, Kant insists, can "be judged morally good only by virtue of that which can be imputed to him as performed by himself," necessarily fails the obligations of self-sufficiency whenever he endeavors to "win favour" through mere worship.[35] Prayer leads man morally astray by persuading him "either that God can make him happy . . . without his having to become a better man . . . or . . . that God can make him a better man without his having to do anything more than ask for it. Yet since, in the eyes of a Being who sees all, to ask is no more than to wish, this would really involve doing nothing at all."[36] By bringing the anxieties of the work ethic to bear upon ethics itself, *Religion* perversely reformulates worship as a form of moral idleness.

If Kant's monumental philosophical labor succeeds in capturing moral agency and the contiguous capacity for social justice as the prerogative of a certain sort of subject—one who is singular, self-identical, self-sufficient, immune, and transcendental—it also simultaneously releases into liberal ethical and political thought an influential bias against what we might call "hybridity": the mongrelization of subjectivity viewed in the body of Kant's work as the unwholesome byproduct of the affectivity which attaches either to desire or to prayer, and which springs from the perils of relationality either with other beings in the world (human, animal) or with God. We might say that in its implicit discourse against hybridity Kantian thought establishes a strange kinship between empiricism (the realm of desire, inclinations) and metaphysics (the realm of prayer, unknowable reality), insofar as it treats them as similar types of threat or temptation to the integrity and agency of the ethico-rational subject.

Over the last few decades a range of anti—or *contra*—Kantian thinkers have attempted to reclaim hybridity as the basis for a more humane and humanizing ethics. Rarely, such theorists argue, does an ethical action or decision proceed from the dictates of a self-sufficient imagination or from the imperatives of a wholly transcendental rationality.[37] Indeed, as Michael Sandel claims in his critique of Kant and Rawls, our capacity for good is in some ways inextricable from our capacity to pluralize ourselves, either through "intrasubjective" self-understanding, which allows "that for certain purposes, the appropriate description of the moral subject may refer to a plurality of selves within a single, individual human, as when we account for inner deliberation in terms of a pull of competing identities, or moments of introspection in terms of occluded self-knowledge," or through "intersubjective" self-understanding, namely the recognition "that in certain moral circumstances, the relevant description of the self may embrace more than a single, individual human being, as when we attribute responsibility or affirm an obligation to a family or community or class or nation."[38]

It is worth noting that much in the spirit of Sandel's anti-Kantian ethical recalculations, the insurrectionary or revolutionary subject of recent "radical" theory is also a constitutively hybrid entity. The disruptive work of queer theory, Judith Butler maintains, is performed by the unstable, incoherent and discontinuous subject of desire who eschews in favor of a "fragmentation in the ranks" all appeal to a preemptive or prescriptive politics of "unity": "unity set[s] up an exclusionary norm of solidarity at the level of identity that rules out the possibility of . . . actions which disrupt the very borders of identity concepts, or which seek to accomplish precisely that disruption as an explicit political aim."[39] Writing in similar terms about the emergence of heterodox new social movements in Britain (especially those that encompass the politics of race), Stuart Hall and Paul Gilroy each document the inauguration of a "subjective moment in politics,"[40] which emanates from "the body as a seat of desires" and from the rich "nexus of interpersonal relationships."[41] And postcolonial theory is increasingly no less determined to track the emergence of radically protean subjectivities whose politics and ethics—produced, as Said would have it, "between domains, between forms, between homes, between languages"[42]—consist principally in exceeding the foundationalism of racial, colonial, nationalist discourse and avoiding capture by its various agents.

This diverse and complex theoretical rapprochement with hybridity, summarily reviewed above, exemplifies a new and urgent sympathy for and belief in the ethico-political worth of the empirical circumstances of human existence. Nevertheless, it does little to revoke the Kantian extradition of worship and metaphysics from the realm of justice. Indeed, all too often postcolonial "authorities" like Salman Rushdie insist that an aesthetics or ethics of hybridity is constitutively opposed to the domain of the sacred. Wedded to a carnivalesque politics of irreverence and demystification, Rushdie's version of hybridity paradoxically delivers, as in Kant, a potent immunity against the threat and temptation of religious belief.[43] Yet unless we wish to make a categorical distinction between "good" and "bad" hybridity, a truly comprehensive critique of Kantian ethics obliges us to remember that the metaphysical (the religious, the mystical) is as much an agent of self-pluralization as the empirical, and that as such, metaphysical hybridities may well (may yet) help furnish the discontinuous, incoherent, unstable, provisional, affective requirements of a queer or a postcolonial justice. This hope or possibility gains serious attention in Derrida's essay "Faith and Knowledge," a long and combative meditation on Kant's *Religion* to which we might briefly turn our attention.

The Kantian discourse against religion, Derrida reminds us in "Faith and Knowledge," makes a crucial distinction between two families of religious belief: the one "dogmatic," the other "reflective." Of these it is only the first (religion of cult) which cannot be accommodated within the limits of reason alone, in that its morally transcendent appeal to "works of grace," as we have seen above, makes for an indolent morality in which doing (being) good is tantamount to doing (being) nothing.[44] Reflective faith, on the other hand, a moral religion entirely amenable to the limits of rationality, enjoins man to action—"good-life conduct"—by scrupulously withholding from him the certain knowledge of divine cooperation.[45] However, and here lies the rub, only Christianity gains, in Kant's eyes, the prerogative of reflectivity: "of all the public religions which have ever existed," he writes, "the Christian alone is moral."[46] And so, this discourse of and for the limit, and against the imaginative and risky hybridity of prayer and desire, starts to limit the field of tolerance itself. According to its formulations, Derrida observes, "the idea of a morality that is pure but non-Christian would be absurd; it would exceed both understanding and reason . . . The unconditional universality of the categorical imperative is evangelical. The moral law inscribes itself at the bottom of our hearts . . . When it addresses us, it either speaks the idiom of the Christian—or is silent."[47] Faced with this impasse, Derrida provocatively redefines Kant's genealogy of religious belief. Reflective faith, when read with deconstructive suspicion, reveals itself as a homogenizing attachment to the "unscathed" (the safe, the sacred, or the saintly), "which produces the same as much as it confirms it . . . a persistent bond that bonds itself first and foremost to itself . . . A resistance or reaction to dis-junction. To ab-solute alterity."[48] Against this, dogmatic faith offers a positive exemplar of the "fiduciary" (trustworthiness, fidelity, credit, belief, or faith), manifest as a moment of "interruptive unravelling" which "exceeds, through its structure, all intuition and all proof, all knowledge."[49] Such a faith, one that refuses to close itself off into a totality and thus leaves itself open to the threat and temptation of the unknown, the unthought, the unseen, is of course already, in the work of a Levinas or Derrida, "the ether of the address and relation of the utterly other."[50] As the scene of self-pluralization and othering, prayer, marked by its fidelity to the ethic of non-knowledge, is also marked by an "invincible desire for justice . . . [that] is not and ought not to be certain of anything, either through knowledge, conscience, forseeability or any kind of program as such."[51] That is to say, contrary to the limits (of reason, tolerance, culture, religion) which circumscribe Kantian morality, a "fiduciary" mentality offers a crucial rehearsal ground for the openness, uncertainty, and inconclusiveness which must underscore any truly utopian expectation of radical inclusiveness. Needless to say, there are many varieties of meaningful politics besides the utopian. So too, there are many reasons for asserting the meaningfulness of utopian politics, as Derrida does variously under the signs of religion, hospitality, and friendship: "For democracy remains to come; this is its essence in so far as it remains: not only will it remain indefinitely perfectible, hence always insufficient and future, but, belonging to the time of the promise, it will always remain, in each of its future times, to come: even when there is democracy, it never exists, it is never present, it remains the theme of the non-presentable."[52]

Let us recapitulate the movement of our discussion so far. In seeking to explore the possible compatibility of religious belief and social justice we have worked our way through two critiques of Kantian morality, both determined to justify a more flexible ethics of and for hybridity: the one, elaborated in the work of Sandel and other recent "radical" theorists, reclaims the pluralizing effects of that which is empirical in human nature; the other, elaborated in the work and philosophical tradition of Derrida, recommends, with equal enthusiasm, the self-pluralizing benefits of that which is, or which craves, the metaphysical in human nature. One group speaks on behalf of desire, the other on behalf of prayer, and both present a challenge to available conceptions of the political and ethical. The protestations of desire or subjective experience, as Gilroy notes, "are unlikely to be able to make the transition to more stable forms of politics."[53] So too, the protestations of prayer, in their wishful address to the realm of the immaterial or unmanifest, herald a social order which, as Colin McCabe complains in a negative review of Derrida's *Friendship*, "can neither be described nor prescribed but only experienced in a transformed future . . . there is no relation between what is to come and what must be done."[54] Held apart despite their common modality and shared recoil from the impassivity of Kantian rationality, can these two critiques be combined in the form of, say, an empirical-metaphysical politics of hybridity—namely, in a politics or ethics that demonstrates the role of the metaphysical in producing or enabling empirically meaningful types of hybridity?

Such, we have been arguing, was the endeavor of many of the fin-de-siècle spiritualists and mystics with whom this chapter is ultimately concerned. And we gain substantial philosophical insight into their efforts to forge an idiom for an empirical-metaphysical hybridity in the writings of William James, the American proto-psychologist, psychical researcher, and pragmatist whose complex and somewhat eccentric oeuvre constitutes, as Charles Taylor maintains, an extended *apologia pro fide sua*, taking direct exception to the proscriptions of Kantian ethics to launch a series of arguments for the admissibility of belief. But where Taylor sees in James's work the rhetoric of a highly affective and individualistic theism inadequately attentive to the more muscular demands of collectivity or sociality, the following discussion proffers a different reading. It is my claim that James's philosophical labors exemplify and clarify the aspirations of his fellow spiritualists in their effort to bring the experience of mystical and metaphysical self-pluralization to bear upon the reformation of relationality in a hierarchical and imperial world. Theism, as James has it, accelerates the dissolution of that sovereign Kantian ego upon which the divisions of self and other, subject and object are predicated, disclosing in place of a separated and disenchanted world a concatenated "multiverse," strung together, in Darwinian fashion, into a horizontal web of relations.

WILLIAM JAMES AND THE WILL TO RADICAL PLURALISM

Composed in the interstices of spiritualism and psychology, William James's oeuvre is distinguished by its insistence upon the ontological and epistemological primacy of experience. His own predilection toward the experiential is gleaned in large part, as he concedes, from the materialism of his era, specifically the overwhelming influence of evolutionary biology upon fin-de-siècle western intellectual life. "It is difficult," he writes in his *Essays in Radical Empiricism*, "not to notice a curious unrest in the philosophic atmosphere of the time . . . Life is confused and superabundant, and what the younger generation appears to crave is more of the temperament of life in its philosophy, even though it were at some cost of logical rigor and of formal purity."[55] But James protests that the pull toward the existential, constitutive of his thought, does not reflect mere intellectual fashion; rather, it responds to a change in the very fabric of the time, as a result of which life and the living of it have come once again to be regarded as a sufficient good. Defending this principle fervently, James sees it as his enterprise to search out conditions under which experience and life can themselves yield the ethical effects reserved, in earlier philosophical systems, for the action of austere and transcendental rationality. It is this effort to distill the substance of a materialist ethics that leads James, it would seem paradoxically, on the path to theism, disclosing, as we will see, the empirical-metaphysical politics of hybridity of which we spoke earlier.

Variously called "pragmatism," "pluralism," and "radical empiricism," James's philosophical credo defines itself against Kant and Hegel, whose allergy to pluralism, contradiction, and experience he holds responsible for the impoverishment of western thought. Where both thinkers—Kant especially—predicate their "systems" upon the solid and clear substance of monism, rationalism, and absolutism to deliver "a world . . . simple, clean and noble . . . a kind of marble temple shining on a hill," James, creature of his epoch, proposes a philosophy that cleaves enthusiastically instead to the "world of concrete personal experiences . . . multitudinous . . . tangled, muddy, painful and perplexed."[56] Seeking a palliative variety of thought less at war with life, he attempts to confer on "being" the philosophical respectability preserved in Kantian thought for reason alone: "The 'I think' which Kant said must be able to accompany all my objects, is the 'I breathe' which actually does accompany them . . . thoughts in the concrete are made of the same stuff as things are."[57]

Any philosophy that thus restricts itself and its postulates to the facticity of experience and the material world, while eschewing types, essences, taxonomies, precedents, and laws, James maintains, deserves the name empiricism, one to which a long line of English and continental philosophers can justly lay claim. But, James goes on to aver, empiricism in its turn can only earn the mantle of radicalism—call itself "radical empiricism"—when it takes being in the world as the condition of possibility for the ethical or the political, conjuring a subject whose moral or cognitive agency is a function of her implication in, rather than autonomy from, the muddy perplexities of desire or relationality. In these terms, the ethical agent according to James is a "conjunctive" subject for whom being in the world meaningfully or well is a function of being in relation to others: "with, near, next, like, from, toward, against, because, for, through."[58] Far from being bound by the dogmatism of absolute teleological unity, or indeed by the dogma of unified subjectivity, the human propensity for good, James argues, accrues precisely from our capacity for provisional coalition, conjunction, and relationality: "It may mean your loyalty to the possibilities of others whom you admire and love so that you are willing to accept your own poor life, for it is that glory's partner. You can at least appreciate, applaud, furnish the audience, of so brave a total world . . . Identify your life therewith; then, through angers, losses, ignorance, ennui, whatever you thus make of yourself, whatever you thus most deeply are, picks its way."[59]

Yet James concedes that for all their ethical potential, the horizontal demands of conjunctive relationality in a pluralistic world deliver a terrifying schema of uncertified cooperation: an obligation to coexist with irreducible difference that few are equipped to handle. Such are the summons that Hegelian thought typically contravenes in the name of "bad infinity," proposing that the "true must be essentially the self-reflecting self-contained recurrent, that which secures itself by including its own other and negating it; that makes a spherical system with no loose ends hanging out for foreignness to get a hold upon; that is forever rounded in and closed, not strung along rectilinearly and open at its ends."[60] What agent, however enamored of the world and the contingent tug of desire, can surrender herself to that conjunctural form of relation in which the other consistently eludes possession, offering no guarantee of reciprocity, no comfort of finality? "Things," James warns, "are 'with' one another in many ways, but nothing includes everything, or dominates over everything. The word 'and' trails along after every sentence. Something always escapes. 'Ever not quite' has to be said of the best attempts made anywhere in the universe at attaining all-inclusiveness. The pluralistic world is thus more like a federal republic than an empire."[61] How, then, might we submit to the psychic hazards of the nonimperial relationality upon which our ethical capacity as experiential beings is predicated? How can you "trust yourself and trust other agents enough to take the risk"?[62]

Suddenly introducing the specter of risk into the benign narrative of pluralistic justice, James brings us face to face again with Kantian thought and its offer of unconditional rational immunity precisely against such terrors of affectivity. For the Kantian, as Martha Nussbaum reminds us, "'irrational' attachments import, more than any others, a risk of practical conflict and so of contingent failure in virtue. And even when passional activities are not deemed in themselves valuable, the passions can still figure as a source of disruption . . . To nourish them at all is thus to expose oneself to a risk of disorder or 'madness.'"[63] But turning away from cautionary morality, James invokes instead the model of the agnostic-theist, whose moral stamina, or ability to live courageously in the midst of empirical humanity, is at least partly an effect of her daily rehearsal of a credulous, cooperative relationship with God, the unseen and unknown "helper, *primus inter pares*, in the midst of all the great shapers of the great world's fate."[64] Here, much like Derrida, James defines the habit, as it were, of God as a habituation to the hazards of alterity. In a characteristic philosophizing through wordplay, Derrida, we might remember, proposes that the phrase "adieu," which signals a moment of departure and separation from all that is familiar, also carries within itself the possibility of an "a Dieu," or a coming-before-God. Or, in reverse, the experience of tentative agnostic-theism is available, etymologically, as a moment of leave taking from certain knowledge and, as such, is indistinguishable from a surrender to the erratic demands of otherness: "The a-dieu [can mean], for God or before God and before anything else or any relation to the other, in every other adieu. Every relation to the other would be, before and after anything else, an adieu."[65]

To enter the culture of belief, in other words, is eo ipso a schooling in the risk of uncertain (uncertified) cooperation: an apprenticeship to those "trusting" philosophies that will equip us existentially for the rigors of a politics of "intimacy."[66] But James offers the qualification that all cultures of belief are not equally amenable to the conjunctive, horizontal, and democratic requirements of this politics. God comes in many shapes and the alienated, authoritarian, remote, "Absolutist" deity of orthodox Christianity, standing outside of history and thus valorized in Hegelian thought, is wholly inadequate to the ethical reformation of empirical relationality. Such is the monarchial deity, dispensing faith as imperial command, whom fin-de-siècle spiritualism endeavors to "reform," the better to guide its own ethico-political imperatives. As James writes, "The vaster vistas which scientific evolutionism has opened, and the rising tide of social democratic ideals, have changed the type of our imagination, and the older monarchial theism is now obsolete or obsolescent. The place of the divine in the world must be more organic and intimate."[67] That is to say, the demands of empirical-metaphysical hybridity, as James sees them, are contingent upon the immanent and heterodox theism realized in his time, positing a new model of God as the cooperative collaborator with life, the divine as "therefore the most intimate of our possessions, heart of our heart, in fact."[68] In this new form of "intimate" theism the actions of prayer become more readily congruent with the actions of desire. God, acting as guru rather than governor, draws the timorous believer-disciple into the necessary temptations of contingency: "I am going to make a world not certain to be saved, a world the perfection of which will be conditional merely, the condition being that each several agent does its own 'level best.' I offer you a chance of taking part in such a world. Its safety, you see, is unwarranted. It is a real adventure, with real danger . . . Will you join the procession?"[69]

The theoretical conjectures thus explored in James's work find greater practical elaboration in the two contiguous fields of early British psychology and socialism: both typical of the fin-de-siècle, and both movements with which James is linked through personal and professional circumstances. In the following pages I would like to assess, first, with reference to Frederic Myers's monumental *Human Personality and Its Survival after Bodily Death* (1903), the impact of spiritualism upon an ethically motivated psychology of intra/intersubjectivity. Second, I will briefly reassess aspects of the thought and career of the socialist, homosexual reformer, and author Edward Carpenter, whom we encountered in another setting in chapter 3, as illustrative of the productive rapprochement between mysticism and radical pluralism which we have been pursuing in this discussion.

AN EMPIRICAL-METAPHYSICAL POLITICS OF HYBRIDITY

In 1882 a group of agnostic Oxbridge intellectuals pioneered the foundation of the Society for Psychical Research (SPR). In the hope of proving the friendliness of the universe, the group, which came to include William James, aimed to study those psychical or paranormal phenomena commonly associated with mid- and late-nineteenth-century spiritualism.[70] Although the SPR's various investigations into table tapping, planchette writing, spirit possession, and thought transference often appeared to reveal a culture of fraudulence, they also brought to less skeptical researchers a growing consciousness that the seemingly singular self was in fact haunted (or susceptible to haunting) by a curious secondary or tertiary consciousness.[71] And of all the phenomena which fell under the scholarly ambit of the SPR, spirit possession especially seemed to point in this direction. During a séance, the medium's otherwise unified self was revealed and performed as an unstable compound of multiple agencies, sometimes of a discrepant age, gender, race, or class.[72] Moreover, as James observes in his writings on the SPR, trance-mediumship exemplified—albeit in bizarre circumstances—a glimpse into the complex web of conjunctive relations or cooperative intersubjectivities not ordinarily visible to the secular eye: "The sitter with his desire to receive, forms, so to speak, a drainage opening or sink; the medium with her desire to personate, yields the nearest lying material to be drained off, while the spirit desiring to communicate is drawn in by the current set up and swells the latter by its own contributions."[73]

Among the SPR's researchers, it was Edmund Gurney and Frederic Myers in particular whose first-hand encounters with spiritualism came to supply the blueprint for a new psychology of "double-consciousness." Convinced that "a single individual lives in turn two (or more) separate existences,"[74] Gurney strongly disavowed the conception of unified subjectivity in a long essay called "Monism," which he published in 1887. The posthumous publication of Myers's *Human Personality* gathered these incipient conjectures into an even more coherent argument, further displacing the notion of "homogenous character" with "the multiplex and mutable character of that which we know as the Personality of man."[75] Thus, spiritualism directly ushered into early British psychology the notion of the variegated self, which in turn, Alex Owen claims, exposed "the paucity of any analysis based on the often unacknowledged notion of the unified subject."[76] But far more important, in its insistent dramatization of self-variety as the intervention of unseen "higher" powers in incarnate life, spiritualism also, though briefly, rescued the multiple personality from abnormal psychology and delivered it to ethics. And it is this, really, which constitutes the contentious principle conjecture of Myers's magnum opus. Addressed in many ways to the discipline of abnormal psychology, *Human Personality* refuses to concede that the "divided" self is symptomatic of disease, degeneration, or criminality, on the grounds that it "affords a path of transition" to the benign "agency of disincarnate minds or spirits," indeed—in the context of spiritualism—to the existence of God and the immortality of the soul itself: "It would be a great mistake to suppose that all psychical upsets are due to vanity, anger, to terror, to sexual passion. The instincts of personal cleanliness and of feminine modesty are responsible for many a breakdown of a sensitive, but not a relatively *feeble* organisation. The love of one's fellow-creatures and the love of God are responsible for many more."[77] Thus self-division may well mark the pathology of the hysteric, but all too often we neglect to observe that the hysteric belongs to the same typology as the reformer whose "moral genius" is in effect a "possession by some altruistic idea which lies at the root of so many heroic lives."[78]

I am not, let me hasten to add, proposing an argument about the necessary credibility of Myers's hypothesis. Rather, my concern is with those subtle processes whereby the mystical and metaphysical is made to collude with ethically founded notions of hybridity. Indeed, while commending Myers's demonstration of the "queer and cactus like nature of the self," William James himself remained seriously unconvinced of Myers's claim that the "Gothic" self was evolutive and moral rather than dissolutive and morbid.[79] Nonetheless, if somewhat more extreme in their enthusiasm, the conclusions of *Human Personality* are not dissimilar in essence from those reached in James's oeuvre. Nor are they dissimilar from the puissant tonic of mysticism and socialism which sustained the culture of contemporary radicalism.

Inattentive to the ethical component of the psychological interventions of Myers and his colleagues, contemporary reappraisals of the SPR frequently underscore the middle-class conservatism of its members.[80] But this was not necessarily the consensus of contemporary observers. In his autobiography, Edward Carpenter offers a much more sympathetic assessment, counting the SPR among those new movements "tending towards the establishment of mystical ideas and a new social order." As he writes: "Hyndman's Democratic Federation, Edmund Gurney's Society for Psychical Research, Mme Blavatsky's Theosophical Society, the Vegetarian Society, the Anti-Vivisection movement, and many other associations of the same kind marked the coming of a great reaction from the smug commercialism and materialism of the mid-Victorian epoch, and a preparation for the new universe of the twentieth century."[81]

It is also worth noting the political affiliations of several individual SPR members: Henry Sidgwick and his wife were serious allies of women's education and deeply involved in the establishment of Newnham College; Myers enjoyed a long association with Josephine Butler, famous for her campaign against the Contagious Diseases Act in the early 1870s; and perhaps most significantly, Frank Podmore was also a member of the socialist-utopian Fellowship of the New Life, founded under the leadership of the itinerant Scottish philosopher Thomas Davidson. An associate of William James, Davidson was typical of his radical contemporaries in his critique of monism.[82] Holding "Kant and Comte" (along with Descartes and Locke) jointly responsible for taking "the sun out of life,"[83] Davidson proposed an early, reparative version of socialism, based on the principles of personal transformation and interpersonal involvement.[84] Formed in 1883, the fellowship boasted a diverse membership which included J. Ramsay MacDonald, Havelock Ellis, Edith Lees, Arthur Ransom, and the humanitarian and animal-rights campaigners Henry and Kate Salt. Perhaps the most influential member of the group was Edward Carpenter, who commemorates his early association with the New Lifers as a period of "hopeful enthusiasms—life simplified, a humane diet and a rational dress, manual labour, democratic ideals, communal institutions."[85]

Involved in one way or another with many of the radical and socialist groups which mushroomed during the 1880s, Carpenter in his career and work sharply exemplifies the creative paradoxes of fin-de-siècle politics. In the words of a contemporary reviewer: "Carpenter . . .

combines in himself the profound repose of Oriental thought with the reforming zeal of the West; he is at once occultist and publicist, dreamer and reformer, exponent of philosophic reverie and of humanitarian zeal."[86] Initiated into socialism through a combination of Marx, acquired through H. M. Hyndman's *England for All* (the first popular exposition of Marxism in English), and metaphysics, acquired through a revelatory reading of the *Bhagavad Gita* in 1881, Carpenter elaborated a program of social justice which promised deliverance from the separation between selves and, contingently, from the notion of singular or unified subjectivity. If Marxism, via Hyndman, clarified the inequities of "the existing competitive system,[87] the *Gita* and other Hindu and Buddhist texts helped diagnose the ill-effects of capitalism as a consequence of the obscuring "clouds between us and others."[88] Carpenter drew these formative insights into a cogent ethics of radical intersubjectivity, which he describes in an explanatory note on his long prose poem *Towards Democracy* (1883): "I . . . immediately saw, or rather *felt*, that this region of Self existing in me existed equally . . . in others. In regards to it the mere diversities of temperament which ordinarily distinguish and divide people dropped away and became indifferent, and a field was opened in which all might meet, in which all were truly Equal. Thus I found the common ground which I wanted; and the two words, Freedom and Equality came for the time being to control all my thought and expression."[89]

Invariably, this mystical-democratic apprehension of interconnectedness is accompanied by a corresponding awareness of intrasubjectivity. In *The Art of Creation* (1904), Carpenter invokes Myers's notion of a "subliminal mind," and with it the central hypothesis of *Human Personality*, to confirm the (metaphysically induced) multiplicity of self: "I do not doubt that the body and its organisation are the scene and the seat of . . . other orders of consciousness—which, though usually hidden from . . . us are still readily operating within and around our minds."[90] Such a belief in the spiritual basis and potentially progressive nature of "mixed" identity produced in Carpenter the informing conviction that the rigid antinomies of species, class, race, and gender could only be resolved through a cultivated hybridization of subjectivity. And turning the pitfalls of his own sexuality to great advantage, he identified the homosexual, we have seen, as an exemplary or inspired figure of such r/evolutionary hybridity, intrinsically self-pluralized and other-directed. His two major works on sexual reform, *Love's Coming-of-Age* and *The Intermediate Sex*, effectively reformulate the homosexual project as an "open coalition," uniquely amenable to intersubjective solidarities and cooperative counterallegiances between disparate and shifting groups.[91] Attributing his own bent toward socialism as an effect of the instinctual sympathy between homosexuals and workers,[92] he also made the case for a natural affinity between male homosexuals and women, combining forces with the Woman's Freedom League (formed in 1908) to further the cause of the suffrage campaign. Active along with Henry Salt in the animal-rights movement, Carpenter was also notable as a passionate anti-vivisectionist and advocate for the establishment of animal sanctuaries.[93]

Returning to the concerns with which we began this discussion: the experiments conducted by the SPR, and the spiritualist components of Edward Carpenter's socialist career, offer historical exemplification of the hypotheses developed in the philosophical work and thought of William James. They also offer a tantalizing glimpse into the constructive availability of religious ideas to social reform at the scene of fin-de-siècle spiritualism, insofar as reform is amenable to a hybrid style of politics. Or, to put this differently, Carpenter and Myers endorse the role of religious ideas in the positive hybridization of the political. By the end of the nineteenth century, however, hybridity went out of fashion (to be reinvented, perhaps, in 1968). In 1892, as mentioned in chapter 2, Max Nordau condemned fin-de-siècle mysticism and socialism, *contra* Myer, as a symptom of degeneration, and it was in the same year that Friedrich Engels, in his *Socialism, from Utopia to Science*, pronounced, *contra* Carpenter, the obsolescence of the "kind of eclectic, average Socialism, which . . . has . . . dominated the minds of most Socialist workers in France and England . . . a mishmash allowing of the most manifold shades of opinion; a mishmash of . . . critical statements, economic theories, pictures of future society by founders of different sects."[94] Through the 1890s, or so historians tells us, spiritualism and spirit familiars also began to disappear from the scene.[95]

In a crucial way, we are the heirs of this shift in attitude, this turning away from the compound enthusiasms of fin-de-siècle spirituality and socialism. While querying this change in our attitudes, however, it has never been my aim in this chapter to proffer late Victorian radicalism, seamlessly, as a model for our own politics. Rather, I have suggested that once we concede the varieties in religious experience, the metaphysical may often prove to have much more in common with those questions of multiculturalism, pluralism, and complex equality which constitute the positive ethical preoccupation of our own time, and much less in common with the "fundamentalisms" and "extremisms" that we fear. The sphere of the "political," as Dipesh Chakrabarty tells us, does not have to be "bereft of the agency of gods, spirits, and other supernatural beings."[96] For each of the figures whom we have reviewed, it is precisely the idea of divine–human coexistence or cooperation which assists in the dissolution of personal limit, of the self-sufficient self-regard, that comes in way of sympathetic identification with those unlike ourselves. Theism may not be indispensable to this enterprise but it was no doubt propitious to Mirra Alfassa's anticolonial socialism, to William James's vision of social-democratic or conjunctive-horizontal relationality, to Myers's altruistic subject, and to the affectional possibilities claimed on behalf of Carpenter's homosexual activist. Belief, in these cases, may annul that hope of individual autonomy with which Kantian thought guarantees safety to its moral agents. But in so doing, by bringing the theme of risk back into the business of justice, it turns the pious face of ethics and politics toward the unknown and unprecedented, making it possible at the very least for the agent to experience, in his or her goodness, the self-endangering pleasures of radical inclusiveness.

6

ART

Aestheticism and the Politics of Postcolonial Difference

STORM IN A TEACUP

On 24 May 1890, in his last year of regular reviewing, Oscar Wilde published in the *Pall Mall Gazette* an affectionate but inconsequential notice for a new volume of poems called *Primavera* brought out by Basil Blackwell earlier that month. Gaining its title from Botticelli's painting, the delicate-looking volume of wan poetry, featuring a Selwyn Image woodcut design of interwoven leaves and flowers on its cover and title page, showcases the early verse efforts of four friends, Laurence Binyon, Arthur Cripps, Manmohan Ghose, and Stephen Phillips—the first three undergraduates at Oxford, the last an aspiring actor recently hailed for his unlikely performance as the Ghost in *Hamlet* at the Globe Theatre. *Primavera* would do surprisingly well given the relative anonymity of its poets, quickly running into a second edition and engaging the jealous gaze of literary London after commendations from John Addington Symonds in the *Academy*, Lionel Johnson in *Hobby Horse*, and perhaps most remarkably the *Cambridge Review*. Of all these, however, Wilde was the first to welcome the new *ephebe* into the house, as it were, of Literature.

Ever susceptible to the charms of youthful Oxford men, especially those with flawed poetic affectations, Wilde praised these "new young singers" in that teasing and hyperbolic vein of which he would write with bitterness some years hence, from Reading Gaol, to Lord Alfred Douglas: "You send me a very nice poem of the undergraduate school of verse, for my approval: I reply by a letter of fantastic literary conceits: I compare you to Hylas, or Hyacinth, Jonquil or Narcisse, or someone whom the great god of Poetry favoured, and honoured with his love . . .

It was, let me say frankly, the sort of letter I would in a happy but wilful moment, have written to any graceful young man of either University, who had sent me a poem of his making."[1] It is thus, as a bemused and charmed older writer, that Wilde, tongue lightly in cheek, celebrates *Primavera* for manifesting "the exquisite art of idleness" so diligently taught by Oxford in its summer term. Bestowing a happy and wilful kindness on each individual writer, he endorsed the volume as one that "undergraduates might read . . . with advantage during lecture-hours."[2]

Standard Wilde. One review in a corpus of similar pieces, justly ignored by Wilde biographers. Yet the postcolonial critic cannot overlook the special favor reserved for the young Indian in the chorus. "Particular interest," Wilde writes, "attaches naturally to Mr Ghose's work. Born in India, of purely Indian parentage, he has been brought up entirely in England and was educated at St. Paul's School, and his verses show us how quick and subtle are the intellectual sympathies of the Oriental mind."[3] Praising Ghose's somewhat deafening lyricism for its "lovely" faults, exemplary influences (Keats and Arnold, mainly), and consummate show of "culture and taste and feeling," Wilde confidently predicts that he "ought some day to make a name in our literature." What merits this attention for which, we must reluctantly concede, Ghose's musical gifts are in themselves insufficient?

There is evidence of a personal acquaintance between Ghose and Wilde, enough to place Ghose at the fringes of the Oxford undergraduate coterie of which Matthew Sturgis writes in *Passionate Attitudes*: an informal group held together only by the magnetism of its guru, clustering around him at private viewings, theater openings, the Café Royal, not so much homosexual as homoaffective, yet defining "the flavour of the *cenacle*" by an unmistakable "deviancy."[4] Manmohan's brother testifies with some exasperation to Ghose's place in such a set, claiming that "at a time Manmohan was almost Wilde's disciple."[5] It is certainly with the flattered incredulity of an unexpectedly favored acolyte that Ghose greets Wilde's notice, recording his pleasure in a letter of 27 May 1890 to his friend Laurence Binyon: "good soul that he is, he praised me so much, so out of proportion to my merits, and gave me a sort of introduction to the public as well. You, by getting the Newdigate, and Stephen as an actor, are already before the public in other ways; but I was quite unknown until Oscar's generous notice of me."[6]

There is doubtless an element of goodness and noblesse oblige in Wilde's minor critical favor to Ghose, not to mention something of that carefully cultivated taste for the exotic and foreign, de rigueur for late Victorian dandyism, and well expressed on its behalf by Lady Henry at the beginnings of *Dorian Gray*: "You have never been to any of my parties, have you Mr Gray? You must come. I can't afford orchids, but I spare no expense in foreigners. They make one's rooms look so picturesque."[7] Explicitly drawn to the sympathies of Ghose's "Oriental mind," Wilde is not alone in his partiality to the younger poet's exoticism. John Addington Symonds, in his review of *Primavera*, likewise confesses that "Mr. Manmohan Ghose's work possesses a peculiar interest on account of its really notable command of the subtleties of English prosody and diction, combined with just a touch of foreign feeling."[8] Yet where Symonds's attention suffers perhaps from too much surprise in the face of Ghose's English-language skills, and from setting too small an aperture for the admission of "foreign feeling" ("just a touch"), we can readily situate Wilde's xenophilia in this instance within his relentless wider critique of imperial narcissism. Recall, for instance, this startling aphorism from the preface of *Dorian Gray*: "The nineteenth-century dislike of Romanticism is the rage of Caliban not seeing his own face in a glass."[9] Some lines from Terry Eagleton's play *Saint Oscar* are also apposite for their critical explication of the fierce antipathy between Wilde's aestheticist xenophilia and his imperialist xenophobia: "You subjugate whole races, you condemn the mass of your own people to wretched toil, you have reduced my own nation to misery and despair . . . You prate of liberty and crush anything that differs from you as soon as it stirs. You look about you and can tolerate no image but your own; the very sight of otherness is intolerable to you."[10] The business of art, in context and in its defiant autonomy, is precisely to interject a countermanding newness or difference into the self-same world. "There steals over us," as Wilde writes of the impulse to creativity, "a terrible sense of the necessity for the continuance of energy in the same wearisome round of stereotyped habits, or a wild longing, it may be, that our eyelids might open some morning upon a world that had been refashioned anew in the darkness."[11]

Thus in celebrating the "sympathies" of Ghose's "Oriental mind," does Wilde observe in his beguiling foreignness the means for importing an estranging idiom into English prosody, the capacity to liberate the "aesthetic" from its nervous conformity to the world, so that it can begin the work of postulating an alternative reality? In "The Decay of Lying," he praises any impulse toward "orientalism" in the decorative arts in such terms, for "its frank rejection of imitation . . . its dislike to the actual representation of any object in nature . . . in which the visible things of life are transmuted into artistic conventions, and the things that life has not are invented and fashioned for her delight."[12] None of these wider tenets of the aestheticist credo are directly explicated in the review in the *Pall Mall Gazette.* They remain as shadowy possibilities whose insistent invocation, of the kind we have been engaged in, generates something of a storm in the unprepossessing teacup of Wilde's incidental piece on yet another incidental volume of fin-de-siècle poetry. There is, however, a single line upon which we might pause a little longer, for it gestures toward the discursive oppositions that are the main business of this chapter.

Once again, drawing upon an aestheticist lexicon in which the signs "art," "poetry," and "culture" stand in one reading for "difference," "freedom," and "alterity," Wilde observes in Ghose's poetic negotiation of the East-West divide a form of relation that might come to dissolve the coercive bonds of imperialism. "His verses," Wilde writes in a rare moment of sobriety in the piece, "suggest how close is the bond of union that might one day bind India to us by other methods than those of commerce and military strength." So here we have some faint battle lines, with the relation of poetry, literature, art on the one side and that of the colonial encounter on the other. Yet how difficult it is to foment a politics out of such discursive content, as it is precisely the oppositions between culture and imperialism, literature and history, aesthetics and materialism that postcolonial thought has so scrupulously trained us to read with suspicion as the first symptom of ideological foul play. Thus in the disarming substitution of imperialism with culture proposed by Wilde, postcolonial analysis is likely to discern only the raw materials of colonial hegemony: that form of "binding" based on methods of consent rather than coercion. Does Wilde's review bring us face to face with that procedure, detailed by Gauri Viswanathan, whereby the transcendental categories "Literature," "Art," and "Culture" always insidiously posit a "mask of conquest"? Or another, predicated upon the belief that only in its radical autonomy—that is, its separation from materialism, historicism, objectivism—does art obtain its powers of dissidence, earn (in context) its anticolonial credentials? To put this more simply, is aesthetic autonomy—the argument for the freedom of art from the realm of the real, an argument inaugurated within western aesthetics by Immanuel Kant's *Critique of Judgement*—a conservative or a radical discourse?

These questions are at the heart of the following discussion, which continues the enquiry into the status of the "political" explicated in chapter 5. In so doing, it will interrogate—this time under the sign of "art"—the constitutively modern demand for realism in politics manifest in other contexts as an allergy to the revolutionary claims of utopian, metaphysical, affective, and "spiritualist" endeavor. Reading Wilde's sentence in praise of Ghose at face value, as simply and radically anticolonial, I wish to disclose some greater variety in forms of the political than modernity allows. Concurrently, it is also my aim to mount a postcolonial defense of poetry, to find a model of aesthetic autonomy that might be recoupable within anticolonial politics and thought. To this end, we must first enter into critical relation with postcolonial orthodoxy, asking how it came to pass that the disciplinary tasks of anticolonial critique took the form of an anti-aestheticist fallacy. Second, pursuing a counter to this bias, we will attempt to locate, at the interstices of Kantian and Hegelian aesthetics, a model of aesthetic autonomy that makes political or anticolonial sense of Wilde's insistent polarization of poetry and empire, one wedded to the belief that sometimes art discloses its radical provenance precisely in its defiant flight from the realm of the real.

MASKS OF CONQUEST

The discursive logic whereby anticolonial thought seeks its contemporary articulation in and as a bias against literary autonomy displays further symptoms of our impoverished understanding of the political that Dipesh Chakrabarty discusses in *Provincialising Europe*. Starkly visible, as we saw, in the prejudices of secularist humanism, to which western political thought is both heir and sentinel, the "straightforward identification of the realist or the factual with the political," as Chakrabarty argues, betrays a disabling generic bias that owes its origins to "the familiar political desire of the modern to align the world with that which was real and rational." Seeking an epistemology always "amenable to historicist and objectivist treatment," and always suspicious of the erratic agency of "vision" and "imagination," modernity iteratively condemns the political to constitutive singularity.[13] Inhospitable to gods, spirits, and other supernatural beings, such territory is also unable, for similar reasons, to house the insistent recourse to a "poetic view" of self-determination that Chakrabarty observes at work in the anticolonial nationalism of a Tagore. In the face of these prejudices the task of restoring semantic plenitude to the category of "the political" demands, Chakrabarty says, that we "breathe heterogeneity into the word 'imagination'—and, we might add, all other terms within the same typology: poetry, autonomy, art, inventiveness, enthusiasm.[14] Contiguously, we must reexamine more critically the realist epistemology to which postcolonialism, among other disciplines in the new humanities, proffers its allegiance.

A favored legatee of the deeper biases of modern political thought, postcolonialism's peculiar anticolonial, antiliterary fallacy owes something to the circumstances in which the discipline emerged, its coarticulation in the late 1970s with the "sociology of literature." Let us consider these circumstances briefly. In 1976, as is well known, the University of Essex inaugurated a series of historic conferences, symposia, and publications under the rubric of the "Essex Sociology of Literature Project." Committed in part to the disciplinary enrichment of sociology, the project was equally—and often rightly—insistent upon the benefits of sociological analysis for the seemingly moribund field of Literary Studies.[15] Informed, John Hall writes, by the conviction "that literature can only be understood in its social context, or that an *external* referent is necessary for any full comprehension of the text," the sociologization of literature delivered complex strategies of reading whose full creativity would be realized in work conducted under the sign of "cultural materialism" in the British academy and "new historicism" in the American. These productive effects notwithstanding, the venture displayed even in its incipience symptoms of an unequal partnership, framed by a zealous tutoring of the "soft" discipline by its hardy, empiricist companion. And in time, what began as an incentive toward methodological reform—

designed to bring materialist analysis within the purview of literary criticism—would give way to a feverish assault on any perceived defense of aesthetic autonomy emanating from within Anglo-American English departments.

This antipathy toward claims for culture's immunity from the "real" were determined, as Stuart Hall explains, by the founding neo-Marxism of scholars within the sociology-of-literature movement.[16] Taking its cue from the work of Lukács, Goldmann, Williams, and Althusser, the subdiscipline might well be explained as an elaborate gloss on that famous passage in *The German Ideology* in which Marx insists that even "the phantoms formed in the human brain" are mere sublimates of a "material life-process," always "empirically verifiable and bound to materialist premises," and that consequently "Morality, religion, metaphysics, all the rest of ideology and their corresponding forms of consciousness . . . no longer retain the semblance of independence."[17] As elaborated in the late 1970s, this Marxist edict against the illusion of ideological independence found itself newly inflected by a politico-philosophical charge against the very theme of "autonomy" in all its discursive incarnations. So where some scholars who were identified with the field under consideration simply dismissed as mythical the motif of "human autonomy," others such as Catherine Belsey discerned in "the knowing autonomous subject" the very "lynch-pin of capitalism," an ideological portent of Thatcherism, right-wing "nouveaux philosophies" in France, and the growth of American neoconservatism and libertarianism.[18] Or as Boyd Tonkin puts it in an essay from this period, "conservative publicity" always "adopts a language . . . of unfettered liberty and of abstract, transcendent subjectivity" to disguise its narrow economic incentives.[19]

This was the basic theoretical agenda which produced the putative "crisis in English" of which Chris Baldick has written in *The Social Mission of English Criticism.* As a result of this sleight of sociological hand, the discipline "English" and its curricular content "Literature" were suddenly identified as repositories, bastions, and safe houses for the conservative trope of autonomy, and neomaterialism became invested with the revolutionary chore of displacing, in Stuart Hall's words, "the notion of the radically autonomous text which had held the centre of English literary studies for so long."[20] On the continent Pierre

Bourdieu's study *La Distinction* (1979) demonstrated this sociological responsibility through an unforgiving identification of aesthetic autonomy as an instrument of bourgeois domination; Anglo-American scholars quickly followed suit, insisting vehemently upon the irremediable symbiosis between "aestheticism" and "conservatism." "Ever since Théophile Gautier launched the idea of 'art for art's sake' in a vicious polemic against the followers of Fourier and Saint-Simon," Jan Birchall writes, explicating the terms of combat, "the idea of the autonomy of art has been a component of conservative ideology."[21]

In one of those curious accidents of disciplinary history, it was in this moment, when "the political" was reined into war against "literature," that we can also witness the emergence of a congenial critical space within the sociological humanities for postcolonial elaborations. For the project that demanded, in its assault against aesthetic autonomy, a counteractive "worlding" of literature was also impelled by a radically pluralizing momentum, bringing art down to level with the empirical variety of human history and sociality. As Catherine Belsey insists, with the advent of the new sociology in the 1970s, it became the task of radical teachers in crisis-ridden English departments to transform "the central ideological apparatus by the introduction of counter-knowledges, counter-meanings which demonstrate the plurality of what might be said and thought and what can in consequence be done."[22] It is not incidental that Edward Said's *Orientalism*, the inaugural articulation of postcolonialism as an unrelenting critique of "disinterested knowledges," appeared in 1978, in the thick of the sociology-of-literature initiative; and Said's work explicitly dovetailed with the initiative in the symposia at Essex in 1984, which resulted in the publication of the influential two-volume study *Europe and Its Others*. Showcasing Said's essay "Orientalism Reconsidered," as well as work by Homi Bhabha, Gayatri Spivak, and Lata Mani, the study demonstrates the housing of a postcolonial problematic within an initiative whose own radical materialism is inextricable, as we have been arguing, from an anti-aestheticist dispensation. To speak the political (postcolonial, feminist, gay and lesbian, Marxist) within this space is already and intractably coded as a speaking against all aspirations to literary and cultural immunity.

How readily visible this bias is in the three founding propositions that structure Said's magisterial *Orientalism*: One, there is no such thing as a pure or disinterested knowledge formation. Two, whenever knowledge protests its purity too much it is a symptom of that knowledge's lack of the very purity to which it lays claim, and the extent of a knowledge's interestedness in power is in direct proportion to its protestations of disinterest or autonomy. And three, most famously, Orientalism is such a form of implicated knowledge posturing as autonomous or disinterested. These themes are further augmented in *Culture and Imperialism*, especially through Said's insistent designation of postcolonial theoretical practice as an effort to take "Western cultural forms . . . out of the autonomous enclosures in which they have been protected," to place them instead "in the dynamic global environment created by imperialism."[23]

So, I suggest, it was as disciplinary participant in the neomaterialist idiom of the new humanities academy in the late 1970s that early postcolonialism yoked its own belated anticolonial imperatives to a sociological refutation or "worlding" of aestheticism, literature, and culture, that it acquired, in other words, the antiliterary fallacy adumbrated in Gauri Viswanathan's *Masks of Conquest*, invoked at the outset of this discussion. To recapitulate the arguments: much in the spirit of Said's oeuvre, Viswanathan insists axiomatically upon imperialism's enmeshment with literary culture, arguing specifically that in an age of empire the rhetoric of literary or cultural immunity is always evidence of an attempt to mask the harsh reality of imperial interests: "The introduction of English Literature marks the effacement of a sordid history of colonialist expropriation, material exploitation, and class and race oppression behind European world dominance. The English literary text functioning as a surrogate Englishman in his highest and most perfect state, becomes a mask for economic exploitation . . . successfully camouflaging the material activities of the coloniser . . . The split between the material and the cultural practices of colonialism is nowhere sharper than in the progressive refinement of the rapacious, exploitative, and ruthless actor of history into the reflective subject of literature."[24]

Against this perceived literary conspiracy, Viswanathan and other like-minded postcolonial scholars have called categorically for armed historical response: unmasking aestheticist protestation to disclose the unpalatable reality of imperial content. Needless to say, there is little space within this theoretical paradigm to read as political or anticolonial

Oscar Wilde's gentle claim that their radical autonomy from the gross, material realities of imperialism are precisely what enable literature and art to proffer a "bond of union that might one day bind India to us by other methods than those of commerce and military strength." There are, however, two routes through which we might attempt a postcolonial recuperation of the ethic hinted at by Wilde. The first is suggested in Priya Joshi's *In Another Country* (2002), a study that counteracts the bias of Viswanathan, Said, and the sociology-of-literature movement against literary autonomy through a subtle shift of scholarly focus from questions of colonial intent to those of colonized reception—that is, from the politics of the colonial literary-cultural-aesthetic commodity to the hitherto occluded archive of colonized consumption. Working very much within the materialist domain of postcolonial sociological analysis, Joshi tells another set of competing stories in a painstaking demonstration of the authority and selectivity with which colonized Indian readers received imperial "literariness," always astutely distinguishing the romance of the English book from the realism of English colonialism. To some extent our own project borrows from this initiative in its effort to delineate the story of Ghose and Wilde as a counternarrative, revealing in it a confident anticolonial negotiation with the claims of western aesthetic and literary autonomy. Yet ultimately it is theoretically unsatisfactory to ascribe our quarrel with postcolonial orthodoxy (in the name of Wilde and Ghose) only to a matter of differing or competing archives, for such a strategy does little to unsettle the foundational claims of that realist epistemology to which our notions of the political have long been hostage. To breathe heterogeneity, as Chakrabarty does, into a "poetic view" of anticolonial self-determination, we must also, and urgently, attempt a radical rehabilitation of the very theme of aesthetic autonomy, pursuing the postcolonial sociologizing of literature into the matrix of its philosophical antipathy to aestheticism. Our aim in so doing is to supplement the counternarrative of colonized readership with a countermodel of literary autonomy that might be congenial, as we have been saying, to the ethico-political demands of anticolonial thought.

To this end, we must negotiate the "problem" of Immanuel Kant's *Critique of Judgement*, a work famously identified by Bourdieu in *Distinction: A Social Critique of the Judgement of Taste* as the source-text for the bourgeois trope of aesthetic autonomy, and one that is guilty as charged of imbricating all subsequent aestheticism with a surreptitious will-to-power. In *Culture and Imperialism*, Said likewise names Kantian aesthetics as the founding paradigm for the motivated lie of cultural immunity in western thought. As he writes, "Cultural experience or indeed every cultural form is radically, quintessentially hybrid, and if it has been the practice in the West since Immanuel Kant to isolate cultural and aesthetic realms from the worldly domain, it is now time to rejoin them."[25] Thus, we might say after Said, in its defining commitment to the "worlding" of culture, sociological postcolonialism is eo ipso a departure from the principles of Kantian aesthetics. Furthermore, given the logic of this flight—from cultural immunity toward cultural materialism—it also tends, theoretically and implicitly, toward the field of Hegelian aesthetics: originary, it will be remembered, in offering "materialism" and "historicism" as a riposte to Kant's appeal for the radical freedom of aesthetic experience. Before Hegel, Kai Hammermeister tells us, "no philosophical attempt had been made . . . to deduce the necessity of historical changes in art from an overarching principle that itself depends on historical unfolding."[26] To choose Hegel over Kant (or vice versa), however, is no simple matter, as we saw earlier, for what look very much like radical differences between the two philosophers often disguise deep and complicating affinities: for example, the Hegelian critique of the solipsistic Kantian subject (re)produces, in the end, the logic of an even more violently solipsistic community. A similar problem, I will argue, attends the implicit choice of Hegel over Kant that guides postcolonialism in its assault on aesthetic autonomy. For where certain appeals to the immunity of aesthetic experience in Kant are generative of that élitist, imperialist subject-of-power condemned by Bourdieu and Said, the countervailing subject of Hegelian materialism does not really deliver an alternative amenable to anticolonial appropriation. Indeed, at least within the limited field of aesthetic theory, closer examination reveals elements within Kantian aestheticism to be far more recoupable for anticolonial use than the harsh postulates of Hegelian materialism. Nonetheless, to be adequately responsive to the complaints of historicism, such a recuperation of Kant can only be effected, as it were, after Hegel—that is, as a post-Hegelian critique of judgment. Such too is the critique in which we might find the political space we are seeking for an adequate reading of Oscar Wilde's review of *Primavera.*

THE SPACE OF AUTONOMY

In *Distinction*, it will be remembered, Pierre Bourdieu charges Kantian aesthetics with a disenchanted negation of the social and ordinary world. The autonomous, "*selbstständig*" sphere of aesthetic experience, or "judgment," is predicated, he argues, upon a constitutive "disgust" with the realm of necessity. Although obscured, strains of nausea and nihilism underscore the ascetic imperatives of Kantian ethics and epistemology, specifically (we argued in chapter 5) in their neurotic reworking of the expressivist dream of freedom as the austere desert of "separation": between the knowing subject and the external world, and between the rational subject and her own unregulated nature. Radical freedom in the Kantian sense, Charles Taylor tells us, "seemed only possible at the cost of a diremption with nature, a division within myself between reason and sensibility more radical than anything the materialist, utilitarian Enlightenment had dreamed, and hence a division with external nature from whose causal laws the free self must be radically independent, even while phenomenally his behaviour appeared to conform."[27] Committed unforgivingly in all his philosophical oeuvre to this self-dividing project, Kant nevertheless offers in his third critique, *The Critique of Judgement* (1790)—although in a manner barely perceptible and quickly recanted—a sudden deflection, *contra* Bourdieu, from the monkishness of his own thought. For where this critique will, in the spirit of its companion volumes, come to found the freedom of the subject of judgment, or of aesthetic experience, upon her uncompromising "separateness" from nature, it will also, if nervously, instantiate a protest. This protest will claim as a salve to the burden of her separateness the subject of judgment's autonomy not only from "sensibility" but also from "reason," not only from "nature" but also from the capturing, universalizing concept-categories of "cognition" and "morality." It is this divided idiom of "autonomy" in Kant's third critique—the baffling liminality of the subject of aesthetic experience—that we need to examine more closely in the following discussion.

The experience of beauty, Kant writes—that is, the faculty of pleasure or displeasure—occurs at the unmarked threshold between knowledge and desire, neither purely a priori nor purely empirical. Registered through the unique "reflective" capacities of the subject, it signals the action of musing "upon the objects of nature with a view to getting a thoroughly interconnected whole of experience."[28] The organicity of understanding to which reflection aspires, however, presupposes, in a Kantian idiom, some action of those universal concept-categories without which the world would remain chronically unintelligible, and on account of which the world must eventually be separated from the desiring self. Yet in this instance—in face of the beautiful—reflective judgment is never entirely captured by the categories of cognition. Tending, in the sensations of pleasure and displeasure, toward the empirical wealth of nature, it can only hope without knowing for sure that nature will yield the "systematic unity" upon which another kind of freedom (from self-division, from the alienating partiality of purely rational knowledge) depends. Thus the subject of judgment gazes upon nature, awaiting what Kant calls the "lucky chance" of intelligibility, always knowing that chance might not prove favorable. "The specific variety of the empirical laws of nature," Kant writes, "might still be so great as to make it impossible for our understanding to discover in nature an intelligible order."[29] The characterizing "confusion" and "heterogeneity" of nature may well thwart any effort "to make a consistent context of experience."[30] Aesthetic experience thus includes in its inception a movement of hazardous surrender to the realm of difference—Kant calls this the "dwelling place," or "domicilium"—designated by nature's ineluctable contingency.[31] Any tenancy within this domicilium, however, is simultaneously and vertiginously a gesture of autonomy from the legislative realm, or *ditio*, ruled over by cognitive concept-categories.[32] So in that initial moment of its exposition which we are interrogating here, Kant's third critique liberates the possibility that the autonomy of aesthetic experience consists at least in part of a capacity to dwell with difference. Let us name this strain of aesthetic autonomy "the ethics of domicilium."

It is only very briefly, however, that Kant surrenders the subject of his critique into the risky ethics of domicilium, quickly recoiling from his tentative compromises with the discourse of radical freedom to coin new terms with which to effect a diremption from nature, thus restoring "autonomy" to the safeguard of "separation." As he notes in a moment of philosophical panic, even though the reflective activity of judgment resists capture by the possessive *ditio* of cognition, its claim to meaningfulness (to philosophic consideration) demands submission of its hitherto whimsical estimate of nature to a project of "finality": "an endeavour to bring, where possible, its heterogeneous laws under higher, though still always empirical, laws."[33] Where outside the realm of concept-categories may we recognize the cohering moment of finality? In the experience of pleasure, Kant avers with perverse circularity: an experience restricted, furthermore, to the subject of judgment, to her faculty of "taste" rather than to any quality in the object(s) being apprehended. Thus, finality does its work by reintroducing a normative breach between subject and object of pleasure: a state of "separation" issuing this time from the irremediably self-protective Kantian subject's newly snobbish credo of "disinterest," a freedom from interest in the materiality or "necessity" of the objects that provoke the subject's pleasure. Herein lies that other ground for the autonomy of aesthetic experience so fiercely condemned, and with such good cause, by Bourdieu: an experience of the beautiful predicated upon a disenchanted and negating break from the material world, uncontaminated by the base perils of want, need, and necessity. As Kant has it, "Of all . . . kinds of delight, that of taste in the beautiful may be said to be the one and only disinterested and *free* delight; for with it, no interest . . . exhorts approval . . . All interest presupposes a want, or calls one forth; and being a ground determining approval, deprives the judgement on the object of its freedom."[34]

The Kantian thematic of disinterest has been justly censured by others besides Bourdieu for introducing a narrative of death into the trope of aesthetic autonomy, indeed into the very experience of the beautiful. In its ascetic brutality Kantian disinterestedness, according to Nietzsche, paralyzes the will, wrenching from its grasp the "promise of happiness" that Stendhal once witnessed in the beautiful.[35] So too, Giorgio Agamben sees in the self-denying criterion of judgment and taste a reduction of the "living body" of art to "an interminable skeleton of dead elements."[36] It is, we might concur, precisely while possessed by this deathly, narcissism that Kantian judgment also declares war on difference, giving rein yet again to a self-englobing subjectivity freely defending, in the name of its own ethical and epistemological safety, the unchecked territorial expansion of its ego. Thus misperceiving, in Terry Eagleton's terms, "the quality of the object" for a "pleasurable co-ordination of its own powers," the disinterested Kantian subject of aesthetic judgment arrives at an imperialist dénouement: "once I am established in . . . autonomy, I can then proceed in the real social world to strip those others of their own equivalent independence."[37] In addition, not only does disinterest potentially liberate in judgment the difference-eradicating territorialism to which other Kantian subjects are prone, it also bestows on the faculty of taste the equally homogenizing action of a civilizing imperative. For those privileged with taste, Kant tells us, are entitled if not obliged to demand consensus: "he must believe that he has reason for demanding a similar delight from everyone" (50); "when he puts a thing on a pedestal and calls it beautiful, he demands the same delight in others" (51); "He judges not merely for himself, but for all men . . . Thus he demands this agreement of them" (52). Let us name this demanding strain of aesthetic autonomy "the colonising imperative of disinterest."[38]

To summarize: we may discern in the vexed fiber of Kant's third critique an idiom stretched between two strains of aesthetic autonomy. The first, which we have called "the ethics of domicilium," construes the experience of beauty as freedom from the possessive concept-categories of cognition and morality, and in so doing releases the subject of judgment into a psychically perilous cohabitation with difference. The second, which we have called "the colonizing imperative of disinterest," recoils from these compromises of reflection to reclaim for judgment an autonomy premised on division from nature. This puts us again in face of a territorializing and civilizing subject, constitutively at war with alterity. To make brief reference to our guiding concerns in this discussion, the first strain of autonomy is clearly amenable to the demands of anticolonial thought, while the second is clearly antithetical to it. Let us issue a tender, in the name of anticolonial imperatives, for some discursive surgery that might amputate the limb of "disinterest"—already lifeless, by the report of Nietzsche et al.—from the body of "domicilium," but let the surgery be delicate enough to preserve, to keep safe, that capacity to live among foreigners, aliens, and strangers that is secreted within the arguments of Kant's third critique.

In Pierre Bourdieu's estimation, disinterest requires urgent materialist operation: a reconnection of aesthetic tissue with social sinew that might reveal the "eye" of taste to be "a product of history," underscored by the belief that "aesthetic perception is necessarily historical."[39] History is thus presumably the "lack" that disinterest enforces within the realm of aesthetics, whose reintroduction will complete the picture, as it were, restoring a lost plenitude to art and to its experiencing subject(s). But in fact, "history," in Bourdieu's sense, is not a reparative, organic agency, seeking to fill in with the excluded stuff of life, nature, and matter the barren spaces of "separation" to which the subject of judgment is condemned. It enters rather the domain of the aesthetic as a self-righteous invading army might: convinced that its encroachments are liberatory, replacing a repressive older regime with a revolutionary alternative. So within the pages of *Distinction*, if the realm of "disinterest," or what Bourdieu calls the "pure aesthetic," stands simply and categorically for bad (conservative) politics, that of materialism, or necessity, is posited as simply a good (revolutionary) alternative. In other words, if aestheticism is a corollary to a life of bourgeois ease, privilege, and domination, then "objectivism," "historicism," and "sociologism" conversely designate a space of and for the oppressed.[40] This is precisely the opposition that we are attempting to complicate, not least because it excuses an unexamined anti-aestheticism in Bourdieu's thought and, concomitantly, the anti-literary fallacy within postcolonial orthodoxy. In *Distinction*, as in Bourdieu's later *The Rules of Art*, the proposition "historicism is better politics than aestheticism" collapses into the adjacent propositions "sociology is better than philosophy," "there is no political value in abstract thought," "the real and the factual are the only acceptable realm for the political," and "history is better than art."[41] Subjecting the "colonising imperative of disinterest" to materialist operation would appear at first glance to be a somewhat drastic procedure that threatens the very space of art, leaving little scope for elaborating the distinctly aesthetic "ethic of domicilium" that we wished to safeguard. But perhaps we might find within the category "history" a similar, indeed improved, ethic, congenial to difference and uncontaminated, as its apostles claim, by the exclusionary prerogatives of Kantian disinterest.

In Hegel's oeuvre, however, originary, as suggested earlier, in its specifically historicist riposte to the terms and conditions of Kantian deontology, the contest between "history" and "art" (objectivism and aestheticism) achieves a strangely colonial dimension, and nowhere more so than in his influential *Philosophy of History*. In this work, zealous as ever in the task of allocating civilizational priority, Hegel makes a crucial distinction between those cultures (good and progressive) that possess history and those (bad and retrogressive) that possess only poetry. "Legends, Ballad-stories, Traditions," he writes, "must be excluded from . . . history. These are but dim and hazy forms of historical apprehension, and therefore belong to nations whose intelligence is but half awakened . . . The domain of reality . . . affords a very different basis in point of firmness from that fugitive and shadowy element, in which were engendered those legends and poetic dreams whose historical prestige vanishes, as soon as nations have attained a mature individuality."[42] Thus India and specifically the "Hindoo" race, although gifted with "treasures of literature," nevertheless has "no history."[43] Only Europe, Hegel insists, with its universal social forms, is equipped to produce the empirically grounded "prose" of history.[44] In its Hegelian detour, the proposition "history is better than art" gathers up as a residuum, and retains a faint trace of, an adjacent proposition: "Europe is better than Asia," a secret code that further complicates the exclusive entitlement to "freedom" of the élite possessors of history and ruthlessly withheld from those limited to poetry. "Universal history," Hegel thunders, "shows the development of the consciousness of Freedom on the part of the Spirit, and of the consequent realisation of that Freedom."[45] Or to inflect this proposition otherwise, as Robert Young does, we might claim that Hegelian world history "not only involves what Fredric Jameson describes as the wresting of freedom from the realm of necessity but always also the creation, subjection and final appropriation of Europe's others."[46]

So what, we might ask, precisely privileges the claims of historical freedom over and above those of aesthetic autonomy? Of Hegelian materialism over those of Kantian deontology? Such autonomy, Hegel contends, as is defended by the monkish, stripped down, and disinterested Kantian subject, is simply misguided in its demand for separation from the external world. Far from being strange to each other, as feared, the subject and object, subjective will and objective laws, are similar and identical, rendered "same" through grace of that shared subjectivity distributed in raw, unrealized form by the itinerant Spirit on its travels. True freedom, in context, obtains from a recognition that the world is a familiar place, but a recognition that can only be liberated within history and as thought—that is, in shape of the cognitive concept-category (which Kant relinquishes in the third critique). In précis: the freedom disclosed within history (through the concept-form) is palpably less self-dividing than the lonely and austere autonomy jealously safeguarded by the disinterested subject of Kantian deontology. Here we may be in face of a claim that might satisfy a Nietzsche or an Agamben, except that in making the business of freedom so much more existentially comfortable for the subject of history, Hegel delivers us at a scene startlingly similar to the one disclosed by "the colonising imperative of disinterest." Hegel's assault on the "separation" upon which "disinterest" is predicated does not, of course, liberate the subject into an "ethic of domicilium" but into an even more radical order of similitude, replacing what Mary Louise Pratt describes as "master-of-all-I-survey" with what Hélène Cixous describes as "the empire of the self-same."[47] "Recognition," we might say, is to a Hegelian idiom what "disinterest" is to a Kantian: close cousins both despite the ostensible differences between their progenitors.

It is upon the stage of history, Hegel writes in his *Introduction to Aesthetics*, that the violent drama of recognition will be performed. Here "man" will bring "himself before himself in whatever is directly given to him, in what is present to him externally, to produce himself and therein to recognise himself. This aim he achieves by altering external things whereon he impresses the seal of his inner being and in which he now finds again his characteristics. Man does this in order, as a free subject, to strip the external world of its inflexible foreignness and to enjoy in the shape of things only an external realisation of himself."[48] What history enables, furthermore, is exacerbated by the difference eradicating "thinking-spirit" or concept-form through "the power and activity of cancelling again the estrangement in which it gets involved."[49] It is precisely in the name of this power to cancel estrangement that colonialism, according to Cixous and Clement, lays its dubious claim to history. In their words, "I saw that the great, noble 'advanced' countries established themselves by expelling what was 'strange'; excluding it but not dismissing it; enslaving it. A commonplace gesture of history: there have to be *two* races—the masters and the slaves."[50]

Are there any means that could puncture the opaque façade of similitude engineered by Hegelian historicism? The surprising answer, to which we must attend very closely, is offered by Hegel himself in his writings on aesthetics. As the chief venue for the drama of recognition, history, Hegel tells us, is assisted in its commitment to the subject's self-perpetuation by a variety of cultural forms—specifically philosophy, religion, and art. Yet if enlisted as a foot soldier to this project, the realm of art or aesthetic experience would appear to fail chronically in its assigned task, refusing containment by historical necessity and by the regulative economy of the concept-category. In Hegel's words: "the beauty of art does in fact appear in a form which is expressly opposed to thought and which thought is compelled to destroy in order to pursue its own characteristic activity."[51] Why? Because, as Kant recognized too well, poised in that liminal space between reason and sensibility, cognition and nature, general and particular, universal and contingent, aesthetic experience is ever susceptible to the heterogeneous terrain marked in each instance by the second term in this series, intransigent in the face of the cultural and civilizational diminishment demanded by Hegelian historicism.[52] Indeed aesthetic autonomy—in Hegel's words, "the *freedom* of production and configurations that we enjoy in the beauty of art"—is a function precisely of art's commitment to the "manifold and variegated appearance" of nature, to its "multiple variety of content," in a word, to difference.[53] Accordingly, because of its conflict with the governing imperatives of history and the thinking spirit, art, as Hegel so infamously demands, must die. Proper fulfilment of the project of recognition demands that we pass "over from the poetry of the imagination into the prose of thought," into the "prose of history."[54]

Let us review the terms of our discussion: searching for some anticolonial ground from which to defend aestheticism (against a historicist and sociological imperative), we found in the nervous inauguration of Kant's third critique a strain of aesthetic autonomy structured by a capacity to reside, nonviolently, with unlikeness. As yet rudimentary and untested, this incipient "ethics of domicilium" was too quickly repressed by the prerogatives of "separation," too closely fettered to—although not entirely eliminated by—the colonizing imperatives of "disinterest." The political potential, for our ends, of aesthetic autonomy, *as in* Kant, thus remained unrealized, deferred indefinitely until discursive circumstances proved more propitious. In large part, it is to historicism and materialism that we owe this disappointed insight into the contaminating perils of Kantian "disinterest." History, we might say, proves better than aestheticism in its demand, following Bourdieu, Said, and Hegel, that art must be "interested" in the world. In pressing its case for "interestedness" (against the separation and estrangement of subject and object), however, Hegelian historicism reverts tiredly to the colonizing undercurrent of Kantian thought, sovereign in its discursive mastery over difference but for the uncontainable heterogeneity of artistic production. Art, we might say, thus presents itself as the "remainder" in both Kantian and Hegelian thought, straining for freedom from the possessive claims of "disinterest" and "recognition," through its intractable congeniality to alterity. Such is the utopian possibility that Theodor Adorno and Martin Heidegger have also beheld in the domain of art and poetry. For both, art, as a realm that simultaneously dwells among and gives dwelling to difference, is a space hospitable to the singular and the nonidentical, one that offers refuge to the ineluctable thingness of things, preserving the rich assortment of the world, its unqualified empiricism, in what Heidegger designates the liberated "interior of the heart's space."[55] It is in this capacity to offer asylum that art lays claim to radical autonomy from the leveling and conservative actions of history and thought, resisting, for Adorno, the difference-eradicating nature of the totalitarian concept and, for Heidegger, the colonizing and separating violence of the thinking-spirit.[56] Let us, in one last act of naming, call this ethics of and for aestheticism—that is, of post-Hegelian domicilium—"the paradigm of interested autonomy."

It is, I suggest, precisely such a form of "interested autonomy" that Manmohan Ghose is likely to have encountered in Oscar Wilde: one demanding liberation from the prosaic sameness of imperial realism and narcissism in its flight toward the numerous strange outcasts variously excluded from the privileged mainstream. In what remains of this discussion we will elaborate this conjecture through a closer look at the story of the brief and accidental convergence between the lives of Wilde, Irish interloper in the imperial metropole, and Ghose, colonial aspirant in the same. Wilde needs little introduction, but what of Ghose? Known principally as one of the brothers of Aurobindo Ghose (the extremist anticolonial revolutionary, poet, philosopher, and mystic, encountered in chapter 5), Manmohan Ghose enjoyed a brief tenancy within the emerging culture of English aestheticism between 1888 and 1894, before returning reluctantly to the inequities of colonial India to take up the post of assistant professor in English at Patna College. Haunted for the remainder of his life by the radical discrepancy of character between his "aestheticist" friends in England and his colonial governors in India—between, we might say, the seemingly disparate worlds of English Literature and English Imperialism—the strangely vexed figure of Manmohan Ghose supplies a means to reengage, microhistorically, both with postcolonialism's insistence upon a necessary collusion of European culture and imperialism and with its consequent allergy to the discourse of aesthetic and cultural autonomy. What was it in a colonial subject like Manmohan Ghose that rendered him—as we will see—so very susceptible to the culture of aestheticism, especially in its Wildean exemplification? What were the costs, the gains, if any, of such susceptibilities for a young Indian foreigner in the heart of Empire? And what might aestheticism have looked like to a subject such as Ghose? Let us engage some of these questions directly.

PORTRAIT OF A FRIENDSHIP

The story of Manmohan Ghose's transactions with aestheticism is framed almost entirely by the narrative of his lifelong friendship with the poet, dramatist, translator, art historian, and critic Laurence Binyon. The two met at St. Paul's in London, overlapped for a while at Oxford, and maintained a correspondence long after Ghose's departure for India. Of these letters only Ghose's survive, documenting in the rich language of affect the emergence of an unlikely intercultural friendship within the nourishing subculture of late Victorian decadence.

Ghose arrived in England in 1879 along with his two brothers Benoybhushan and Aurobindo, all summarily removed from India to achieve the English education and comportment devoutly wished for them by their father, Kristo Dhone Ghose, then civil medical officer of Rangpur in northeastern Bengal. In time, the harsh features of imperialism would substantially diminish that love for England with which the elder Ghose had been afflicted during his medical training at Aberdeen University. However, as yet in that state of uncomplicated anglophilia to which cultured men of his generation were prone, he deposited his sons into the care of the Manchester congregational minister William H. Drewett, leaving strict instructions that they be disallowed "the acquaintance of any Indian or . . . any Indian influence."[57]

In September 1884, after a few years of erratic study at the Manchester Grammar School, Manmohan and Aurobindo were enrolled at St. Paul's in London, where Laurence Binyon had been unhappily in residence as a foundation scholar from May 1881. Instantly drawn into friendship with the exotic Ghose, Binyon records his compelling attraction to Ghose's rare "capacity to be intoxicated by poetry."[58] And it was poetry—its earnest reading and adolescent outpouring—that was the chief matter of Ghose's relationship with Binyon. Exchanging animated letters about new literary discoveries, the boys extended passionate support to each other's early verse efforts. "You are the only one," Ghose proclaimed in 1887, "who gives me any encouragement to write; and I am sure it cannot all be in vain for I know you would tolerate nothing but true poetry."[59] Such interchange would result in the shared authorship of *Primavera*, and in years to come, after Ghose had left for India in 1894, Binyon would remain committed to promoting and publishing his poetry.[60]

Intensely literary in their affect, what was it that accounted for the expressive singularity of poetry, of art, for these two young men at the historical moment in which they came to face each other as schoolboys and as undergraduates? What, in other words, was so rare about that mutual capacity for poetic intoxication of which, Binyon laments, he "found no trace" in his classmates, and that Ghose would find distressingly displaced in favor of athletics at Oxford? "The sole success of all attempts at union is in Athletics," Ghose wrote. "I have no grudge against athletics . . . But it grieves me to see such fine physical endowments and activities lacking what would so enhance their pleasure and value—a little more of reflective and appreciative powers."[61]

In Binyon's case the category "poetry" emerges and does its work in equal and opposite reaction to the category "prose," shorthand in his dialect for Victorian utilitarianism, insularity, inflexibility—in a word, "philistinism."[62] To these categories and their antagonism he returned throughout his life, once describing the boyhood trauma of St. Paul's shift in location from the erratic and impractical bylanes of Cheapside to an expanse of well-ordered sports grounds as a move "to Hammersmith and prose."[63] An essay of 1912, "The Return to Poetry," elaborates the theme, acclaiming the twentieth century for auguring the triumph of a "poetic view" over the Newtonian "prose view of the world" where "all is fixed, matter is finality."[64] In this essay, poetry's conquest of "prose" is enabled by, indeed predicated upon, the admission of nonwestern or "oriental" knowledges within the monochromatic plains of western epistemology: "The secret of this art is all in the paradoxes of Lao-tzu, and in his doctrine of the Tao,—the Way,—the ever-moving, ever-changing, eternal and universal rhythm of life."[65] So too, if more simply, does Binyon conceive of "poetry" in his boyhood, as a space of and for the foreign, and as such embodied in and conjured by his friend Manmohan Ghose. In a memoir published as an introduction to Ghose's posthumous *Love Songs and Elegies*, he recalls how Ghose's capacity for poetic intoxication instantly brought with it "a breath from a world outside the world of habit," his passionate recitations of Shakespeare quintessentially foreign to the prosy sameness of Hammersmith: "The legendary East seemed suddenly to have projected a fragment of itself into our little world of everyday things and humdrum studies, disturbing it with colour, mystery, romance."[66] In adult life it is the ethics of "poetry," thus envisioned, that would lead Binyon into a career pioneering in its commitment to introducing and promoting nonwestern art and thought within the western world. In forty years at the British Museum he would consolidate Oriental art collections, write and lecture extensively on nonwestern philosophies and religions, and adapt a range of Asian legends for the English stage.

For Binyon, then, the category "poetry" amplifies a muted but principled idiom devoted to an internal critique of empire: breaching its prosaic realism to receive, gratefully, the romance of artful strangers. Working this same taxonomy through the somewhat more fraught experience of colonization, Ghose in turn uses the antinomy of poetry and prose to quarantine the best from the worst of Europe; thus "poetry," far from occluding the material, prose realities of imperial force, brings them starkly into relief. It is always the agency of remembering rather than forgetting, a gesture of refusal rather than submission, a means of exposing rather than masking the bad faith of colonial conquest. Here we must emphasize that in Ghose's usage (as also in Binyon's) the series poetry-art-culture inhabits a transcendental and utopian rather than geohistorical or civilizational schema. Incontrovertible proof of an improved ethical or existential capacity, it belongs to no culture in particular and is by no means the monopoly of the West. A "reflective" ability to enjoy Shelley (rather than de Quincey) or Simonides (rather than Mimnermus) does not testify to the cultural triumph of a putative civilizing mission. So Ghose attests in a highly strung letter to Binyon in 1887: "People have a mistaken idea: they think England has brought civilisation to India. India had a civilisation when the English were barbarians, and it was there just the same when England negotiated India into her hands (I won't say conquered, for India was never conquered by the English . . .). We do not want our civilisation done away with, and European civilisation brought in."[67] In the same letter, concerned in the main with praise of Binyon, Arnold, and Lodge (in that order), Ghose moves with ease, and without any apparent contradiction, into the sharp rhetoric of anticolonial polemic, excoriating the Raj for "the devilishness of their machinery of tyranny," and as a "system of government . . . rotten to the core . . . everything . . . in favour of the rulers and to the destruction . . . of the ruled."[68] In the course of his long tenure as assistant professor of English in a variety of Indian institutions, Ghose would continue to advance the cause of English Literature as a gesture against the lapsed imagination of the imperial project. An obituary from one of his students, Nirendranath Roy, foregrounds Ghose's pedagogic ability to summon "poetry" as a force with which to countervail rather than obscure colonial rapacity, conjuring for his students "not the West of economic exploitation and diplomatic dodges with which we are too familiar—but the . . . West represented by Sophocles and Shakespeare . . . Raphael and Velazquez, Beethoven and Mozart. It was in the atmosphere of this Europe that Professor Ghose lived, moved and had his being."[69]

Some lineaments of the "prose" versus "poetry" theme animating the friendship of Ghose and Binyon show up in the pages of *Primavera*, largely in an unmodulated elegiac register, lamenting at large the impassable if unoriginal chasm between the ideal world of youth, love, and beauty on the one hand and the real world of time, loss, and mortality on the other. Every now and then, however, a more accomplished note strikes home, as in Binyon's "Youth," turning adolescent cliché into the language of social complaint: "How keep unquench'd / and free / "Mid others" commerce and economy / Such ample visions, oft in alien air / Tamed to the measure of the common kind?"[70]

Although peculiar to the temperaments and circumstances of the friendships it puts to song, *Primavera* was also finally a creature of its time, expressing, as John Addington Symonds observed in his notice for the *Academy*, the unmistakable "note of the latest Anglican aesthetic school," with, we might add, its doctrinal commitment to the autonomy of art. From its beginnings in 1884 the compact between Ghose and Binyon was ripe for aestheticist elaboration, consistently manifesting those seemingly paradoxical tastes and symptoms that would find their apotheosis and proper political charge, as we will see, in the figure of Oscar Wilde. Thus while their voracious reading was dominated by Swinburne, direct in intellectual line of descent from Théophile Gautier, it was equally possessed by Walt Whitman, sage of late Victorian radicalism, especially in its homosexual and vegetarian protestations.[71] Worshipful of Arnold, the much berated object of postcolonial critique, they also maintained an intellectual diet that turned hungrily to the vague socialist tracts characteristic of the era.[72] In February 1888, true to the spirit of this bibliography and while still a schoolboy, Binyon controversially supported a motion in favor of socialism at a debate organized by St. Paul's Union Society; and in 1891 he supported another at Oxford's Gryphon Club proposing "that it is the opinion of this House that the principle of Nationality is pernicious."[73] Expressing strong solidarity with his friend's political views, Ghose writes disparagingly from Oxford in May 1888 about the inability of his privileged (and overly athletic) Christ Church peers to appreciate the noble socialist sentiments expressed in Binyon's early poem "John Averill": "I found that only two, both of democratic temper, could really enter into it. What can you expect from people who shudder as tho' from instinct at the name of 'socialist' and believe that it hoards all the foulest meanings in the language? They roll above as in a sphere that absolutely disdains any conception of the divine passions and crimes of the multitude."[74] Clearly, we might note as a theme to which we will return, both friends understood that the élite "sphere" of political disengagement was not only distinct from but in some way antithetical to the equally empyrean "sphere" of aesthetic autonomy.

Interleaved by the variegated subculture of their times, the friendship of Ghose and Binyon found its proper aestheticist provenance within the secret enclaves of Pater's Oxford into which Binyon arrived in July 1888, one year after Ghose; this was also the year in which the third edition of *The Renaissance*, the unofficial bible of English aestheticism, appeared, this time with a modified portion of its controversial conclusion restored.[75] After dining quietly with Pater on 24 March 1892, Binyon left with a gift from the great man, typifying the peculiar aesthetic of fin-de-siècle decadence: "a little box of incense our talk having chanced on old-fashioned scents, gums & spices."[76] It was in Oxford that both Binyon and Ghose widened their social sphere to include mutual acquaintances who led them inexorably, Ghose in particular, into the unremarked fringes of Oscar Wilde's circle. Yet the trajectory that gives the name "aestheticism" to their embryonic negotiations of the opposition of "prose" and "poetry" was also one that broached the first signs of strain between the friends, Ghose's excitable temperament having responded rather more fervently than Binyon's quieter nature to the new influences around them.

The fault lines appear in a set of some three letters from Ghose to Binyon between 18 February and 27 February 1888, each protesting, almost in the same breath, the twinned pressures of an inchoate and unspeakable passion on the one hand and—in a sublimating register—the desire more actively to take up arms on behalf of Literature on the other. "You are the only company to me," Ghose writes on 18 February, "I triumph in the thought of this. The only doubt and dread that crosses my mind is that I may suffer some strange resurrection of the passion I have smothered to death . . . I wish to be an ascetic."[77] Some nine days later, a letter agreeing to "let all this rest, and talk no more about it" speaks instead, and volubly, of a will to turn aestheticist crusader: "Art has not the barest representation . . . As for Literature, we have no centre for it whatever: it is my hope—or fond delusion, perhaps—that we may be able in the future to create one, or at least the germs of one . . . I want a centre from which and a sphere in which to act."[78]

While the question of an incipient homosexuality qua homosexuality in Ghose (or between Ghose and Binyon), is strictly speaking irrelevant to the main plot of our discussion, there is considerable interest in the psychic dislocation of his aestheticist designs within a nervously articulated homoerotic thematic. For it is this association between homosexual deviance and aestheticism, subtle but unmistakable, that finally rescues the fin-de-siècle cult of aesthetic autonomy from such charges of élitism as, say, Camille Paglia levels against Wilde and his followers, placing the cult at least tentatively on the side of renegade outcasts.[79] It is in many ways precisely in its covert homoerotic performativity that decadent aestheticism plays out its defiant, self-marginalizing strategies of complaint and satire. So, for instance, the effete dandyism of the movement, as Regina Gagnier and others persuasively contend, is available to reading as an aestheticist riposte to the productivity and industry of the imperial bourgeoisie. "The dandy," Gagnier writes, "showed the gentleman what he had sacrificed: eccentricity, beauty, camaraderie . . . 'Art' was the magical, fetishized term dandies deployed to replace the losses of the age of mechanical reproduction."[80] To such sexually dissident dandyism Ghose subscribed readily, developing, in his brother's account, an expensive taste in "velvet suits, not staring red but aesthetic . . . to visit Oscar Wilde in."[81] In June 1891 his name also appeared in a list of potential contributors to *The Book of the Rhymers Club*, confirming his implication in that group of tragic aesthetes of whom Yeats writes so vividly in *The Trembling of the Veil*, and linking their conscientious, anti-bourgeois "turn from every kind of money making that prevented good writing" to a perverse ethic of sexual ambivalence, "a refusal of domestic life."[82]

Other evidence points likewise to the homoerotic dispensation under the aegis of which Ghose and Binyon began their fractured approach to Wilde's circle. Friendship with the New College poet Lionel Johnson, the man responsible for introducing Bosie to Wilde, provided access to the Hobby Horse House in Fitzroy, creative center in London of the arts and crafts revivalism professed by the Century Guild. It was there that Binyon first met Wilde in full conversational flight on the subject of female emancipation.[83] The friendship with Johnson was productive in other ways. An early admirer along with Wilde of *Primavera*, he reviewed the book for *Hobby Horse*, inscribing on the flyleaf of his personal copy an unpublished poem celebrating the friendship of Ghose and Binyon for its affective and poetic credo:

Now is there any love at all
In all England left, for simple song?
Let all such lovers hear your call:
You have a strain, shall charm them long . . .
And fair befall you both! And may
Your friendship hold all grace in store:
Friends in one art: and, day by day,
True sons of Arnold's, more and more.[84]

Ghose and Binyon were further drawn into a Wildean milieu through association with the painter-engraver Charles Rickett and his lifelong partner Charles Shannon, generous hosts of the Vale in Chelsea—to which Wilde was a regular visitor—and editors of the *Dial*, for some time the house journal of English aestheticism, especially in its peculiar commerce with the artful expressions of contemporary French anarchism.[85] Of these new associates, perhaps none was more visibly infatuated with Ghose than Ernest Dowson, the highly strung poet and Rhymer who in Ellmann's reading may well have become Wilde's lover for a brief period in 1897.[86] Describing his new Indian attachment to Arthur Moore in September 1890 as "the beautiful lotus-eyed Ghose" and two months later to Charles Sayle as "the Primavera poet: a divinely mad person," Dowson bears witness to the aestheticist, decadent company that Ghose was keeping at the beginning of the mauve decade.[87] Writing to Moore on 9 October 1880, he reports thus on the malingering ill-effects of a hard night in the company of Ghose and Wilde among others: "How are you after our potations on Tuesday morning? I am a little decayed from that & subsequent up-sittings. I had a charming night again on Tuesday at Johnson's & at Horne's. Oscar was on show and was quite charming, & in very good form: also Shannon, (the artist & editor of The 'Dial': that mad, strange art review (!): also the prototype of the artist in 'Dorian.')—Ghose and Image."[88] Of such meetings Ghose himself wrote excitedly to Binyon, reporting consistently on

Wilde's gentle patronage. A letter of 4 August 1890 speaks of the older man's advice that the younger pursue plans for an Indian fairy tale: "He was quite charmed with my design for a short Indian tale. 'I should advice you,' he said 'to make a bold bid for the public favour . . . Write this tale and make it rich, striking and concentrated and send it to me: I will get it into the Quarterly Review or some other Magazine for you.' I am going to France for a week or so, and then we shall be able to take counsel together and carry out our little plans. I hope to see much more of you then."[89] Responding a few days later to a possible note of possessive peevishness from his old friend, Ghose penned a gentle defense of his new mentor: "You musn't say anything bad of Oscar . . . now I know him well, I love him very much. He is a wonderful and charming being. You are inclined to think him superficial, I know. You should know him as I do; and then you would feel what depth and sagacity there is behind his delightful mask of paradox and irony and perversity."[90]

The question of what Ghose might have found behind Wilde's "delightful mask" is of central concern to our discussion, since we are searching precisely for the sober imperatives that might have structured Wilde's celebration of Ghose's estranging aestheticism as a counter to the homogenizing violence of empire. There is little in Ghose's letters that immediately betrays the more serious lessons learned and endorsed at the feet of Saint Oscar. He speaks increasingly in the high pitch of Wildean camp, addressing Binyon as "a dear boy" who must "tolerate" Ghose's "wickedness," just as Ghose tolerates Binyon's "goodness," and berating his sober friend with other infuriating aphorisms: "When I see feet of clay, I feel as if I could embrace a man. I see my own sins imaged in him, and yearn toward him in fellow-feeling"; "Perfection, my dear Laurence, is a dangerous virtue; we pay for practising it by cooling our warmer feelings"; "Practice a little passion, a little levity; and I will adore you," ad nauseam.[91] Predictable stuff, and yet even in its derivative talk of "fellow-feeling," "warmer feelings," and "passion," it expresses something of the insistent humanizing quotient at the perverse heart of Wildean aestheticism. Perhaps Ghose's clearest elaboration of this instruction comes in a quarrelsome letter of August 1890 to Binyon, strongly dissociating the impulse toward "self-containment" or "disinterest" from the free exercise of poetry. "But why do you wish so much to come to such a state of self-content," he asks. "It is only a few rare and beautiful souls, who are rich enough in themselves to afford to give without asking to receive back again: and these are never poets."[92] True aestheticism, he avers in an evocatively Darwinian register, demands "that 'relish of passion,' that frailty which is the touch of nature making the whole world kin."[93] Here we have some hint at that paradigm of "interested autonomy"—quintessentially relational and cosmopolitan in its defiant will-to-difference—that we arrived at in our detour through Kantian and Hegelian aestheticism. To the possible amplification of this paradigm in the work of Oscar Wilde let us now briefly turn.

ART FOR THE SAKE OF OTHERS

By the late nineteenth century, Gene H. Bell-Villada writes in his study of European aestheticism, Kant's *Critique of Judgement* "came to be viewed as *the* sourcebook for Art for Art's Sake."[94] This identification was a consequence of the gallicizing of Kant begun in the years of Napolean's dictatorship by French exiles in Germany such as Mme. De Staël and Victor Cousin, and then transmitted to Théophile Gautier, J. K. Huysmans, and others.[95] Oscar Wilde is likely to have made his own first encounters with German philosophy on native soil.[96] As early as 1874, while at Oxford, his commonplace book shows an easy acquaintance with Kant and Hegel. And the chances are that his initial exposure to German thought came from his teacher Walter Pater, whose work displays the contours of Kantian aestheticism, especially as mediated through the writings of J. G. Fichte.[97] Nonetheless, given his extensive commerce with Parisian aestheticism, there is reason to emphasize the distinctly French complexion of Wilde's "Germanism"—and this not for reasons of historical pedantry but rather because in its French transmission the doctrine of aesthetic autonomy kept, in certain circles, very close company with the credo of anarcho-socialism.[98] And it is in some ways the telling proximity and coarticulation of anarchism and aestheticism, socialism and art, in Wilde's thought that accounts for his subtle modifications of Kantianism proper—along the lines hinted at earlier—to produce a discourse of "interested aestheticism."

Contemporary France certainly accommodated these two seemingly paradoxical inheritances in Wilde's work. In certain quarters of Paris he was, David Sweetman writes, "*Mister* Oscar Wilde, the dandyish poet and poseur," drawn up by Toulouse-Lautrec in white tie and tails, complete with a much-too-conspicuous flower in his buttonhole. But in other quarters, better known as "*Monsieur* Oscar Wilde," he received acknowledgment in another panel by Toulouse-Lautrec, once displayed at the Foire du Trone in east Paris, showing Wilde shoulder to shoulder with Félix Fénéon, editor of the radical journal *La Revue blanche* and notorious anarchist, once charged with causing an explosion in a restaurant in Paris.[99] While relatively unacknowledged, Wilde's links with continental anarchism translated into strong sympathy with the indigenous subcultures of late Victorian radicalism, especially in their utopian-socialist exemplification. He was associated with Peter Kropotkin, who began his British exile in 1886, and whom he describes in *De Profundis* as a paradigm, along with Verlaine, of the perfectly aestheticized life.[100] In a review in 1889 of *Chants of Labour: A Song-Book of the People*, edited by Edward Carpenter, the impulses of art likewise combine with those of revolution to praise contemporary socialism for its gift of song: "Nero fiddles while Rome was burning—at least, inaccurate historians say he did; but it is for the building up of an eternal city that the Socialists of the day are making music, and they have complete confidence in the art instincts of the people."[101] In Wilde's own work anarcho-socialist sentiments are explored in his first performed play, *Vera, or, The Nihilist*, a sincere if clumsy critique of "tyranny," potent in the context of contemporary reports about the repressive regime of Czar Alexander II. Of this play, and the politics informing its construction, he would write thus to the actress Mary Prescott: "I have tried in it to express within the limits of art that Titian cry of the peoples for liberty, which in the Europe of our day is threatening thrones, making governments unstable from Spain to Russia, and from north to southern seas."[102] A more sophisticated elaboration of these themes comes in the essay "The Soul of Man under Socialism," first published in July 1890 and possibly the clearest exposition of the symbiosis between aestheticism and socialism in Wilde's idiom. Postulating both art and socialism as complementary demands for freedom from the tyranny of the mainstream, Wilde claims art as an apotheosis of the socialist dream: "For what it seeks to disturb is monotony of type, slavery of custom, tyranny of habit, and the reduction of man to the level of a machine."[103] The significance of these direct political utterances notwithstanding, the anarcho-socialist components of Wilde's aestheticism are as readily visible in the paradoxes and perversities of his apparently less serious oeuvre, pointing consistently to the will-to-difference, and against indifference, that emerges in the interstices of Kantian and Hegelian aesthetics.

The theme of aesthetic autonomy is spoken in Wilde's work in a series of closely orchestrated registers. Art asserts its freedom, in the main, from the strictures of Victorian utilitarianism and industry, the realm of the "real" to which belong the inducements of commerce, economy, and force falsely binding India and other imperial possessions to Britain. In language much like that of Ghose and Binyon, he designates this capturing region the "prose of life" or "the prison house of realism," and it is to this space of imaginative confinement that he will condemn Bosie while passing his own sentence of time behind the impermeable walls of Reading Gaol: "Don't you understand now that your lack of imagination was the one really fatal defect of your character"; "With very swift and running feet you had passed from Romance to Realism."[104] Cleaving from the "real" in a charged generic preference for "romance" and "imagination," art also takes flight from the homogenizing systematicity of a priori, universal concept-forms, preserved and enforced in "the standard of one's age," "the cheap severity of abstract ethics."[105] Two consequences attend this doubled departure from the realm of historicity and the real and from the possessive *ditio*, we might say, of cognition and morality. First, the liberated space of art manifests a radical hospitality to what Adorno calls "the singular" and "non-identical" and Wilde, before him, calls "the new" or "uncommon." It is into the estranging sphere of such perverse ethics that Dorian Gray, for example, is initiated by Sir Henry: "in his search for sensations that would be at once new . . . and possess that element of strangeness that is so essential to romance, he would often adopt certain modes of thought that he knew to be really alien."[106] Second, as "The Soul of Man under Socialism" makes clear, the aesthetic impulse toward difference, against similitude, belongs firmly to an aetiology of "disobedience," refusing the leveling, legislative mediations of the State for the sake of a "true" freedom that "will not always be meddling with others, or asking them to be like itself. It will love them because they will be different."[107] The autonomy of art becomes, in context, the critique of governmentality that we encountered in an earlier chapter—a strongly anarchist strain emerging, in this case, from a poetic view of the world in which the artist voices her refusal of external authority: "People sometimes enquire what form of government is most suitable for an artist to live under. To this question there is only one answer. The form of government that is suitable to the artist is no government at all."[108]

Never a doctrine of self-containment or separation from necessity, Wildean aestheticism always attaches forcefully to a critique of disinterest, amplified particularly in his fairy tales as a discourse against isolation and selfishness. So many of these stories begin with the ethical and existential confinement of privileged but solipsistic characters, who must be trained into affective exchange with the seemingly foreign and alien world from which, we might recall, the Kantian subject recoils in horror and which the Hegelian subject cancels, negates, erases. Thus the isolated "young king" will learn of the dispossessed citizens who labor to produce his luxury; the antipathetic "star child" will recognize as his mother the loathsome beggar-woman; the "happy prince" will make belated reparations, as a statue, for the cloistered life that once preserved him from all the ugliness and misery of his city; and the selfish giant will restore spring to his wintry garden through a gesture of invitation to trespassing children.[109] In Wilde's lexicon (shared in this instance with the fin-de-siècle animal welfare groups encountered in chapter 4), it is the motif of "sacrifice" that supplies the most effective antidote for the ethical petrifaction of his selfish and isolated characters. Always a self-endangering gesture for the sake of others, the aesthetics of sacrifice realize themselves perhaps most vividly in the figure of Wilde's Christ, invoked in *De Profundis* as an exemplar of imaginative sympathy: "He realised in the entire sphere of human relations that imaginative sympathy which in the sphere of art is the sole secret of creation. He understood the leprosy of the leper, the darkness of the blind . . . he was the first to conceive the divided races as a unity."[110] Sacrifice, we could say, is the substance that yokes the discourse of Wildean "interestedness" to the thematic of "relationality." Indeed, such relationality tends toward what Derrida calls "heteroaffection": the tendency toward the entirely other, manifest in the conjuncture of those strange and sudden kinships that animate most of

Wilde's stories—between fishermen and mermaids, swallows and statues, nightingales and roses, giants and children, and last but not least, Irish dandies and Indian poets.

Did Manmohan Ghose recognize entirely the radical fibers of "interested autonomy" that rendered Wilde's work and thought amenable to anticolonial appropriation? Did he find in his master a more refined reworking of those tentative oppositions between "prose" and "poetry" that he had rehearsed through his shared adolescence with Laurence Binyon? Is it to such recognition that we might attribute his praise of the sagacity masked behind Wilde's paradoxes, of the generous hospitality to difference cloaked beneath his perversities? Perhaps. We have little record outside Ghose's correspondence with Binyon of his response to the culture of English aestheticism that he left behind in his departure for India in 1894, where he would spend the rest of his days teaching Indian undergraduates the crucial distinction between English culture and imperialism before his death in 1923. We can, however, infer a little more about the import of Wilde's aestheticist politics for an Indian audience in the writings of Ghose's considerably more brilliant brother Aurobindo—a witness, as we have seen, to his older sibling's infatuation with the Irish poet.

Between 1890 and 1892, while reading classics at King's College, Cambridge, Aurobindo wrote a series of dramatic dialogues in Wildean style, praising the pursuit of beauty as a revolutionary counter to the commercial spirit of the contemporary West, and, celebrating Oscar Wilde as a patron saint of poetic radicalism. "I think," he writes in an early defense of poetry, "that the soul of the Ithacan Ulysses has not yet completed the cycle of transmigrations, nor would I wrong the author of Hippias by ignoring his conclusions. Or why go to dead men for an example? The mould has not fallen on the musical lips of the Irish Plato nor is Dorian Gray forgotten on the hundred tongues of Rumour."[111] In years to come Aurobindo would speak with greater circumspection about Wilde, indeed scarcely remembering him as he embarked upon the extraordinary career of anticolonial extremism and radical mysticism of which we spoke in chapter 5. In these years—along the lines of his early faith in the liberating idiom of "art"—he would come to privilege spirituality as the specifically Indian locus for autonomy from, among other things, the prose of empire. Nonetheless, committed throughout his yogic life to the writing of poetry and its encouragement in his disciples, between 1917 and 1920 Sri Aurobindo composed a series of articles devoted to another, this time more substantially elaborated, defense of poetry, published in 1953 as *The Future Poetry*. The book, a selective appreciation of English and European literary history, proclaims the familiar encomium to poetry as a zone of freedom from the real, crucial for the rehearsal of spiritual endeavor. But once again, despite the intervening passage of time, we hear reiterated a clear identification of the European impulse toward art as being simultaneously an impulse of internal critique, dismantling from within that prison house of imperialism in which India was incarcerated. There are many favorites to whom Sri Aurobindo accords special favor (Shelley, A. E., Whitman), but at the outset of his discussion he notes that the European impulse toward poetry (as against prose) is "purest" in its "Irish form," in which it manifests a particularly defiant "preference of the lyrical . . . and of the inwardly suggestive."[112] Belated thanksgiving? More, we could say, an acknowledgment of collaboration, conceding the worth of the different "bond of union" that could one day bind India to Europe "by other methods than those of commerce and military strength." Perhaps it is time for postcolonial thought to offer similar acknowledgment to a poetic view of the world, conceding its claim to the hitherto singular space of the political. To refuse this gesture, and here is the burden of this chapter, is to surrender the political to the joylessness of a utilitarian dispensation, condemned eternally to counter the prose of imperialism in the derivative prose of anti-aestheticist anticolonialism.

7

CONCLUSION

An Immature Politics

While there is not much on the face of it that seems to connect the diverse and disparate subcultures of fin-de-siècle anti-imperialism examined in this book, each of them, I have been suggesting, obtained something of its energies and distinct political style from the overriding grammar of contemporary utopian socialism, especially in its second efflorescence during the 1880s. Thus, we have seen, where anticolonial contestations in the name of homosexual exceptionalism achieved their discursive and ideological commerce with socialism through the efforts of Edward Carpenter, those performed under the sign of animal welfare were molded into socialist shapes by, among others, Henry Salt, a founder-member along with Carpenter of Thomas Davidson's influential socialist-utopian Fellowship of the New Life. So too, albeit more obliquely, aestheticism found itself drawn into the unlikely suburbs of contemporary anarcho-socialism under the perverse guidance of Oscar Wilde. And late Victorian spiritualism, emerging in the wake of orthodox faith, likewise gained its particular status as an alternative or countercultural "religion of socialism."

Ever hybrid and eclectic—a "superb mixture," as the theosophists J. H. and M. E. Cousins once observed, "of all the heterodoxies, dietetic, political, social, intellectual, aesthetical and religious"—utopian socialism conferred upon its various affiliates a distinct style of coalition and collaboration marked by apparent disregard for what we now know as "identity" or "single-issue" politics, thus enabling the easily transferable sympathies and promiscuous alliances that we have witnessed among unlikely ideological bedfellows (for example, bringing the affective urgencies of zoophilia or homosexual asceticism productively to bear upon the cause of the colonized races).[1] Yet where once the disorderly catalogues and creative mutations of utopian politics were celebrated as a unique means of showing society, in Carpenter's words, "the wealth and variety of affectional possibilities which it has within itself," it was precisely this quality of chaotic admixture that came to signal the impoverishment of utopianism as a viable and effective form of socialist politics, disclosing in place of political versatility an incoherent dilettantism. This charge is best captured in George Orwell's mordant description of late-nineteenth-century utopianism as an undiscriminating "magnetic field" that drew toward itself "every fruit-juice drinker, nudist, sandal-wearer, sex-maniac, Quaker, 'Nature-cure' quack, pacifist and feminist in England."[2]

What, I wish to ask in this concluding chapter, explains the progressive political disqualification of utopianism to which Orwell so sharply bears witness, one that renders invisible, for our purposes, the minor anticolonial agitations conducted under its impossibly copious umbrella? How might we best contest this debarment: by launching counterclaims for the "competence" of utopian political forms or, as I will propose, by arguing that it is precisely their ineligibility for the drama of mainstream politics, their lexical inadmissibility within a "developed" or established political vocabulary, that is the crucial revolutionary ingredient of utopian socialism?

NEWS FROM NOWHERE

Deemed entirely disreputable by the time Orwell was writing *The Road to Wigan Pier* (1937), fin-de-siècle utopianism was subject to systematic if discontinuous political disqualification across a period bookended by Friedrich Engels's *Socialism, Utopian and Scientific* (1892) and Lenin's *"Left-Wing" Communism: An Infantile Disorder* (1920), both texts that attest to the lamentable "immaturity" of utopian political forms. Commanding socialism to abandon its playground anarchism (its "eclectic mish-mash") for the science of "conscious organization on a planned basis," Engels's epochal pamphlet forcefully corroborated the anti-utopian sentiments expressed in the same year by Robert Blantchford, editor of the popular socialist paper the *Clarion*, in his *Merrie England* (1892). Demanding a distinction and evolutionary hierarchy between "ideal" and "practical" socialism, Blantchford's work categorically dismissed the former as the uncoordinated childhood of adult political consciousness: "Really they are only part of one whole; ideal socialism being a kind of preliminary step towards practical socialism, so that we might with more reason call them elementary and advanced socialism."[3] Such charges of "childishness" or "primitivism" slowly attaching to utopianism gained yet another substantial if unexpected endorsement in 1892 with the publication of Max Nordau's opus *Degeneration*, a book intent on anathematizing the culture of fin-de-siècle radicalism as "the extreme silliness of . . . the brain of a child or savage."[4] Summarily consigned to the wastebin of history, utopianism suffered a further blow with the formation of the Independent Labour Party (ILP) in 1893. The ILP was committed from the outset to placing labor candidates within Parliament, and it firmly, some might say irrevocably, adopted the path of respectable, organized, single-issue politics. Socialism, as H. M. Hyndman, leader of the SDF, is reputed to have observed, could no longer remain "a depository of odd cranks: humanitarians, vegetarians, anti-vivisectionists anti-vaccinationists, arty-crafties . . . sentimentalists. They confuse the story."[5]

Despite these efforts discursively to cleanse socialism of its unwholesome utopian accretions, however, something of the legacy of Edward Carpenter et al. found a new lease of life within the incipient communist movement in England and on the Continent. Increasingly dissatisfied with the dull compromises of parliamentary politics, early-twentieth-century British communism drew upon the inspiration of its anarcho-utopian predecessors to resist the unification and homogenization of aims fast becoming the hallmark of the labor movement. Something of this mood is conveyed in a contemporary dispatch from one W. Gallacher of the Scottish Workers Council in Glasgow: "The rank and file of the I.L.P. in Scotland is becoming more and more disgusted with the thought of Parliament . . . This is very serious, of course, for the gentlemen who look to politics for a profession, and they are using any and every means to persuade their members to come back into the parliamentary fold. Revolutionary comrades *must not* give any support to this gang."[6] It was as a rejoinder to this unexpected communist recalcitrance in face of the project of "practical" or "scientific" socialism that Lenin wrote his influential and irascible *"Left-Wing" Communism: An Infantile Disorder* in 1920, updating Engels's recommendations for the political circumstances of the new century and conclusively recouping "adulthood" and "science" as the distinguishing marks of "the political."

Sound revolutionary politics, Lenin asserts, must conform to the protocols of realism in two ways: first, through a rigorously pragmatic view of revolutionary ends, conceding the adulteration and suspension of ideals within the compromised and bourgeois form of parliamentary democracy; and second, through an equally rigorous curtailment of revolutionary means and adoption of an ascetic regimen of "perseverance . . . discipline, firmness, inflexibility . . . unity of will . . . strictest centralisation and iron discipline . . . [an acceptance of] Marxism, as the only correct revolutionary theory . . . *scientific* principles . . . a single Communist Party."[7] By contrast, any pseudo-revolutionary posture that dares contravene the generic obligations of realism, thus defined, constitutes an "infantile disorder," "a piece of childishness that is even difficult to take seriously."[8] Nominating "immaturity" as the single pathological flaw within any politics remotely redolent of utopianism, Lenin simultaneously captures "the political" as the privilege and expression of mature adulthood, decisively recasting the old opposition between "utopian" and "scientific" socialisms as a conflict between "immature" and "adult" politics.

Although startling for the sharp tone in which they are pronounced, the tropes deployed by Lenin and his immediate predecessors to discredit utopianism are scarcely original. In each instance the hierarchies of adulthood and infantilism or science and immaturity designate politics as a zone of enlightenment—the exit from immaturity into the asylum of adult rationality forcefully endorsed by Kant on behalf of his philosophical generation in his famous essay "What Is Enlightenment?" (1784). Kant's influential conception of adulthood, informed by the imperatives of his wider ethical philosophy, is elaborated once again as a fantasy of autonomous subjectivity: the picture of a unitary and sovereign Self armored affectively against the defenselessness of human existence. "To come of age," in Kant's understanding, demands that men secure their "release from . . . self-incurred tutelage . . . becoming capable of correctly using their own reason . . . with assurance and free from outside direction."[9] The "freedom" with which "adulthood" is made synonymous in "What Is Enlightenment?" takes shape, we have seen in previous chapters, in a philosophy that severs the ethical subject's access to all external influences, be they divine, human, or animal, rendering Kant's hypostasized adult into a being wholly immune to the distractions of faith, nature, desire, and inclination. By contrast, the "immature" escapee from the prison house of enlightenment rationality remains a creature of contingency, mired, as Martha Nussbaum has written in another context, "in the 'barnacles' and 'seaweed' of passion," ever "messy, needy, uncontrolled, rooted in the dirt and standing helplessly in the rain."[10]

Drawing upon a recognizable Kantian conception of adulthood, Lenin's play of generational metaphors in *"Left-Wing" Communism* maps the fantasy of autonomous subjectivity upon the space of "the political," substituting unity of purpose for a profusion of aims: centralization and singularity of organization for coalition and collaboration; premeditation for conjuncture; detachment and focus for affective irregularity. By 1920 a politics of spontaneism officially vanishes into the horizon of necessity, and socialism, as Chantal Mouffe and Ernesto Laclau have written elsewhere, is reified into a series of fixed a priori arrangements in which "the concrete is reduced to the abstract. Diverse subject positions are reduced to manifestations of a single position; the plurality of differences is either reduced or rejected as contingent; the sense of the present is revealed precisely through its location in . . . a succession of stages."[11]

The passage of disciplinary thought between Engels and Lenin summarily reviewed above, aiming at a purification of "the political," doubtless exemplifies an incontrovertible commitment to revolutionary efficacy, one underscored by the sound conviction that social transformation demands a certain measure of disinterestedness and moral rigor from its agents. Yet, we are arguing, this endeavor is simultaneously manifest as a form of disqualification: a homogenization and "normalization" of the field of politics that can only announce itself along the axis of a disabling hierarchy of knowledges. So Foucault avers through the course of his lectures at the Collège de France in 1975–76, maintaining that elaborating any thought system in the name of reason, adulthood, and "science" necessarily betrays the impulse to "minorize" and "subjugate" adjacent thought systems, perhaps most vividly in the discursive trajectory of modern socialism: "You know how many people have been asking themselves whether or not Marxism is a science for many years now, probably for more than a century . . . The question or questions that have to be asked are: 'What types of knowledges are you trying to disqualify when you say that you are a science? What speaking subject, what discursive subject, what subject of experience and knowledge are you trying to minorize when you begin to say: "I speak this discourse, I am speaking a scientific discourse, and I am a scientist." What theoretico-political vanguard are you trying to put on the throne in order to detach it from all the massive, circulating, and discontinuous forms that knowledge can take?' "[12]

As will be remembered, it is against this will to epistemic sovereignty that Foucault discloses the counteractive operations of "genealogy": the "attempt to desubjugate historical knowledges, to set them free, or in other words to enable them to oppose and struggle against the coercion of a unitary, formal, and scientific theoretical discourse."[13] Yet, and here Foucault's interjections become most apposite to our concerns, the genealogical "desubjugation" of knowledges consistently runs up against its own desire to postulate a competing and self-defeating enthronement or "majorization" of "minor" thought systems: "if we try and protect the fragments we have dug up, don't we run the risk of building with our own hands, a unitary discourse?"[14] In other words, apropos of the present discussion, how might we recognize and refuse the modalities whereby fin-de-siècle utopianism is occluded or delegitimized through the tropes of "science," "adulthood," and "maturity" without succumbing to the temptations of genealogical reconstruction? Perhaps, and further to Foucault, we might proceed by giving credence to the notion that the synonyms of "immaturity" leveled at utopianism by its detractors signal the mutually contradictory actions of debarment and recognition: the identification of property as much as lack; a making visible while occluding; an inadvertent gesture of qualification that also supplies the basis for disqualification. In other words, inasmuch as the charge of "immaturity" that we have been pursuing so far masks the "minor" anticolonialisms and socialisms enacted by the likes of Carpenter, Salt, Wilde, and Alfassa, it discloses equally the constitutive conditions of possibility for such a politics. Let us briefly consider some lenses, theoretical and historical, through which these "conditions of possibility" might come more clearly into view.

AN IMMATURE POLITICS

Read positively, the association of "immaturity" and "utopianism" carries the force of genuine theoretical insight, for in any of the affiliated forms of fin-de-siècle radicalism that we have encountered in this book it is precisely the qualities of disorganization, provisionality, coincidence, and conjuncture that make up the fabric of a utopian politics of inventiveness, bearing within itself the mutually complementary gestures of refusal and relationality; these gestures, in their turn, are intensely amenable to the imperatives of anticolonial thought. In this regard late Victorian utopian socialism can best be explained as a politics of the "event," a trope celebrated in one tradition by a long line of thinkers, from Jean-Paul Sartre to Alain Badiou, as the revolutionary or epistemic ability to instantiate the new.[15] Predicated upon a formative movement of departure or disobedience, the event announces itself, Badiou argues, as a "de-suturation," or break from that which already exists, be it in the form of Law, Truth, or Criteria.[16] This action invariably begins as an initial moment of rebellious "no-saying," but it is maintained uniquely through the event's constitutive auto-immunity to "substantializing" or "absolutizing." Marked, as it were, by an irremediable immaturity—"chance and confluence, coincidence and conjuncture"—an event is eo ipso a procedure "onto which no knowledge can 'pin' its name, or discern beforehand its status"; "it cannot, therefore, in any way . . . fall under the remit of knowledge."[17] So it is that the event "by definition begins something new."[18] So too, for reason of its chronic immunity to substantializing, its intransigence in the face of all structure, law, axiom, and generality, it posits a radical inclusiveness, "offered to all, addressed to everyone, without a condition of belonging being able to limit this offer, or this address."[19] That is to say, the structural features supporting the event's incalculable inventiveness—its will to bring forth such things as never were before—also buttress its conjunctural inclusivity. At once the scene of "pure difference," as Foucault has observed, "devoid of any grounding in an original, outside of all forms of imitation, and freed from the constraints of similitude," an evental politics is, we might say, atavistically inclined toward a theater of alterity.[20] It dramatizes, to borrow Jacques Rancière's formulation, a political opening to otherness, with "the other" not so much representing the figure of a reified victim or beneficiary as naming a relation, or putting forth relationality as the characteristic feature of an immature politics and rendering politics into a performance of strange alliance, unlikely kinships, and impossible identification: the elaboration, to recall an earlier trope from this book, of Derridean philoxenia.[21]

Manifesting thus a space of unpremeditated relationality, immature politics simultaneously discloses (and refuses) the crisis of nonrelation upon which juridico-transcendental and universalizing forms of power, especially in their totalitarian, imperialist guise, are predicated. It struggles against the profound contradiction at the heart of modern political life—diagnosed by thinkers like Hannah Arendt and more recently Giorgio Agamben—by which the "mature" promise of collectivity, solidarity, and inclusion is premised perversely upon a logic of caesura, exception, and exclusion. This principle is crystallized in what Agamben calls a relation of abandonment or ban, consigning those without recognizable political attributes to the desert of "bare life" at the margins of organized sociality: "The ban is essentially the power of delivering something over to itself, which is to say the power of maintaining itself in relation to something presupposed as non-relational. What has been banned is delivered over to its own separateness."[22] Such is the logic of nonrelation that Agamben (like Arendt before him) discerns in predicating citizenship upon the abandonment of the refugee, and that Foucault discerns in the racism secreted within the modalities of the modern state, which expresses itself precisely as a power of exclusion, ban, and separation.[23] In his words: "racism is inscribed as the basic mechanism of power, as it is exercised in modern States. As a result, the modern State can scarcely function without becoming involved with racism at some point . . . It is a way of separating out the groups that exist within a population . . . exposing someone to death, increasing the risk of death for some people, or, quite simply, political death, expulsion, rejection, and so on."[24] Concealed in this way beneath the everyday veneer of civil society, the law of exception, or *exceptio*, analyzed by Foucault and Agamben acquires a pathological dimension in conditions of totalitarianism and imperialism—the forms of power whose purpose it is, according to Hannah Arendt, "to ruin[s] all relationships between men," dissolving thereby the being-together or being-in-common that should be the basis of political existence.[25]

The antirelational basis of imperialism is precisely what Carpenter and his colleagues aimed to expose and contradict through an inchoate, provisional, and incoherent form of politics that might show society its wealth of affectional possibility. The discrete studies in this book have endeavored to detail some varieties of dissident relationality characteristic of the "minor" politics that came briefly into its own at the last fin-de-siècle. While much of this history, further to its occlusion at the hands of "scientific" and "adult" socialism, has since all but disappeared from view, something of its enterprise can be illuminated with reference to the political energies unleashed by the events of May 1968 in France, as well as the more recent demonstrations against the World Trade Organization at Seattle in December 1999 and others still unfolding in the name of contemporary anticorporatism.

It is not that 1968 and 1999 bring, through revealing actions of imitation or repetition, the struggles of the 1880s and 1890s into greater coherence or "scienticity," but rather, to borrow some themes from Kristen Ross, that they represent in some way an "afterlife" to utopian socialism, creating "a new optic" on its "immaturity." So, for instance, nearly half a century after the first nail is hammered into the unwieldy coffin of utopian socialism, Daniel and Gabriel Cohn-Bendit pose a direct rejoinder to Lenin's *"Left-Wing Communism"* in their hastily composed book *Le Gauchisme: Remède à la maladie sénile du communisme*, which announces "immaturity" as the governing trope for the style of revolutionary politics newly summoned by the epochal events of May 1968. *Le Gauchisme* testifies to the youthful composition and concerns of that brief revolution, led by student leaders and involving the mass mobilization of thousands of schoolchildren. Several commentators have read May '68 as archetypal: a replay on a larger scale of the perennial caviling of youth against the cant of the adult world, an insurrection, à la Pink Floyd, against the petty tyrannies of education, timetables, and parental scrutiny. For the Cohn-Bendit brothers, however, the generational conflicts of May '68 appear rather more acutely historical than psychodynamic. By directly evoking and reversing the title of Lenin's pamphlet, they situate May '68 within a peculiar history in which the hierarchy of adulthood and childhood also refers, as we have seen, to the conflict between two types of resistance, two varieties of socialism: the one enshrined (this time round) in the organizational determinism and electoral aspirations of the "adult" Left, the other reawakened and defended through the unstructured and disorganized spontaneity of student revolutionaries. On this occasion, though, it is adulthood that is discredited through the brutal metaphor of senility.

Historians and sociologists have often pointed to the thematic similarities between the socialisms which overcame Britain in the 1880s and Paris in 1968. Diana Burfield notes in both movements an affinity with avant-garde ideas; Keith Nield discerns a common emphasis on personal transformation or "individual liberation . . . from capitalist work disciplines, from sexual stereotypes and suffocating moralities"; and Alain Touraine has directly claimed 1968 "as an expression of utopian communism" which inherited from the utopian socialisms of the nineteenth century a "global opposition to a specific civilisation and a form of social power."[26] Such accounts of continuous aspirations are crucial for our genealogy. But it is perhaps even more important to recognize, as the actors and participants of May 1968 did so vividly, that the utopian flavor of their movement obtained (as it did for its predecessors) from its defiant immaturity. For many writers, such as Touraine, the May revolution "failed," in the final analysis, on account of its "undefined . . . disorganised . . . confused" procedures, its lack of any developed "theory, party, or policy."[27] Yet "disorder" is precisely what Daniel Cohn-Bendit affirms as the positive condition "that lets men speak,"[28] and the absence of leaders, manifestos, institutions, agendas, and aims is what he celebrates in *Le Gauchisme* as a creative possibility for radical democracy that would make the edenic "beach under the paving stones" "open to all." As he puts it: "If a revolutionary movement is to succeed, no form of organisation whatever must be allowed to dam its spontaneous flow. It must evolve its own forms and structures . . . We support everything that widens the struggle."[29] Taking its cue from 1968, contemporary anticorporatism likewise ascribes its energies to a constitutive disorganization, describing its own revolutionary events as productively accidental, coincidental, and temporary. "It is often said disparagingly," Naomi Klein writes in *No Logo*, "that this movement lacks ideology, an overarching message, a master plan. This is absolutely true, and we should be extraordinarily thankful."[30]

For the Cohn-Bendit brothers and Klein, provisionality is privileged as the condition of evental inclusivity that we spoke of earlier, unexpectedly giving shape to a subversive coalitional modality, and gathering seemingly disparate causes under the same umbrella. Thus the "mixed streets" of Paris in 1968 stage complex and shifting alliances between students, workers, peasants, doctors, churchmen (Jews, Protestants, Catholics, Arabs), scientific statisticians, museum directors, and footballers.[31] Here we might also emphasize the uniquely international dimension of the movement, determinedly combining workers' causes with those of anticolonial aspirants in Vietnam and Algeria.[32] Something of this disposition is conveyed in Hervé Bourges's first-hand account in June 1968: "From this point, strictly political commitments may be more or less far-reaching in their different directions, but they must be conceived in terms of priorities and in original forms, even in France, with an acute awareness that this battle is the best way to unite with anti-imperialist struggles everywhere, the best way to oppose the detour of neo-colonialism, to support the resolute struggles of the Vietnamese, Palestinian and Latin American people . . . This international open-ness, which is not in contradiction with the declared intention of fighting on a limited terrain, is demonstrated in the generous cosmopolitanism of the Sorbonne, open to all the hopes of the Third World . . . blending in posters and unexpected meetings of ethnic and political minorities . . . Utopia, or tomorrow's reality?"[33]

Much like Cohn-Bendit, Bourges is at pains to underscore the movement's commitment to a discourse of "open-ness," and it is in this iterative defense of an uncovered, permeable, unknown, undisclosed future that 1968 gathers within itself a critical momentum of relationality. Giving expression in part to the "situationism" associated with Guy Debord and his followers, the young revolutionaries associated with the movement consistently pose a critique to that commercialization of human relations held in place by a "society of the spectacle," in which the triumph of commodity fetishism, or the supersession of use by exchange value, comes to interrupt all direct relations between subject and object, self and other, by means of various alienating mediations. Intent on transforming the punitive "separations" of spectacular society through the alchemy of compact and communication, May '68 exemplifies, as several commentators tell us, an explosion of talk and association. The "most effective political forms and actions the movement could develop," Ross writes, "were those that attempted what has variously been called the 'dialogue,' 'meeting,' 'relay,' 'alliance,' 'solidarity,' or even 'alloy' (*alliage*)."[34]

Similar imperatives resurface in the politics of Seattle '99. Distinguished by its resolute identification of global corporatism with neo-imperialism, the movement insists upon a continuum between protests against the WTO and those against the putative war on terror.[35] Its declared aim in so doing is to refute the compartmentalization of causes and specialization of interests so characteristic of the anti-relational style of global or corporate governance, a style determined by the culture of "branding" and its devastating mediative modality. In context, activists associated with the movement consistently profess the desire to build "real global connections," seeking "the ultimate anti-commodity . . . [in] human communication, between friends, inside communities of trust."[36]

Does a politics of relationality—the conjunctive modality that William James once described as the distinguishing feature of radical empiricism—ever change the world? Does it successfully dispatch imperial governments and occupying armies from native soil? Lead a disenfranchised people into the promise of self-determination? Mitigate in any way the burdens of a colonial inheritance? Certainly not with anything like the speed and efficiency of those better organized and better focused (and more mature) revolutionary movements less inclined to found social change upon the painstaking labor of personal transformation. Yet precisely because of its inability to work its effects at industrial speed and scale, the politics that we have been pursuing in this discussion often alter the genetic structure of the societies in which they eventuate, subtly varying for future use their ethical, epistemic, and political composition. Thus the drama of "impossible identification" nags unobserved at the reformation of subjectivity, substituting the aggressions contingent upon the rarefactions of psychic sovereignty with the creative if messy and tangled ecologism of intra- and intersubjectivity. We can observe this work of subjective, ethical, and psychic reconstitution in Paris on Wednesday 22 May, when in response to the information that the part-German Cohn-Bendit had been banned from France, a crowd of student protesters, some of them young Arabs from Algeria, marched onto the heavily guarded National Assembly shouting, "We don't give a damn about frontiers! We are all aliens! We are all German Jews!"[37]

We have encountered this language of self-estrangement before: in the fierce anti-imperialism of Sheffield workers in the 1880s; the pro-suffrage activism of late-nineteenth-century homosexuals; the anarcho-socialism of fin-de-siècle vegetarians. And we have seen it since: on the streets of Seattle in December 1999, in current American dissidence against the government's neo-imperialism, in the philoxenic actions of anonymous multitudes giving notice to their own governments and communities of belonging on behalf of vulnerable strangers. In each of these instances we are witness to that critical conjuncture when some of the selves who make up a culture loosen themselves from the security and comfort of old affiliations and identifications to make an unexpected "gesture" of friendship toward all those on the other side of the fence. There is no finality in this action, no easily discernible teleological satisfaction. Just the expression, to end with Giorgio Agamben, "of a mediality . . . a process of making a means visible as such."[38] A breach, that is, in the fabric of imperial inhospitality.

NOTES

CHAPTER 1 Affective Communities

1 For an engrossing account of British anti-imperialism see Jonathan Schneer, *London 1900: The Imperial Metropolis* (New Haven: Yale University Press, 1999). A complementary perspective, drawing attention to the analogy between imperialism's domestic and foreign prejudices, is offered in David Cannadine, *Ornamentalism: How the British Saw Their Empire* (New York: Oxford University Press, 2001).

2 Schneer, *London 1900*, 162.

3 Ibid., 13.

4 Said, *Culture and Imperialism* (London: Chatto and Windus, 1993), xxviii, 36.

5 Homi Bhabha, *The Location of Culture* (London: Routledge, 1994), 193.

6 Karl Marx, *The People's Paper*, cited in Terry Eagleton, *Marx and Freedom* (London: Phoenix, 1997), 44.

7 Bhabha, *The Location of Culture*, 196.

8 These arguments are famously offered in Edward Said's *Culture and Imperialism* and Gauri Viswanathan's *Masks of Conquest: Literary Study and British Rule in India* (London: Faber and Faber, 1989).

9 Said, *Culture and Imperialism*, 19

10 See Eric Hobsbawm and Terence Ranger, eds., *The Invention of Tradition* (Cambridge: Cambridge University Press, 1983), and Partha Chatterjee, *Nationalist Thought and the Colonial World: A Derivative Discourse?* (London: Zed, 1986).

11 Bhabha, *The Location of Culture*, 175, 91, 95.

12 Bhabha vigorously and persuasively contests the charge of determinism leveled against his work by Marxist interlocutors. His essay "The Postcolonial and the Postmodern: The Question of Agency," in *The Location of Culture*, is apposite here in its insistence that the narratives of hybridity and interstitiality postulate another model of agency, privileging performative and intersubjective elements over deliberative and individuated elements. As he writes, "the moment of the subject's individuation emerges as an effect of the intersubjective . . . This means that those elements of social "consciousness" imperative for agency—deliberative, individuated action and specificity in analysis—can now be thought outside that epistemology

that insists on the subject as always prior to the social or the knowledge of the social as necessarily subsuming or sublating the particular 'difference' in the transcendent homogeneity of the general" (185).

13 Also noteworthy, in context, is Susan Stanford Friedman's demand for a new feminist geopolitical literacy more keenly attentive to "the role of intercultural exchange and symbiosis in all cultural formations, and the heterogeneity of both 'the West' and 'the Rest.'" *Mappings: Feminism and the Cultural Geographies of Encounter* (Princeton: Princeton University Press, 1998), 6.

14 Ashis Nandy, *The Intimate Enemy: Loss and Recovery of Self under Colonialism* (Delhi: Oxford University Press, 1983), 36.

15 See Ashis Nandy, "Oppression and Human Liberation: Toward a Post-Gandhian Utopia," Thomas Pantham and Kenneth L. Deutsch, *Political Thought in Modern India* (New Delhi: Sage, 1986), 438.

16 Nandy, *The Intimate Enemy*, 36.

17 *Beehive*, 1 October 1864, cited in Henry Collins and Chimen Abramsky, *Karl Marx and the British Labour Movement* (London: Macmillan, 1965), 34–35. For a more partisan account of the anticolonial motivations of the First and Third Internationals see William Z. Foster, *History of the Three Internationals: The World Socialist and Communist Movements from 1848 to the Present* (New York: Greenwood, 1968). Although the anticolonial agenda of the Second International is considered somewhat less robust by its critics, an engaging account of its motivations and achievements is offered in James Joll, *The Second International, 1889–1914* (New York: Harper Colophon, 1966).

18 The historical and ideological links and continuities between the utopianism and anarchism that so fruitfully combined within the culture of fin-de-siècle radicalism have been well observed by a variety of scholars. We might note especially E. H. Carr's observation in *Michael Bakunin* (London: Macmillan, 1937), 434, that nineteenth-century anarchism was "the logical conclusion of the romantic doctrine."

19 E. M. Forster, *Two Cheers for Democracy* (London: Edward Arnold, 1951), 66.

20 Edward Carpenter, "Empire in India and Elsewhere," *Humane Review* 1 (1900): 207.

21 Michael Hardt and Antonio Negri, *Empire* (Cambridge: Harvard University Press, 2000), 215. Hardt's and Negri's configuration of posthumanism and communism within the "new" anti-imperialism is powerfully evocative of the peculiar conjunctions of late-Victorian and western anti-imperialism. Note, for example, further to the theme of fin-de-siècle animal rights as a critique of empire, their valorization of Saint Francis of Assisi as a paradigmatic anti-imperialist: "Francis in opposition to nascent capitalism refused every instrumental discipline, and in opposition to the mortification of the flesh (in poverty and in the constituted order) he posed a joyous life, including all of being and nature, the animals, sister moon,

brother sun, the birds of the field, the poor and exploited humans, together against the will of power and corruption. Once again in postmodernity we find ourselves in Francis's situation, posing against the misery of power the joy of being" (413).

CHAPTER 2 Anticolonial Thought

1 St. Stephen's College was founded in 1881 by the missionary Society for the Propagation of Gospel (SPG), also the main sponsor of the Cambridge Mission. It was as a representative of the mission that Andrews first came to India.

2 See Susan Visvanathan, "S. K. Rudra, C. F. Andrews, and M. K. Gandhi: Friendship, Dialogue and Interiority in the Question of Indian Nationalism," *Economic and Political Weekly*, 24 August 2002, 3532–41.

3 C. F. Andrews, "Letter from Natal," *Modern Review*, March 1914, cited in Hugh Tinker, *The Ordeal of Love: C. F. Andrews and India* (Delhi: Oxford University Press, 1998), 84.

4 Ibid.

5 Early in 1919 the imperial administration had issued the infamous Rowlatt Bill, prescribing harsh punishment and a secret trial for anyone under suspicion of "terrorist" activity. To protest the legislation Gandhi, now resident in India, appealed for a nationwide *satyagraha* campaign. The recommended modes of nonviolent civil disobedience soon dissolved into violence, however, and on 10 April 1919 riots broke out in the city of Amritsar. No significant reprisals occurred on the day. But on 13 April, as is well known, a company of British forces led by the infamous General Dyer emptied machine-gun fire into a crowd of some twenty thousand peaceful protesters gathered in an enclosed park, Jallianwala Bagh, killing hundreds and wounding thousands.

6 C. F. Andrews, *Christ in Silence* (London: Hodder and Stoughton, 1933), 96. The Sikh, we are told, gave his pardon, conceding that "the past had all been forgotten and forgiven" (ibid.).

7 While this book consistently favors those figures who prevented Indian anticolonialism from resolving itself into a stance of pure oppositionality, it is not in any way my intention to advance the cause of some "enlightened" cosmopolitanism at the expense of anticolonial nationalism or, for that matter, to posit a stark opposition between a global and a local discourse; between internationalism and nationalism; between cosmopolitanism and culturalism. Not only would such a contrast be simplistic; it would also be inaccurate. There are countless varieties of cosmopolitanism, and where some take the form of transnational solidarity, others, in countries like India, take the form of transregional, transreligious, cross-linguistic affinity. In this regard I owe especially to Dipesh Chakrabarty the understanding that even in its most oppositional and "culturalist" manifestation Indian nationalism, among others,

was never without its own varieties of cosmopolitan practices, albeit ones perhaps internal to the subcontinent.

8 M. K. Gandhi, *Collected Works of Mahatma Gandhi* (Delhi: Ministry of Information and Broadcasting, 1976), 16:312–14.

9 Ibid., 33.

10 C. F. Andrews, *The True India: A Plea for Understanding* (London: George Allen and Unwin, 1939), 15.

11 Ibid., 234.

12 Letter from C. F. Andrews to Munshi Ram, 30 April 1913. Cited in Tinker, *The Ordeal of Love*, 31.

13 C. F. Andrews, *What I Owe to Christ* (London: Hodder and Stoughton, 1932), 77.

14 Rabindranath Tagore, Foreword, C. F. Andrews, *The Sermon on the Mount* (London: George Allen and Unwin, 1942), xi.

15 Cited in Krishna Kripilani, "Andrews, Gandhi and Tagore," Deenbandhu Memorial Papers, St. Stephen's College Library.

16 R. N. Bose, "Two Friends, Gandhi and Andrews," Deenbandhu Memorial Papers.

17 In a letter to Andrews dated 7 July 1921, Tagore is especially emphatic in his negative reading of desire: "I know that the idea which I have in mind requires the elimination of all passions that have their place in the narrow range of life; but most people believe that these passions are the steam-power which gives velocity to our motives. They quote precedents; they say that pure idea has never achieved any result. But when you say that the result is not greater than the idea itself, then they laugh at you." Rabindranath Tagore, *Letters to a Friend* (London: George Allen and Unwin: 1928), 178–79.

18 Many of the obituaries of Andrews and commemorations of him invoke the language of friendship, in these terms, to establish the "unofficial" and "unassuming" nature of Andrews's politics. The following lines from the *Times of India*, 12 February 1971, are typical: "Andrews did not hold any office or preside over the Indian National Congress. He preferred to remain in the background as a friend, philosopher and constructive critic."

19 C. F. Andrews, *The Good Shepherd* (London: Hodder and Stoughton, 1940), 94.

20 Andrews, *The Sermon on the Mount*, 50.

21 Andrews, *What I Owe to Christ*, 129.

22 Andrews, *The Good Shepherd*, 7. J. H. Cousins and M. E. Cousins, in *We Two Together* (Madras: Ganesh, 1950), 339, are among many contemporaries struck by Andrews's bisexual nature: "College routine was enlivened by new events and occasional visitors. A very distinctive visitor was the Reverend C. F. Andrews (Charlie to

his friends). He came goodness knows why, and left goodness knows when. In the meantime, having only one pair of socks with him, he washed them and dried them in the sun. He was travelling light, he said, but, for all the little he carried, I have seen no one who could make a more fantastic litter of clothes and bedding and newspapers in an hour or two. I did some tidying up for him, and he confided in me that what he had always wanted was a wife. I had a private idea that what he needed was a husband, for he appeared to me to be a big-hearted woman who had got mixed in his incarnation."

23 Andrews, *The True India*, 235.

24 Cousins and Cousins, *We Two Together*, 125. The Cousinses testify to Andrews's involvement with Indian theosophical circles, giving account of his lectures to large theosophical gatherings.

25 Friedrich Engels, *Socialism, from Utopia to Science*, trans. Edward Aveling (1892; New York: New York Labor Press, 1968), 21.

26 Michael Hardt and Antonio Negri, *Empire* (Cambridge: Harvard University Press, 2000).

27 Jacques Derrida, *Politics of Friendship*, trans. George Collins (London: Verso, 1997), 306.

28 Jean-Luc Nancy, in *The Inoperative Community*, trans. Peter Connor, Lisa Garbus, Michael Holland, and Simona Sawhney (Minneapolis: University of Minnesota Press, 1991), 1, conceives of community in similar terms as being "at once beyond social divisions and beyond subordination to technopolitical dominion, and thereby beyond such wasting away of liberty, or speech, or of simple happiness as comes about whenever these become subjugated to the exclusive order of privatisation."

29 Ibid., 27. Martin Buber, in his classic study of the ethics of relationality, *I and Thou*, trans. Walter Kaufmann (1970; New York: Simon and Schuster, 1996), 62, voices a similar resistance to universalism and foundationalism in the business of community: "The relation to You is unmediated. Nothing conceptual intervenes between I and You, no prior knowledge and no imagination; and memory itself is changed as it plunges from particularity to wholeness. No purpose intervenes between I and You, no greed and no anticipation . . . Every means is an obstacle. Only where all means have disintegrated encounters occur."

30 Ibid., 29. Buber also privileges the "between as such," valorized by Nancy as "a marginal exorbitance of the act of relation: the relationship itself in its vital unity is felt so vehemently that its members pale in the process: its life predominates so much that the I and the You between whom it is established are forgotten" (ibid., 135). But where Buber's discourse discloses irreducible "between-ness" as the space of fusion, Nancy vehemently elides the fusional aspects of community, insisting at every move upon a "sharing" that in some way exceeds the logic of fusion.

31 Giorgio Agamben, *The Coming Community*, trans. Michael Hardt (Minneapolis: University of Minnesota Press, 2001), 85.

32 Nancy, *The Inoperative Community*, 25.

33 See Drucilla Cornell, *The Philosophy of the Limit* (New York: Routledge, 1992).

34 Alasdair MacIntyre, in his *After Virtue: A Study in Moral Theory*, 2d edn (London: Duckworth, 1997), 261, convincingly claims a Kantian patrimony for both modern liberals and Marxists: "The key intellectual opposition of our age . . . is that between modern liberal individualism and some version of Marxism or neo-Marxism. The most intellectually compelling exponents of this view are likely to be those who trace a genealogy of ideas from Kant and Hegel through Marx . . . Marxists have always fallen back into relatively straightforward versions of Kantianism or utilitarianism. Nor is this surprising. Secreted within Marxism from the outset is a certain radical individualism." Chantal Mouffe, in *The Return of the Political* (London: Verso, 1993), 13, likewise asserts the continuities between liberalism and Marxism, arguing that "neither liberalism with its idea of the individual who only pursues his or her own interest, nor Marxism, with its reduction of all subject positions to that of class can sanction, let alone imagine," the "entirely new perspectives for political action" ushered in by new social movements.

35 For a thoughtful account of socialist feminism's stigmatization of female subjectivity as anarchic and regressive, see Cora Kaplan, "Pandora's Box: Subjectivity, Class and Sexuality in Socialist Feminist Criticism," *Making a Difference: Feminist Literary Criticism*, ed. Gayle Greene and Coppelia Kahn (London: Methuen, 1985), 146–76.

36 Georges Bataille, *Oeuvres Completes* (Paris: Gallimard, 1970), 8:353, cited in Nancy, *The Inoperative Community*, 16. It is in sympathy with Bataille's critique of the existential costs of the sovereignty of "production" in orthodox Marxism that Nancy endeavors to dissociate affective community from the discourse of work and production: "This is why community cannot arise from the domain of *work*. One does not produce it, one experiences it or one is constituted by it as the experience of finitude . . . Community necessarily takes place in what Blanchot has called 'unworking,' referring to that which, beyond or before the work, withdraws from the work, and which, no longer having to do either with production or with completion, encounters interruption, fragmentation, suspension . . . Communication is the unworking of work that is social, economic, technical and institutional" (31).

37 Ernesto Laclau and Chantal Mouffe, *Hegemony and Socialist Strategy: Towards a Radical Democratic Politics*, trans. Winston Moore and Paul Cammack (London: Verso, 1985), 177.

38 Arguments for the irremediable neonihilism of postmodern thought are provided in Luc Ferry and Alain Renault, *French Philosophy of the Sixties: An Essay on*

Antihumanism, trans. Mary H. S. Cattani (Amherst: University of Massachusetts Press, 1990). An earlier study, Raymond Aron's *The Elusive Revolution: Anatomy of a Student Revolt*, trans. Gordon Clough (New York: Praeger, 1969), attributes the alleged nihilism of postmodern thought to the political style of the May 1968 revolution. Both readings, needless to say, are contentious and debatable.

39 Chantal Mouffe, *The Return of the Political*, 181. The language of postmodern nihilism is freely invoked, for example, by Judith Butler in *Gender Trouble: Feminism and the Subversion of Identity* (New York: Routledge, 1990), 14–15: "The insistence in advance on . . . 'unity' as a goal assumes that solidarity, whatever its price, is a prerequisite for political action . . . Perhaps also part of what dialogic understanding entails is the acceptance of . . . breakage, splinter, and fragmentation." Butler's work is always scrupulously attentive to the need to imagine new political configurations out of the ruins of the old. But postmodern thought in general, as Žižek complains in *The Ticklish Subject: The Absent Centre of Political Ontology* (London: Verso, 2000), 171, frequently tends toward an absurdist reduction of the political: " 'dispersionists' condemn politics as unifying, totalitarian, violent, and so on, and assume the position of ethical critics who reveal (or voice) the ethical Wrong or Evil committed by politics, without engaging in an alternative political project."

40 Laclau and Mouffe, *Hegemony and Socialist Strategy*, 189.

41 In *Hegel* (Cambridge: Cambridge University Press, 1975), 154, Charles Taylor suggests that the relation of master and slave in Hegel's notes on 'Lordship and Bondage' is in effect that of consumer and producer: "The relation of the master to what surrounds him is that of a pure consumer; the hard task of transforming things and preparing them for consumption is that of the slave."

42 Nancy, *The Inoperative Community*, 32.

43 Paul Gilroy, *There Ain't No Black in the Union Jack: The Cultural Politics of Race and Nation* (London: Hutchinson, 1987), 227.

44 Michel de Certeau, *The Practice of Everyday Life*, trans. Steven Rendall (Berkeley: University of California Press, 1984), xix.

45 Against such objections to the ethical limits of consumerism, Bataille, as Nancy points out in *The Inoperative Community*, 37, valorizes erotic consumption as appropriate countermand to the acquisitiveness of the State: "he . . . represented them as a society, as another society, one that harbours the impossible and communal truth that simple society despairs of attaining: 'Love unites lovers only in order to expend, to go from pleasure to pleasure, from delight to delight: their society is one of consumption, the inverse of the State's, which is one of acquisition.' " Yet despite this apparent endorsement, Nancy's writing consistently seems to postulate untrammeled "consumption" as the limit point of "communication," as the juncture at which the thinking of community is forestalled.

46 Hardt and Negri, *Empire*, 156. Žižek, *The Ticklish Subject*, 220, among many

other critics from the left, raises similar objections to hybridity and the hybrid subject: "It is easy to praise the hybridity of the postmodern migrant subject, no longer attached to specific ethnic roots, floating freely between different cultural circles. Unfortunately, two totally different sociopolitical levels are condensed here: on the one hand the cosmopolitan upper- and upper-middle-class academic, always with the proper visas enabling him to cross borders without any problem in order to carry out his (financial, academic . . .) business, and thus able to 'enjoy the difference'; on the other hand the poor (im)migrant worker driven from his home by poverty or (ethnic, religious) violence, for whom the celebrated 'hybridity' designates a very tangible traumatic experience." The particular relevance to my argument of the critiques by Žižek and others is that the postmodern subject of desire draws even the "real" traumas of hybridity into a principally libidinal vector as a form of defiant "enjoyment." This subject faces the world as one might a supermarket bearing an excess of choices, homes, identities, opportunities. Yet if salutary, the objections to hybridity and the politics of desire prove ultimately unsatisfactory because of their inevitable reversal to the language of asceticism; reinstating the tired opposition between politics and desire, ethics and affect, etc. In contrast, our project, via Derrida, Nancy, and Blanchot among others, is to affirm the possibility of an anti-renunciatory politics of desire and ethics of affect that does not succumb to the self-regarding hedonism or reckless consumerism—the "appetite," simply—of the hybrid subject.

47 Charles Taylor, *Hegel* (1975; Cambridge: Cambridge University Press, 1999), 156.

48 The phrase is borrowed out of context from Seamus Deane, Introduction, *Nationalism, Colonialism and Literature* (Minneapolis: University of Minnesota Press, 1990), 8.

49 Maurice Blanchot, *The Unavowable Community*, trans. Pierre Joris (Barrytown: Station Hill Press, 1988), 5. Compare Jacques Derrida, *Of Hospitality: Anne Dufourmantelle Invites Jacques Derrida to Respond*, trans. Rachel Bowlby (Stanford: Stanford University Press, 2000), 3: "before being a question to be dealt with, before designating a concept, a theme, a problem, a program, the question of the foreigner is a question *of* the foreigner, addressed *to* the foreigner. As though the foreigner were first of all *the one who* puts the first question or *the one to whom* you address the first question. As though the foreigner were being-in-question, the very question of being-in-question, the question-being or being-in-question of the question. But also the one who, putting the first question, puts me in question."

50 Blanchot's designation of subjective insufficiency as the catalyst for community is reiterated in Nancy's *The Inoperative Community* as the theme of "finitude": "Being *in common* means . . . *no longer having, in any form, in any empirical or ideal place, such a substantial identity, and sharing this* (narcissistic) '*lack of identity*.' This is what philosophy calls 'finitude' . . . Finitude, or the lack of infinite identity, if we can risk such a formulation, is what makes community" (xxxviii).

51 Michael Sandel, "Liberalism and the Limits of Justice," *What Is Justice?*, ed. Robert C. Solomon and Mark C. Murphy (Oxford: Oxford University Press, 1990), 354.

52 Taylor, *Hegel*, 153.

53 For a fuller discussion of the dream of equality secreted within Hegelian recognition see Charles Taylor, "The Politics of Recognition," *Multiculturalism: Examining the Politics of Recognition*, ed. Amy Gutmann (Princeton: Princeton University Press, 1994), 25–74.

54 Blanchot, *The Unavowable Community*, 3.

55 K. Anthony Appiah, "Identity, Authenticity, Survival: Multicultural Societies and Social Reproduction," *Multiculturalism*, ed. Gutmann, 163.

56 For a compelling defense of "chosen" or "voluntary" communities see Marilyn Friedman, *What Are Friends for: Feminist Perspectives on Personal Relationships and Moral Theory* (Ithaca: Cornell University Press, 1993).

57 Edward Said's thoughts on "affiliation" in *The World, the Text, and the Critic* (Cambridge: Harvard University Press, 1983), 22–23, are apposite here: "The affiliative order . . . surreptitiously duplicates the closed and tightly knit family structure that secures generational relationships to one another. Affiliation then becomes in effect a literal form of re-presentation, by which what is ours is good, and therefore deserves incorporation and inclusion in our programs of humanist study, and what is not ours in this ultimately provincial sense is simply left out."

58 Agamben, *The Coming Community*, 85.

59 Emmanuel Levinas, "Peace and Proximity" (1984), *Emmanuel Levinas: Basic Philosophical Writings*, ed. Adrianna T. Peperzak, Simon Critchley, and Robert Bernasconi (Bloomington: Indiana University Press, 1996), 165.

60 Horst Hutter, *Politics as Friendship: The Origins of Classical Notions of Politics in the Theory and Practice of Friendship* (Waterloo, Ont.: Wilfrid Laurier University Press, 1978), 2.

61 Derrida, *Politics of Friendship*, viii.

62 See Said's discussion of "filiation" in *The World, the Text, and the Critic*, 111–25.

63 Aristotle, *The Ethics of Aristotle: The Nichomachean Ethics*, trans. J. A. K. Thomson (Harmondsworth: Penguin, 1955), 258. All subsequent references are to this edition.

64 Aristotle's *Ethics* was composed at a time when, following from the expansionism of Philip and Alexander, the small and culturally self-contained city-state was being compelled to join the ever-expanding circle of a wider, more impersonal, imperial community.

65 Derrida, *Politics of Friendship*, 35.

66 Cited in Benjamin Farrington, *The Faith of Epicurus* (London: Weidenfeld and Nicolson, 1967), 31.

67 Giorgio Agamben, *Homo Sacer: Sovereign Power and Bare Life*, trans. Daniel Heller-Rouen (Stanford: Stanford University Press, 1998), 7, 11.

68 This point is made by Marios Constantinou, "Spectral *Philia* and the Imaginary Institution of Needs," *South Atlantic Quarterly* 97, no. 1 (winter 1998): 156–57: "Epicurean ethics is . . . confronted with a paradoxical difficulty: the altruistic bond of friendship entails vulnerability to dependency on external attachment. Does not altruistic friendship interfere with, even disrupt, the self-sufficient state of *ataraxia*." Phillip Mitsis raises similar concerns in his *Epicurus's Ethical Theory: The Pleasures of Invulnerability* (Ithaca: Cornell University Press, 1988), 124: "A . . . difficulty confronts Epicurus's account of friendship . . . Epicurus claims, for instance, that for the sake of friendship we should run risks, *dei de kai parakinduneusai charin philias* . . . It is unclear, however, that he can justify any risk-taking given his model of pleasure and rational agency."

69 Constantinou, "Spectral *Philia* and the Imaginary Institution of Needs," 156.

70 E. M. Forster, *Two Cheers for Democracy* (London: Edward Arnold, 1951), 66.

71 Derrida, *Of Hospitality*, 123.

72 See Blanchot, *The Unavowable Community*, 7: "a communion . . . a fusion . . . a unity (a supra-individuality) would expose itself to the same objections arising from the simple consideration of the single individual, locked in its immanence." In his "The Other in Proust" (1947), in *The Levinas Reader*, ed. Sean Hand (Oxford: Basil Blackwell, 1989), 164, Levinas makes a similar point, arguing that most projects of communication fail on account of their misguided aspiration for "fusion": "If communication bears the mark of failure of inauthenticity . . . it is because it is sought as a fusion."

73 Butler, *Gender Trouble*, 14.

74 Donna J. Haraway, *Simians, Cyborgs, and Women: The Reinvention of Nature* (New York: Routledge, 1991), 154.

75 E. M. Forster, *A Passage to India* (1924; Penguin: Harmondsworth, 1978), 289.

76 In his *Perpetual Peace: A Philosophical Sketch*, ed. Lewis White Beck (1794; Indianapolis: Bobbs-Merrill, 1957), Kant paradigmatically draws cosmopolitanism within the rubric of his moral philosophy. Written to commemorate the Treaty of Basel, this occasional tract endorses the new peace between Prussia and France, while courageously hinting at the author's republicanism in its celebration of the hard-won accord between the monarchial states of Europe and the French Republic. This notwithstanding, Kant's ethico-political rubric is intensely susceptible to the prescriptive universalism of colonial thought, consistently nominating cosmopoli-

tanism as the decisive marker of European rationality and civility. In recent years various theorists have attempted productively to rehabilitate the discourse of cosmopolitanism, wresting it from its neocolonial Kantian ascriptions to disclose instead a project of radical democracy. See especially Jacques Derrida, *On Cosmopolitanism and Forgiveness*, trans. Mark Dooley and Michael Hughes (London: Routledge, 2001), and Sheldon Pollock, Homi K. Bhabha, Carol A. Breckenridge, and Dipesh Chakrabarty, eds., "Cosmopolitanisms," *Public Culture* 12, no. 3 (2000).

77 Derrida, *Of Hospitality*, 77.

78 Vikram Seth, *Mappings* (Delhi: Viking Penguin, 1994), 70.

CHAPTER 3 Sex

1 Edward Carpenter, *Towards Democracy* (1883; London: GMP, 1985), 373.

2 Ibid., 373–74.

3 H. M. Hyndman, "Shall We Fight for India," *Justice*, March 1885, 4.

4 Although not strictly interchangeable, anti-imperialism and the critique of western civilization are inextricable in Carpenter's thought, as in that of his contemporaries.

5 Edward Carpenter, "Empire in India and Elsewhere," *Humane Review* 1 (1900): 207.

6 Gilbert Beith, *Edward Carpenter: In Appreciation* (London: George Allen and Unwin, 1931), 110.

7 Cited in Hugh David, *On Queer Street: A Social History of British Homosexuality 1895–1995* (London: Harper Collins, 1997), 50–52.

8 E. M. Forster, *Maurice* (1971; Harmondsworth: Penguin, 2000), 213.

9 Ibid., 208.

10 Gayle Rubin, "Thinking Sex: Notes for a Radical Theory of the Politics of Sexuality," *The Lesbian and Gay Studies Reader*, ed. Henry Abelove, Michele Aina Barale, and David M. Haleperin (New York: Routledge, 1993), 35.

11 Leo Bersani, *Homos* (Cambridge: Harvard University Press, 1995), 59, 61, 67.

12 Housman, untitled essay, *Edward Carpenter: An Appreciation*, by Gilbert Beith (London: George Allen and Unwin, 1931), 111.

13 Eve Kosofsky Sedgwick, *Epistemology of the Closet* (Harmondsworth: Penguin, 1994), 1, refers to the fundamental contradiction "between seeing homo/heterosexual definition on the one hand as an issue of active importance primarily for a small, distinct, relatively fixed homosexual minority (what I refer to as a minoritising view), and seeing it on the other hand as an issue of continuing, determinative importance in the lives of people across a spectrum of sexualities (what I refer to as a universalising view)." Compare with Monique Wittig, *The Straight Mind and Other Essays* (Boston: Beacon, 1992), 64: "A text by a minority writer is effective only if it

succeeds in making the minority point of view universal, only if it is an important literary text. *Remembrance of Things Past* is a monument of French Literature even though homosexuality is the theme of the book. Barnes's oeuvre is an important literary oeuvre even though her major theme is lesbianism . . . the work of these writers has transformed, as should all important work, the textual tissue of our times."

14 Sedgwick, *Epistemology of the Closet*, 2.

15 Ibid.

16 Michel Foucault, *The History of Sexuality: An Introduction*, trans. Robert Hurley (Harmondsworth: Penguin, 1984), 1:49.

17 Ibid. 18. Emphasis in original.

18 Ibid., 48.

19 Ibid., 45.

20 Slavoj Žižek, *The Ticklish Subject: The Absent Centre of Political Ontology* (London: Verso, 1999), 256.

21 Foucault, *The History of Sexuality*, 101.

22 Michel Foucault, "What Is Enlightenment," *The Foucault Reader: An Introduction to Foucault's Thought*, ed. Paul Rabinow (Harmondsworth: Penguin), 48.

23 Ibid., 42.

24 Judith Butler, *Gender Trouble: Feminism and the Subversion of Identity* (New York: Routledge, 1990), 9.

25 James O'Higgins, "Sexual Choice, Sexual Act: An Interview with Michel Foucault," *Salmagundi* 58–59 (fall 1982–winter 1983): 22.

26 Ibid.

27 Ibid.

28 Foucault, *The History of Sexuality*, 108.

29 Ibid., 106.

30 Ibid., 108.

31 Foucault's philosophical preference for a politics of gay relationality over the politics of gay sex acts is comprehensively discussed in David M. Halperin, *Saint Foucault: Towards a Gay Hagiography* (New York: Oxford University Press, 1995), 15–125.

32 Foucault, *The History of Sexuality*, 96.

33 Edward Carpenter, *Love's Coming of Age: A Series of Papers on the Relation of the Sexes* (1896; London: George Allen and Unwin, 1948), 181. In my efforts to prepare the theoretical ground for a rehabilitation of Edward Carpenter and his kind I have set up a somewhat polemical opposition between pro-sex and pro-relationality gay and lesbian theorists. Needless to say the oppositions are not always so stark (nor am I proposing a puritanical assault on sex acts and their complex pleasures). In recent years, especially, queer theory in all its variants has generally come to concur

with the Foucauldian emphasis on reimagining community either through or without the accompanying performance of sex. For example, Leo Bersani, in *Homos*, 7, seeks in an enthusiastic exploration of "gay desire" a radical "redefinition of sociality." And on the other side, while insisting that "queers" do not want "just sex," Michael Warner inaugurates the anthology *Fear of Queer Nation: Queer Politics and Social Theory* (Minneapolis: University of Minnesota Press, 1993), xxi, with a declaration of resistance against heterosexual culture's privileging of itself "as the elemental form of association." In the end my proposed exploration of the sort of politics exemplified by Carpenter gains its cue from queer theory's generic turn toward issues of community, association, and kinship rather than its turn away from the performance of homo-sex.

34 In his interview in 1982 Foucault refuses to answer this question on the grounds that "if the relationships to be created are as yet unforeseeable, then we can't really say that this feature or that feature will be denied." O'Higgins, "Sexual Choice, Sexual Act," 22.

35 See Edward Carpenter, *The Intermediate Sex: A Study of Some Transitional Types of Men and Women* (Cambridge: MIT Press, 1993), 48; Havelock Ellis, *Sexual Inversion* (1897), *Studies in the Psychology of Sex* (New York: Random House, 1942), 1:32–33; and John Addington Symonds, *The Life of Michelangelo* (1893; Philadelphia: University of Pennsylvania Press, 2002). References to Michelangelo's exemplary homosexuality continued well into the twentieth century. A famous "citing" of Michelangelo comes from a letter that Sigmund Freud wrote in 1935 to an American female correspondent who was distraught at the discovery that her son was homosexual. In his characteristically humane reply Freud attempts to allay her anxieties by placing her erring son in distinguished company: "Many highly respectable individuals of ancient and modern times have been homosexuals, several of the greatest among them (Plato, Michelangelo, Leonardo da Vinci etc.). It is a great injustice to persecute homosexuality as a crime and a cruelty too. If you do not believe me, read the books of Havelock Ellis." "A Letter from Freud," *American Journal of Psychiatry*, April 1951, 786.

36 Ellis, "Sexual Inversion," 33.

37 Symonds, *The Life of Michelangelo*, 540–41.

38 David Finn and Frederick Hartt, *Michelangelo's Three Pietàs: A Photographic Study* (New York: Harry N. Abrams, 1975), 108.

39 John 19:39–40.

40 Luca Landucci, *Florentine Diary from 1450 to 1516*, trans. Alice de Rosen Jervis (London: J. M. Dent and Sons, 35). Also cited in Finn and Hartt, *Michelangelo's Three Pietàs*, 19.

41 Judith Butler, *Antigone's Claim: Kinship between Life and Death* (New York: Columbia University Press, 2000).

42 Ibid., 57, 22, 62.

43 Ibid., 55.

44 The profound influence of *The Descent of Man* upon Darwin's contemporaries is powerfully asserted in Gillian Beer, *Darwin's Plots: Evolutionary Narrative in Darwin, George Eliot, and Nineteenth-Century Fiction* (1983; Cambridge: Cambridge University Press, 2000), xxiv.

45 Ibid., 8.

46 Darwin, *The Descent of Man and Selection in Relation to Sex* (1871; Princeton: Princeton University Press, 1981), 173.

47 Ibid., 178.

48 Frank J. Sulloway, *Freud, Biologist of the Mind: Beyond the Psychoanalytic Legend* (New York: Basic, 1979), 252.

49 Darwin, *The Descent of Man*, 253.

50 Ibid., 324.

51 Ibid., 323.

52 Ibid., 343.

53 Ibid., 356.

54 The impact of Darwin's *Descent* upon the construction of Victorian womanhood is comprehensively analyzed in Cynthia Russett, *Sexual Science: The Victorian Construction of Womanhood* (Cambridge: Harvard University Press, 1989). See also Beer, *Darwin's Plots*.

55 Iwan Bloch, *The Sexual Life of Our Time, in Its Relations to Modern Civilisation*, trans. M. Eden Paul (London: Rebman, 1908), 534.

56 The most comprehensive recent survey of nineteenth-century sexology can be found in Lucy Bland and Laura Doane, eds., *Sexology Uncensored: The Documents of Sexual Science* (Cambridge: Polity, 1998), and Lucy Bland and Laura Doane, eds., *Sexology in Culture: Labelling Bodies and Desires* (Cambridge: Polity, 1998).

57 R. von Krafft-Ebing, *Aberrations of Sexual Life after the Psychopathia Sexualis of R. v. Krafft-Ebing, Brought Up to Date and Issued by Alexander Hartwich*, trans. Arthur Vivian Burbury (London: Staples, 1959), 9.

58 August Forel, *The Sexual Question: A Scientific, Psychological, Hygienic and Sociological Study*, trans. C. F. Marshall (New York: Medical Art Agency, 1906), 450, 451.

59 Bloch, *The Sexual Life of Our Time*, 6.

60 Patrick Geddes and J. Arthur Thomson, *The Evolution of Sex* (London: Walter Scott, 1889), 267–70.

61 Havelock Ellis, *Man and Woman: A Study of Human Secondary Sexual Characteristics* (London: Walter Scott, 1894), 13. For other examples see Bland and Doane, eds., *Sexology Uncensored*, 201–30. It is worth noting the geographical indeterminacy of the term "savage." While used more often than not to designate nonwestern

"primitive" peoples, savagery simultaneously covered a spectrum of attributes which could be identified among criminals, prostitutes, and the underclass generally. In sexological analyses each of these subgroups was charged with inadequate sexual differentiation. Thus Ellis points to symptoms of sexual ambivalence in criminals and "men of lower classes" (*Sexual Inversion*, 23), and the Italian criminologist Lombroso likewise attests to "the virility underlying the female criminal type" (Caesar Lombroso and William Ferrero, *The Female Offender* (New York: D. Appleton, 1898), 112.

62 Ellis, *Sexual Inversion*, 79–80.

63 For more on the discourse of degeneration see Daniel Pick, *Faces of Degeneration: A European Disorder* (Cambridge: Cambridge University Press, 1989), J. Edward Chamberlin and Sander L. Gilman, eds., *Degeneration: The Dark Side of Progress* (New York: Columbia University Press, 1985), and Greta Jones, *Social Darwinism and English Thought: The Interaction between Biological and Social Theory* (Sussex: Harvester and Humanities, 1980).

64 Forel, *The Sexual Question*, 246–47.

65 Bloch, *The Sexual Life of Our Time*, 13.

66 Ibid.

67 Ibid., 40.

68 David Hilliard, "Unenglish and Unmanly: Anglo-Catholicism and Homosexuality," *Victorian Studies* 25, no. 2 (1982): 187.

69 Bland, "Trial by Sexology? Maud Allan, *Salome* and the 'Cult of the Clitoris' Case," *Sexology in Culture*, ed. Bland and Doane, 193.

70 Sir Richard Burton, *Plain and Literal Translation of the Arabian Nights' Entertainment, Now Entitled, The Book of the Thousand and a Night* ([London:] Burton Club For Private Subscribers Only, 1886), 10:206–27.

71 Ibid. See 226, 232, 236, 237.

72 Ibid., 207, 65.

73 The complex subject of homosexual orientalism is addressed by, among others, Christopher Lane, *British Colonial Allegory and the Paradox of Homosexual Desire* (Durham: Durham University Press, 1995), Parminder Kaur Bakshi, "Homosexuality and Orientalism: Edward Carpenter's Journey to the East," *Prose Studies* 13, no. 1 (1990): 151–77 [special issue: *Edward Carpenter and Late-Victorian Radicalism*, ed. Tony Brown], and Joseph A. Boone, "Vacation Cruises; or, The Homoerotics of Orientalism," PMLA 110 (1995): 89–107.

74 Bloch, *The Sexual Life of Our Time*, 547, 549.

75 Forel, *The Sexual Question*, 244

76 William James, *The Principles of Psychology* (London: Henry Holt, 1890), 2:438.

77 Magnus Hirschfeld, *Racism*, trans. Eden and Cedar Paul (London: Victor

Gollancz, 1938), 150–51. A pioneer in the German movement for homosexual rights in the late nineteenth century and the early twentieth, Hirschfeld came directly under attack in Nazi Germany. Between October 1920 and February 1923 his lectures were disrupted by Nazi youth, leaving him seriously injured on one occasion. In May 1933 his Institute for Sexual Science in Berlin was attacked by storm troopers, who consigned some ten thousand books from the institute's library to a fire, along with a bust of Hirschfeld. It is worth remembering, in context, that tens of thousands of homosexuals from Germany and Nazi-occupied countries were sent to concentration camps in Germany and Austria.

78 Judith P. Butler, *Subjects of Desire: Hegelian Reflections in Twentieth-Century France* (New York: Columbia University Press, 1987), 9.

79 Jean-Luc Nancy, *The Inoperative Community*, trans. Peter Connor, Lisa Garbus, Michael Holland, and Simona Sawhney (Minneapolis: University of Minnesota Press, 1991), 19.

80 See Jean-Luc Nancy, *Hegel: The Restlessness of the Negative*, trans. Jason Smith and Steven Miller (Minneapolis: University of Minnesota Press, 2002), 55.

81 See Giorgio Agamben, *Language and Death: The Place of Negativity*, trans. Karen E. Pinkus and Michael Hardt (Minneapolis: University of Minnesota Press, 1991), xiii. Agamben's definition of *ethos* as the place of sociality and communication is relevant here: "The *ethos*, humanity's own, is not something unspeakable or *sacer* that it must remain unsaid in all its praxis and human speech. Neither is it nothingness, whose nullity serves as the basis for the arbitrariness and violence of social action. Rather it is social praxis itself, human speech itself, which have become transparent to themselves" (106).

82 Nancy, *The Inoperative Community*, xxxviii. See also Nancy, *Hegel*, 36, 37, 39, on the experience of ontological insufficiency as a bridge over into radical or other-directed community:

> Philosophy is thus the self-knowing of negativity even as it is the knowing for the negativity of the self . . . The only presupposition of the *self* is that it cannot presuppose itself . . . "self" is nothing that preexists "for itself" and being "for itself" is to be for this absolute non-preexistence. To let this "for" stand on its own as such is to liberate the self—which also means to liberate freedom itself. For this is to unbind the self from every determination to which it would be attached: that of a substance or that of a subject in the sense of a given political identity, that of an individual or a people, that of some essence or of a symbol, of a signification, of a form, or of a figure. But it is not to unbind the self from all attachment so as to let it float, abstract, in an indetermination that would still only be in the void of the "I = I." It is to operate its unbinding and its liberation right at singularity and for singularity. That I am unbound myself so as to be precisely this one, such a one exposed to others and surging up at my empty place . . . Thus "I = I" means

> nothing, or only this: passage and leap into the other of what was never in itself. The leap is unsettling twice over: in the agitation of its movement, where there is no continuity that would not also be the location of a burst of light, and in the nonknowing of the other that thus makes up all of self-knowing.

In another variation on these themes, negativity also performs its work on behalf of *ethos* and sociality in the use to which Heidegger puts it while mapping the itinerary for *Dasein*, whose actualization as a subject is at once the moment of its dissolution in death, and therefore best deferred in favor of the empirical and life-giving distractions of self-alienating relationality.

83 Nancy, *Hegel*, 59.

84 Monique Wittig, *The Straight Mind and Other Essays*, 5, 40. Wittig's thesis has been notably "updated" by, among others, Judith Butler in *Gender Trouble*, 22–23: "The institution of a compulsory and naturalised heterosexuality requires and regulates gender as a binary relation in which the masculine term is differentiated from a feminine term, and this differentiation is accomplished through the practice of heterosexual desire. The act of differentiating the two oppositional moments of the binary results in the consolidation of each term, the respective internal coherence of sex, gender, desire."

85 In Wittig's words, "For the category of sex is a totalitarian one . . . we must destroy it and start thinking beyond it if we want to start thinking at all, as we must destroy the sexes as a sociological reality if we want to start to exist" (*The Straight Mind and Other Essays*, 8).

86 Ibid., 30.

87 See also Marjorie Garber's notion, in *Vested Interests: Cross Dressing and Cultural Identity* (Penguin: Harmondsworth, 1993), of the third space of the transvestite, "which questions binary thinking and introduces crisis" (11).

88 See Wittig, *The Straight Mind and Other Essays*, 45: "breaking off the heterosexual social contract is a necessity for those who do not consent to it. For if there is something real in the ideas of Rousseau, it is that we can form 'voluntary associations' here and now, and here and now reformulate the social contract as a new one, although we are not princes or legislators. Is this a mere utopia? Then I will stay with Socrates's view and also Glaucon's: If ultimately we are denied a new social order, which therefore can exist only in words, I will find it in myself."

89 Butler, *Gender Trouble*, 16.

90 Wittig, *The Straight Mind and Other Essays*, 32.

91 See Michel Foucault, *The Uses of Pleasure: The History of Sexuality*, vol. 2, trans. Robert Hurley (Penguin: Harmondsworth, 1987), 72–77.

92 Cited in *Saint Foucault: Towards a Gay Hagiography* (New York: Oxford University Press, 1995), 78.

93 Karl Heinrich Ulrichs, *The Riddle of "Man-Manly" Love: The Pioneering Work on Male Homosexuality*, trans. Michael A. Lombardi-Nash (Buffalo: Prometheus, 1994), 1:36.

94 Ibid., 2:547.

95 Carpenter, *Love's Coming of Age*, 54–55.

96 Ibid., 61.

97 Butler, *Gender Trouble*, 16.

98 Carpenter, *The Intermediate Sex*, 114–15.

99 Edward Carpenter, *Love's Coming-of-Age: A Series of Papers on the Relations of the Sexes* (1896; London: George Allen and Unwin, 1948), 181. True to the ethical inducements of homosexuality as he saw it, Carpenter's own sympathies were consistently expansive and inclusive. In addition to his vehement anti-imperialism, he endeavored—through a Whitmanic rhetoric of democratic comradeship—to draw the "worker" into the campaign against public school masculinity. Likewise, convinced of a natural affinity between women and homosexuals, he combined forces with the Women's Freedom League, formed in 1908, to further the cause of the suffrage campaign. Carpenter was also active with Henry Salt in the animal rights movement. The rejection by Carpenter and others of sexual binarism as the prerequisite for radical, inclusive, utopian community was taken up in the early years of the twentieth century by the editors of the pro-homosexual journal *Urania* (1915–40). Declaring their aim to abolish all distinctions of sex and gender, each issue announced the following utopian project: "Urania denotes the company of those who are firmly determined to ignore the dual organisation of humanity in all its manifestations. They are convinced that this duality has resulted in the formation of two warped and imperfect types. They are further convinced that in order to get rid of this state of things no measure of 'emancipation' or 'equality' will suffice, which do not begin with a complete refusal to recognise or tolerate the duality itself."

100 Edward Carpenter, *Intermediate Types among Primitive Folk: A Study in Social Evolution* (London: George Allen and Unwin, 1914), 82, 71–72.

101 Carpenter, *Love's Coming-of-Age*, 16, 17, 19, 21.

102 J. A. Symonds, *A Problem in Greek Ethics* (1883), repr. in *Male Love: A Problem in Greek Ethics and Other Writings* (New York: Pagan Books, 52).

103 Magnus Hirschfeld, *The Homosexuality of Men and Women*, trans. Michael A. Lombardi-Nash (1914; New York: Prometheus, 2000), 114.

104 "Anomaly," *The Invert, and His Social Adjustment* (Baltimore: Williams and Wilkins, 1929), 137.

105 Carpenter, *Love's Coming-of-Age*, 55, 56.

106 Ibid., 106.

107 Ibid., 95, 122, 174, 164.

108 Ibid., 145.

109 Edward Carpenter, *Ioläus, an Anthology of Friendship* (Manchester: S. Clarke, 1902), 177–78.

110 Symonds, *A Problem in Modern Ethics* (1896), repr. in *Male Love*, 99, 101.

111 Edward Carpenter, *From Adam's Peak to Elephanta: Sketches in Ceylon and India* (London: George Allen and Unwin, 1921), 174.

112 Edward Carpenter, *Civilisation: Its Cause and Cure* (London: S. Sonnenschein, 1897), 47.

113 Ibid., 49.

114 M. K. Gandhi, *Hind Swaraj and Other Writings* (1910; Cambridge: Cambridge University Press, 1997), 34.

115 Carpenter, *Civilisation*, 105.

116 See Ashis Nandy, *The Intimate Enemy: Loss and Recovery of Self under Colonialism* (Delhi: Oxford University Press, 1983).

117 The anxious anticolonial recuperation of a lost native masculinity is attested, for instance, in Swami Vivekananda's claim that the salvation of Hindus depended on the three Bs—beef, biceps and Bhagvad-Gita (in a sharp departure from the easy eclecticism and aspirational androgyny of his guru Sri Ramakrishna)—and Nathuram Godse's assassination of Mahatma Gandhi in the name of a "re-masculated" Hindu polity. A substantial treatment of masculine anxieties in nationalist India may be found, among others, in Mrinalini Sinha, *Colonial Masculinity: The "Manly Englishman" and the "Effeminate Bengali" in the Late Nineteenth Century* (Manchester: Manchester University Press, 1995), Revathi Krishnaswamy, *Effeminism: The Economy of Colonial Desire* (Ann Arbor: University of Michigan Press, 1998), and Kate Teltscher, "'Maidenly and Well Nigh Effeminate': Constructions of Hindu Masculinity and Religion in Seventeenth-Century English Texts," *Postcolonial Studies* 3, no. 2 (2000): 159–70.

118 M. K. Gandhi, cited in Ved Mehta, *Mahatma Gandhi and His Apostles* (London: Deutsch, 1977), 191, 192.

119 M. K. Gandhi, *Self-Restraint versus Self-Indulgence* (Ahmedabad: Navjivan, 1928), 105.

120 Henry Salt to M. K. Gandhi, 2 December 1929, *The Savour of Salt: A Henry Salt Anthology*, ed. George Hendrick and Willene Hendrick (Fontwell, Sussex: Centaur, 1989), 175.

121 Sigmund Freud, *On Sexuality*, ed. Angela Richards (Harmondsworth: Pelican, 1977), 56–57 n. 1.

122 Sigmund Freud, "Leonardo da Vinci and a Memory of His Childhood" (1910), *Five Lectures on Psychoanalysis: Leonardo da Vinci and Other Works*, ed. James Strachey (London: Hogarth, 1910), 131. For an excellent account of Freud's medical

bias against the homosexual repudiation of sex for the sake of "love" see Suzanne Rait, "Sex, Love and the Homosexual body in Early Sexology," *Sexology in Culture*, ed. Bland and Doane, 135–49.

123 Freud, *On Sexuality*, 80.

124 See Sigmund Freud, *The Future of an Illusion, Civilisation and Its Discontents and Other Works*, ed. James Strachey (London: Hogarth, 1927–31), 15.

125 Sigmund Freud, *Civilisation and Its Discontents*, trans. James Strachey (London: W. W. Norton, 1989), 31.

CHAPTER 4 Meat

1 M. K. Gandhi, *Collected Works of Mahatma Gandhi* [hereinafter CWMG], 1:9.

2 Ibid., 1:42.

3 Ibid., 1:50–51.

4 Ibid., 1:79.

5 M. K. Gandhi, *An Autobiography, or the Story of My Experiments with Truth*, trans. Mahadev Desai (Ahmedabad: Navjivan, 1927), 36–37.

6 Ibid., 39.

7 Ibid., 40.

8 Bhiku Parekh, ed., *Bentham's Political Thought* (London: Croom Helm, 1973), 67. For a description of Gandhi's early and unfavorable encounter with Bentham and utilitarian philosophy see Gandhi, *An Autobiography*, 40.

9 Jeremy Bentham, *An Introduction to the Principles of Morals and Legislation*, ed. J. H. Burns and H. L. A. Hart (Oxford: Clarendon, 1996) 17–18.

10 Gandhi, *An Autobiography*, 38.

11 Ibid., 41.

12 CWMG, 1:98.

13 Ibid. In a later reminiscence Gandhi recounts that he chose porridge for the first course and a pie for the second: "I saw the 'Central' restaurant, and went there and had some porridge for the first time. I did not at first enjoy it, but I liked the pie I had for the second course." CWMG, 1:49.

14 Stephen Winsten, *Salt and His Circle* (London, 1951), 118.

15 George Hendrick, *Henry Salt: Humanitarian Reformer and Man of Letters* (Urbana: University of Illinois Press, 1977), 111–12.

16 Gandhi, *An Autobiography*, 41. Gandhi confirms this debt to Salt in a letter of 6 October 1931 written to an E. Dolby Shelton, another English vegetarian: "I was a born vegetarian, but I had lapsed from my vegetarianism owing to foolish companionship in youth. On coming to London I became a convinced vegetarian, through having read Mr. Salt's essay. Is this quite clear?" CWMG, 48:114.

17 Gandhi, *An Autobiography*, 41.

18 CWMG, 1:22.

19 Ibid., 1:37.

20 Ibid., 1:49.

21 Stephen Hay, "The Making of a Late-Victorian Hindu: M. K. Gandhi in London, 1888–1891," *Victorian Studies*, autumn 1889, 97.

22 Rajmohan Gandhi, *The Good Boatman* (Delhi: Viking, 1995), 63.

23 CWMG, 1:81.

24 See Gandhi, *An Autobiography*, 55.

25 CWMG, 1:81.

26 Rosina Visram provides an instructive account of Indian colonial traffic to England in *Ayahs, Lascars and Princes: Indians in Britain, 1700–1947* (London: Pluto, 1986).

27 E. M. Forster, *Two Cheers for Democracy* (London: Edward Arnold, 1951, 66).

28 CWMG, 1:125.

29 Marios Constantinou, "Spectral *Philia* and the Imaginary Institution of Needs," *South Atlantic Quarterly* 97, no. 1 (winter 1998): 156.

30 Jacques Derrida, *Of Hospitality: Anne Dufourmantelle Invites Jacques Derrida to Respond*, trans. Rachel Bowlby (Stanford: Stanford University Press, 2000), 124–25.

31 Donna J. Haraway, *Simians, Cyborgs, and Women: The Reinvention of Nature* (New York: Routledge, 1991), 173. My exploration in this chapter of fin-de-siècle human–animal sociality, especially in its anticolonial manifestation, also takes its cue from Haraway's detailed exploration of colonialism as anthropocentrism in *Primate Visions: Gender, Race and Nature in the World of Modern Science* (New York: Routledge, 1989). The anticolonial dimensions of Haraway's thought have recently been explicated in Michael Hardt and Antonio Negri, *Empire* (Cambridge: Harvard University Press, 2000), 91–92, 214–18. In a maneuver related to Haraway's thinking on these subjects, if different for its tone of harsh skepticism, John Gray in his book *Straw Dogs: Thoughts on Humans and Other Animals* (London: Granta, 2003) also foregrounds human–animal sociality as a means of dismantling the rapacious imperial subject, *homo rapiens*, unleashed by the forces of western humanism.

32 *The Vegetarian*, 13 June 1891, 320.

33 Gandhi, *An Autobiography*, 47. The anarchist emphasis on "mutual aid" that Gandhi gleaned from the company of fin-de-siècle vegetarians well anticipates the idea of interspecies relationality, and the politics thereof, that Donna Haraway recommends in her recent *The Companion Species Manifesto: Dogs, People, and Significant Otherness* (Chicago: Prickly Paradigm, 2003), 12: "There cannot be just one companion species, there have to be two to make one. It is in the syntax; it is in the flesh. Dogs are about the inescapable, contradictory story of relationships—co-constitutive relationships in which none of the partners pre-exist the relating, and

the relating is never done once and for all. Historical specificity and contingent mutability rule all the way down, into nature and culture, into naturecultures. There is no foundation; there are only elephants supporting elephants all the way down."

34 See Keith Thomas, *Man and the Natural World: A History of the Modern Sensibility* (New York: Pantheon, 1983), 295.

35 For a basic historical background to the tradition of English vegetarianism see Thomas, *Man and the Natural World*, James Turner, *Reckoning with the Beast: Animals, Pain and Humanity in the Victorian Mind* (Baltimore: Johns Hopkins University Press, 1980), Harriet Ritvo, *The Animal Estate: The English and Other Creatures in the Victorian Age* (Cambridge: Harvard University Press, 1987), Christine Kenyon Jones, *Kindred Brutes: Animals in Romantic-Period Writing* (Aldershot: Ashgate, 2001), and Timothy Molton, *Shelley and the Revolution in Taste: The Body and the Natural World* (Cambridge: Cambridge University Press, 1994).

36 See Kenyon Jones, *Kindred Brutes*, 110 n. 6.

37 An important and sympathetic discussion of romantic orientalism is offered in John Drew, *India and the Romantic Imagination* (Delhi: Oxford University Press, 1987). Nigel Leask provides a rather more familiar postcolonial critique of this tendency in *British Romantic Writers and the East: Anxieties of Empire* (Cambridge: Cambridge University Press, 1992).

38 Contemporary accounts of the Vegetarian Society and its affiliates appear in *The Vegetarian Messenger* 6 (1856): 89 and Howard Williams, *The Ethics of Diet*, rev. edn (London: Humanitarian League, 1896), 424n.

39 E. Mason, ed., *Oscar Wilde on Vegetarianism: An Unpublished Letter to Violet Fane* (Edinburgh: Tragara, 1991).

40 Pyarelal, *Mahatma Gandhi: The Early Phase* (Ahmedabad: Navjivan, 1965), 240.

41 Henry Salt, ed., *The New Charter: A Discussion of the Rights of Men and the Rights of Animals* (London: George Bell and Sons, 1896), 9. This volume of essays reveals the ideological diversity of contemporary vegetarian opinion, encompassing scientists, secularists, theosophists, socialists, and evolutionists.

42 H. S. Salt to Gandhi, 8 October 1932, Gandhi National Museum and Library, New Delhi.

43 *Humane Review* 1 (1901): 2.

44 See Richard French, *Antivivisection and Medical Science in Victorian Society* (Princeton: Princeton University Press, 1975), and Coral Lansbury, *The Old Brown Dog: Women, Workers, and Vivisection in Edwardian England* (Madison: University of Wisconsin Press, 1985).

45 Cobbe writes in detail about the *Zoophilist* and *Le Zoophile* in her *Life of Frances Power Cobbe as Told by Herself* (London: S. Sonnenschein, 1904), 670–71.

46 See James Hunt, *Gandhi in London* (Delhi: Promilla, 1993), 33, and Gandhi, *An Autobiography*, 114.

47 Ritvo, *The Animal Estate*, 162.

48 *Vegetarian*, 29 January 1898.

49 *Almonds and Raisins*, 1886, 4; *Animal's Friend*, August 1895, 238.

50 *Vegetarian*, 2 April 1898, 215.

51 Behramji Malabari, *The Indian Eye on English Life* (Westminster: A. Constable, 1893), 45.

52 *Vegetarian Messenger* 1 (1887): 3–4.

53 T. B. Macaulay, *Critical and Historical Essays* (London, 1843), 3:345.

54 John Rosselli, "The Self-Image of Effeteness: Physical Education and Nationalism in Nineteenth-Century Bengal," *Past and Present* 86 (1980): 123–24.

55 Swami Vivekananda, *Selections from the Complete Works of Swami Vivekananda* (Calcutta: Advaita Ashram, 1986), 530.

56 Gandhi, *An Autobiography*, 17.

57 Ibid., 18.

58 Ibid.

59 The case for the long association of beef and virility in English nationalism is made, variously, in Thomas, *Man and the Natural World*, and Ritvo, *The Animal Estate*.

60 *Almonds and Raisins*, 1886, 4; Anna Kingsford, *The Perfect Way in Diet: A Treatise Advocating a Return to the Natural and Ancient Food of Our Race* (London: Kegan Paul, Trench, 1881), 16–17.

61 See Henry Light, *Common-Sense Vegetarianism* (Manchester: Vegetarian Society, 1929), 96–97.

62 Ernest Crosby and Elisée Reclus, *The Meat Fetish: Two Essays on Vegetarianism* (London: A. C. Fifield, 1905), 15.

63 *Vegetarian*, 8 March 1902, 94.

64 *Vegetarian*, 18 February 1899, 78.

65 *The Brutalitarian: A Journal of the Sane and Strong* 1, no. 1 (1904): 4.

66 Henry Salt, *Killing for Sport: Essays by Various Writers* (London: George Bell and Sons, 1919), 150.

67 CWMG, 68:265.

68 CWMG, 85:266–67.

69 Henry Salt, *Life of Henry David Thoreau*, ed. George Hendrick, Willene Hendrick and Fritz Oehlschlaeger (1890; Fontwell, Sussex: Centaur, 1993), 130.

70 Salt to Gandhi, 18 September 1929, Gandhi National Museum and Library, New Delhi.

71 Gandhi to Salt, 12 October 1929, Gandhi National Museum and Library, New Delhi.

72 *The Parliamentary Debates from the Year 1803 to the Present Time* [hereinafter *Debates*], n.s. 7 (London: Hansard, 1825): 758.

73 For a history of the RSPCA see Arthur Moss, *Valiant Crusade: A History of the RSPCA* (Cassell: London, 1961).

74 F. R. Leavis, *Mill on Bentham and Coleridge* (Cambridge: Cambridge University Press, 1950), 13.

75 Thomas, *Man and the Natural World*, 175.

76 Peter Singer, *Practical Ethics* (Cambridge: Cambridge University Press, 1979), 13.

77 Peter Singer, *Animal Liberation*, 2d edn (London: Pimlico, 1975), 204.

78 Bentham, *An Introduction to the Principles of Morals and Legislation*, 282–83.

79 Immanuel Kant, *Lecture on Ethics*, trans. L. Infield (New York: Harper, 1963), 239–40.

80 *Debates*, 14:555.

81 Thomas Taylor, *Vindication of the Rights of Brutes*, ed. Louise Shultz Boas (Gainesville: Scholars Facsimiles and Reprints, 1960), vii.

82 Bentham, *An Introduction to the Principles of Morals and Legislation*, 282.

83 Elie Halevy, *The Growth of Philosophical Radicalism* (London: Faber and Faber, 1928), 27.

84 Bentham, *An Introduction to the Principles of Morals and Legislation*, 285.

85 Halevy, *The Growth of Philosophical Radicalism*, 27.

86 Michel Foucault, *Discipline and Punish: The Birth of the Prison*, trans. Alan Sheridan (Penguin: Harmondsworth, 1987), 209.

87 Ibid., 221.

88 See for example Thomas, *Man and the Natural World*, 186–88, and Ritvo, *The Animal Estate*, 133–36. Another perspective on the intimate relation between "imperial government" and the "management" of nature is offered in Richard Drayton's study of the rise of the botanical garden—and thereto, the growing compact between Victorian naturalists and administrators—in *Nature's Government: Science, Imperial Britain, and the "Improvement" of the World* (New Haven: Yale University Press, 2000).

89 *Debates*, 35:204.

90 Ibid., 35:202.

91 See *Debates*, 36:847, 36:848, n.s. 16:560, n.s. 16:561.

92 Cited in Ritvo, *The Animal Estate*, 135.

93 The theme of "vigilance" is ubiquitous in most RSPCA writings. See especially Moss's *Valiant Crusade*.

94 S. S. Monro, *Hints: To Workers in the Cause of Humanity* (Tunbridge Wells, 1890), 1.

95 See Moss, *Valiant Crusade*, 53.

96 John Stuart Mill, *Principles of Political Economy with some of their Applica-*

tions to Social Philosophy, ed. W. I. Ashley (New York: Augustus M. Kelley, 1965), 958–59.

97 Cited in Asa Briggs, *The Age of Improvement: 1783–1867* (London: Longman, 1959), 2.

98 Jeremy Bentham, *A Fragment on Government*, ed. J. H. Burns and H. L. A. Hart (Cambridge: Cambridge University Press, 1988), 40.

99 J. S. Mill, *Utilitarianism, On Liberty, Essay on Bentham*, ed. Mary Warnock (Glasgow: Collins, 1962), 135–36.

100 James Mill, *The History of British India*, ed. John Kenneth Galbraith (New York: Chelsea House, 1968), 1:337, 124.

101 Rudyard Kipling, *The Jungle Books* (Harmondsworth: Penguin, 1987), 146.

102 Eric Stokes, *The English Utilitarians and India* (Oxford: Clarendon, 1959), 49, 80, 320. The case for historical links between nineteenth-century utilitarianism and colonial government in India is also pursued in Lynn Zastoupil, "J. S. Mill and India," *Victorian Studies*, autumn 1988, 31–54. For arguments about the structural similarities between utilitarian thought and colonial governmentality see Ranajit Guha, "Dominance without Hegemony and Its Historiography," *Subaltern Studies* 6 (1989): 210–309, and Timothy Mitchell, *Colonising Egypt* (Cambridge: Cambridge University Press, 1988).

103 Pyarelal, *Mahatma Gandhi*, 133.

104 Foucault, *Discipline and Punish*, 199, 200.

105 Ibid., 219–20.

106 Bentham, *A Fragment on Government*, 40.

107 John Durham Peters, *Speaking into the Air: A History of the Idea of Communication* (Chicago: University of Chicago Press, 1999), 16.

108 Bentham, *An Introduction to the Principles of Morals and Legislation*, 21.

109 See ibid., 16.

110 John Stuart Mill, *Autobiography* (London: Longmans, Green, Reader, and Dyer, 1873), 67.

111 *Animal Liberation*, x, opens with Singer's excoriating critique of "feeling" as something irrelevant and deleterious to animal welfare. Recalling a student encounter that he and his wife had with a hypocritical, ham-eating, English animal lover, he launches into the following fulminations: "we were not especially 'interested in' animals. Neither of us had been inordinately fond of dogs, cats, or horses in the way that many people are. We didn't 'love' animals. We simply wanted them treated as the independent beings that they are, and not as a means to human ends—as the pig whose flesh was now in our hostess's sandwiches had been treated . . . The assumption that in order to be interested in such matters one must be an 'animal-lover' is itself an indication of the absence of the slightest inkling that the moral standards

that we apply among human beings might extend to other animals." Singer offers his most coherent defense of the "separation" between animals and humans, once again in a startlingly utilitarian idiom, in his ficto-critical reflection upon J. M. Coetzee's *The Lives of Animals* (Princeton: Princeton University Press, 1999), 85–91.

112 Bentham, *An Introduction to the Principles of Morals and Legislation*, 282.

113 *Debates*, 36:845.

114 See John Kipling (1891) *Beast and Man in India* (London: Macmillan, 1904).

115 Haraway, *Simians, Cyborgs, and Women*, 177, 378. Similar sentiments are repeated in Haraway's paen to human-dog relationality in *The Companion Species Manifesto*, 2–3: "We are training each other in acts of communication we barely understand. We are, constitutively, companion species. We make each other up, in the flesh. Significantly other to each other, in specific difference, we signify in the flesh a nasty developmental infection called love."

116 Henry Salt, *Cruelties of Civilisation: A Program of Humane Reform* (London: William Reeves, 1984), vi–vii.

117 *Humanitarian*, n.s. 2, no. 44 (October 1905): 172.

118 *Animals' Friend*, June 1894, 2.

119 Arthur Broderick Bullock, *"The Basis of Morality": Schopenhauer's View of Ethics* (London: S. Sonnenschein, 1903), 4, 2, 5.

120 *The Brutalitarian: A Journal of the Sane and Strong*, 1.

121 Henry Salt, *Seventy Years among Savages* (London: George Allen and Unwin, 1921), 48.

122 Henry Salt, *Shelley as a Pioneer of Humanitarianism* (London: Humanitarian League, 1902), 14. Salt's numerous writings on Shelley include *Shelley's Principles: Has Time Refuted or Confirmed Them: A Retrospect and Forecast* (London: William Reeves, 1892), *A Shelley Primer* (London: Reeves and Turner, 1887), and *Percy Bysshe Shelley: A Monograph* (London: S. Sonnenschein, 1888).

123 Frances Power Cobbe, *Darwinism in Morals and Other Essays* (London: Williams and Norgate, 1872), 6.

124 Cobbe, *False Beasts and True: Essays on Natural and Unnatural History* (London: Ward, Lock and Tyler, 1900).

125 Cobbe, *The Divine Law of Love and Its Application to the Lower Animals* (London: Pewtress, 1895), 3.

126 Anna Kingsford, *Dreams and Dream Stories*, ed. Edward Maitland (London: George Redway, 1888), 24, 45.

127 See Anna Kingsford, *Pasteur: His Method and Its Results: A Lecture* (London: North London Anti-Vivisection Society, 1886), 11.

128 Edward Maitland, *Anna Kingsford: Her Life, Letters, Diary and Work* (London: John M. Watkins, 1913), 2:268.

129 The discourse of contemporary utopian socialism was also entirely hospitable to the sentimental apologia of radical zoophilia on account of its own unique privileging of sentiment and concomitant focus, as Sheila Rowbotham and Jefferey Weeks have observed in *Socialism and the New Life: The Personal and Sexual Politics of Edward Carpenter and Havelock Ellis* (London: Pluto, 1977), 9, on "the inter-connections between the transformation of personal life and wider external radical social change." So, in his *Love's Coming-of-Age: A Series of Papers on the Relation of the Sexes* (1896; London: George Allen and Unwin, 1948), we find Edward Carpenter celebrating socialism as the politics most appropriate to "love's coming of age," and in a similar vein, Henry Salt endorses socialism for its unique quality of "heart." As he writes in *The Heart of Socialism* (London: Independent Labour Party Publication Department, 1928), 62: "We need . . . in politics—and Socialism alone seems to be able to bring it—'a change of heart' . . . without this change of heart neither religion, nor science, nor statesmanship, will avail to liberate us from our bondage."

130 Henry Light, *Common-Sense Vegetarianism*, 96.

131 Cobbe, *The Friend of Man, and His Friends—the Poets* (London: George Bell and Sons, 1889), 33.

132 Salt, ed., *The New Charter*, 20.

133 See Salt, *Seventy Years among Savages*, 153–55.

134 Salt, *Killing for Sport*, vi.

135 Tolstoy *The First Step: An Essay on the Morals of Diet* (1892), trans. Aylmer Maude (Manchester: Vegetarian Society, 1902), 50, 31.

136 Kingsford, *The Perfect Way in Diet*, 61.

137 E. Nesbit, *The New Treasure Seekers* (Harmondsworth: Puffin, 1982), 209.

138 Ibid., 217.

139 *Vegetarian Messenger*, 1856, 43–45.

140 Thomas Mansell, *Vegetarianism and Manual Labour* (Manchester: Vegetarian Society, 1897).

141 *Animal's Friend* 1 (June 1894): 1.

142 Kingsford, *Unscientific Science: A Lecture* (1883; Edinburgh: Andrew and Elliot, 1915), 29.

143 *Zoophilist*, 2 April 1888, 56.

144 Charles Darwin, *Voyage of the Beagle: Charles Darwin's Journal of Researches*, ed. and abridged by Janet Browne and Michael Neeve (Harmondsworth: Penguin, 1989), 2.

145 Ibid., 9.

146 Ibid., 376.

147 Ibid., 183–84.

148 Charles Darwin, *The Origin of Species, by Means of Natural Selection or the Preservation of Favoured Races in the Struggle for Life* (1859; New York: Modern Library, 1998), 5.

149 Ibid., 610–11.

150 Ibid., 578.

151 Cited in James J. Sheehan and Morton Sosna, *The Boundaries of Humanity: Humans, Animals and Machines* (Berkeley: University of California Press, 1991), 31.

152 Henry Salt, *The Creed of Kinship* (London: Constable, 1935), 8.

153 See J. Howard Moore, *The Universal Kinship* (London: George Bell and Sons, 1906).

154 *Vegetarian*, 1 April 1899.

155 Darwin, *The Origin of Species*, 627.

156 Haraway, in *The Companion Species Manifesto*, 9, draws attention to the anarchism, or mistrust of sequestering categories, implicit in the web of affinities postulated by Darwin: "And like the productions of a decadent gardener who can't keep good distinctions between natures and cultures straight, the shape of my kin networks looks more like a trellis or an esplanade than a tree. You can't tell up from down, and everything seems to go sidewise. Such snake-like, sidewinding traffic is one of my themes. My garden is full of snakes, full of trellises, full of indirection. Instructed by evolutionary population biologists and bioanthropologists, I know that multidirectional gene flow—multidirectional flows of bodies and values—is and has always been the name of the game of life on earth. It is certainly the way into the kennel."

157 Peter Kropotkin, *Mutual Aid: A Factor of Evolution* (London: William Heinemann, 1910), 57.

158 Ibid., 226–27.

159 The peculiarities of fin-de-siècle English anarchism are comprehensively described in Hermia Oliver, *The International Anarchist Movement in Late-Victorian London* (London: Croom Helm, 1983). Generally speaking, anarchism's influence upon and presence within the culture of fin-de-siècle English socialism was both tenuous and tenacious. As is well known, growing tensions between Marx and Bakunin caused the First International to split in 1872, with the Bakunists "officially" expelled. Despite the "formal" triumph of Marxism in this conflict, however, the anarchists continued to meet under the aegis of a Bakunist International between 1872 and 1877, and in 1881 some leading anarchists, among them Kropotkin and Reclus, organized a "black international" with branches in France, Italy, and the United States. Taking root more strongly in France, Italy, and Spain—countries, that is, with weaker industrialization and a smaller urban and working-class population—anarchism never quite managed to become a mass trans-European movement. Nonetheless, and through all of their vexed negotiations with the dominant Marxist orthodoxy in the first two Internationals, anarchists maintained a hold on the international socialist movement at least until they were officially purged from the Second International in 1896. So too, against expectation they managed to find several hospitable pockets within the various subcultures of late Victorian radicalism. And in the

popular imagination, as Joll observes in *The Second International*, 56, socialism and anarchism remained almost indistinguishable: "When ordinary people in Europe thought about international Socialists, it was not the disciplined mass parties, the solid, bearded, self-improving working men of the German or Belgian Socialist Parties or the British trade unions that came to mind. The figure that had captured the imagination was the Anarchist with the smoking bomb in his pocket, whose outrages could be regarded either as the gallant defiance of an oppressive and materialist social system or as the senseless protest of a deranged individual."

160 Edward Carpenter, *Prisons, Police and Punishment: An Inquiry into the Causes and Treatment of Crime and Criminals* (London: A. C. Fifield, 1905), 104, 113.

161 Henry Salt, *Animal Rights Considered in Relation to Social Progress*, rev. edn (London: G. Bell and Sons, 1922), 16–17.

162 Henry Salt, *Cum Grano* (Berkeley Heights, N.J.: Oriole, 1931), 119.

CHAPTER 5 God

1 See Parama Roy, *Indian Traffic: Identities in Question in Colonial and Postcolonial India* (Berkeley: University of California Press, 1998), 123–24: "She was necessary for the consolidation of his nationalism, his guruness, his masculinity, his heterosexuality . . . One might speculate that Nivedita's fervent defence of Hindu gender orthodoxy is also a meditation on her own discipleship."

2 For Adorno, mystical, occultist, and spiritualist practices are inherently antithetical to the project of social justice because of their affinity to authoritarianism. See for example his reading of astrology columns in *The Stars Down to Earth and Other Essays*, ed. Stephen Cook (London: Routledge, 1994), 38, 43: "Under present conditions, the astrological system can function only as 'secondary superstition,' largely exempt from the individual's own critical control and offered authoritatively . . . Indulgence in astrology may provide those who fall for it with a substitute for sexual pleasure of a passive nature. It means primarily submission to unbridled strength of the absolute power." Compare Anthony Storr, *Feet of Clay: A Study of Gurus* (London: Harper Collins, 1997), xiii: "Gurus tend to be elitist and anti-democratic, even if they pay lip-service to democracy. How could it be otherwise? Conviction of a special revelation must imply that the guru is a superior person who is not as other men are . . . Once established, gurus must exercise authority, which . . . precludes making friends on equal terms." While the guru-disciple relationship is necessarily bound by hierarchical obligations, it is absurd to invoke dictatorship as the only model for the enactment of such obligations. Consider the relationship between the inspirational teacher and his students, the revolutionary leader and her followers, etc.

3 Ashis Nandy, *The Intimate Enemy: Loss and Recovery of Self under Colonialism* (Delhi: Oxford University Press, 1983), 95. It is worth noting that Nandy reserves his

suspicion for Mirra Alfassa while remaining deeply sympathetic to Sri Aurobindo's spiritualist politics.

4 Kumari Jayawardene, *The White Woman's Other Burden: Western Women and South Asia during British Rule* (New York: Routledge, 1995), 225.

5 Evelyn Roy, "Mahatma Gandhi: Revolutionary or Counter-Revolutionary?," *Labour Monthly*, September 1993, 158, also cited in Jayawardene, *The White Woman's Other Burden*, 229.

6 Throughout this book I have been treating the terms "politics" and "ethics" as intimate and contiguous. While this enterprise leaves itself open to the charge that it renders "politics" and "ethics" in some way indistinguishable or identical, my insistence upon the contiguity of these two terms does not in any way assume their synonymity. Such insistence is a strong—some might say characteristic—feature of the postmodern philosophies to which this book is indebted, finding utterance variously in the tradition linking Levinas, Lyotard, the late Foucault, and most compellingly the late Derrida. So too, the transactive or symbiotic nature of the "ethical" and the "political" was typical of the historical figures with whom I am concerned in this study: both on the western side (Carpenter, Salt, Mirra Alfassa, Oscar Wilde) and on the nonwestern, most notably in the case of Gandhi.

7 Dipesh Chakrabarty, *Provincializing Europe: Postcolonial Thought and Historical Difference* (Princeton: Princeton University Press, 2000), 16.

8 See Georges Van Vrekhem, *The Mother: The Story of Her Life* (New Delhi: Harper Collins, 2000), 125: "Aurobindo was named by some British authorities as 'the most dangerous man in India,' and 'dangerous' is an epithet attached to his name again and again in the letters of the highest office bearers, including the Viceroy Lord Minto." Although Sri Aurobindo had amnesty from British laws in Pondicherry, both he and his visitors were closely watched by locally placed spies for the British administration. In 1911 one of these visitors, Alexandra David-Neel, the first European woman to enter Tibet and a close friend of the Richards through theosophical circles, was officially reprimanded by British intelligence in Madras for her contact with Sri Aurobindo. For an account of Sri Aurobindo's political extremism in the context of Indian anticolonial nationalism see Peter Heehs, *The Bomb in Bengal: The Rise of Revolutionary Terrorism in India, 1900–1910* (Delhi: Oxford University Press, 1993).

9 Cited in Sujata Nahar, *Mother's Chronicles: Mirra Meets the Revolutionary* (Paris: Institut de Recherches Évolutives, 1997), 5:580.

10 Sri Aurobindo, *Record of Yoga—I* (Pondicherry: Sri Aurobindo Ashram, 2001), 10:1402.

11 The Mother, *Prayers and Meditations* (Pondicherry: Sri Aurobindo Ashram, 1978), 1:291.

12 See Peter Heehs, *Sri Aurobindo: A Brief Biography* (Delhi: Oxford University Press, 1989), 83–84.

13 See A. B. Purani, *Evening Talks with Sri Aurobindo*, 2d edn (Pondicherry: Sri Aurobindo Society, 1995), 52 –53. The meeting between Devdas Gandhi and Sri Aurobindo was not a success. In addition to their strong differences on the admissibility of violence in revolutionary struggle, Devdas's Gandhian recoil from Sri Aurobindo's smoking habit did not raise him in the estimation of the distinctly antipuritanical yogi. An amusing account of the encounter is given by Nirodbaran in *Twelve Years with Sri Aurobindo*, 2d edn (Pondicherry: Sri Aurobindo Ashram, 1972), 13: "A cigar was almost always between his lips. Once Devdas Gandhi, son of Mahatma Gandhi, visited him and saw the inevitable cigar. He shot the question, 'Why are you so attached to smoking?' At once came the retort, 'Why are you so attached to non-smoking?' "

14 *Sri Aurobindo Archives and Research*, December 1994, 237. For a fuller discussion of the suspicion with which the British imperial administration regarded the Richards, see Van Vrekhem, *The Mother*, 160–61.

15 *Sri Aurobindo Archives and Research*, December 1994, 240. See also Van Vrekhem, *The Mother*, 169–91.

16 See Van Vrekhem, *The Mother*, 173.

17 Nirodbaran, *Twelve Years with Sri Aurobindo*, 161.

18 See Logie Barrow, "Socialism in Eternity: Plebian Spiritualists, 1853–1913," *History Workshop: A Journal of Socialist Historians* 9 (spring 1980): 63.

19 Etienne Balibar, "Irrationalism and Marxism," *New Left Review* 9 (January–February 1978): 10, is instructive in his claim that the reaction against theology (or irrationalism) frequently resolves itself in a preference for empiricism rather than rationalism: "Certain variants are altogether paradoxical. Thus, rationalism may take on the shape of a 'rational theology'; while, at the same time, the struggle against theology may assume another compromise for, setting against Faith not Reason, but its 'opposite': Experience, Feeling and Life." For the mid-Victorian turn to empirical methods and empirical investigation, and the enthusiastic reception of John Stuart Mill's *Logic* (1843), see Alan Gauld, *The Founders of Psychical Research* (New York: Schocken, 1968), 46–65.

20 For a more detailed account of the links between Theosophy and late Victorian radicalism see Diana Burfield, "Theosophy and Feminism: Some Explanations in Nineteenth-Century Biography," *Women's Religious Experience: Cross-Cultural Perspectives*, ed. Pat Holden (London: Croom Helm, 1983), 27–56.

21 Cited in Barrow, "Socialism in Eternity," 38, 49.

22 See Annie Besant, *Why I Became a Theosophist* (London: Freethought, 1889).

23 Cited in Stephen Yeo, "A New Life: The Religion of Socialism in Britain, 1883–1896," *History Workshop Journal*, autumn 1977, 5–6.

24 Cited in Stephen Winsten, *Salt and His Circle* (London: Hutchinson, 1951), 64.

25 See Eugen Weber, *France, Fin de Siècle* (Cambridge: Harvard University Press, 1986).

26 See The Mother, *Words of Long Ago* (Pondicherry: Sri Aurobindo Ashram Trust, 1978), 2:40–41, 2:98–99: "error lies in the belief that a thing in the universe may be our own possession. Everything belongs to all, and to say or think, 'This is mine,' is to create a separation, a division which does not exist in reality . . . It is true that some people command great material possessions. But in order to be in accord with the universal law, they should consider themselves as trustees, stewards of these possessions. They ought to know that these riches are administered to them so that they may administer them for the best interests of all."

27 See ibid., 2:12. The left leanings of the Richards were also visible within France on account of Richard's public membership in 1905 in the pro-Dreyfus group Ligue des Droits de l'Homme et du Citoyen and his continuing support for it.

28 J. H. Cousins and M. E. Cousins, *We Two Together* (Madras: Ganesh, 1950), 352.

29 The Mother, *Mother's Agenda: 1968* (Paris: Institut de Recherches Évolutives, 1981), 9:146.

30 The Mother, *Prayers and Meditations*, 4, 5, 129.

31 The Mother, *Words of Long Ago*, 91.

32 Sri Aurobindo, *Record of Yoga–I*, 279. For experiments in thought sharing see 120, 121, 135, 169, 171, 195.

33 My discussion of Kantian ethics here draws upon my earlier *Postcolonial Theory: A Critical Introduction* (Sydney: Allen and Unwin, 1998), 139–140. Compare Michael Sandel's gloss on Kantian anti-empiricism in *Liberalism and the Limits of Justice* (Cambridge: Cambridge University Press, 1982), 7: "Were I wholly an empirical being, I would not be capable of freedom, for every exercise of will would be conditioned by the desire for some object. All my choice would be heteronomous choice governed by the pursuit of some end."

34 Kant entered into conflict with the Prussian State after an edict in 1788 threatened civil punishment and dismissal from office to all those employees under the jurisdiction of the department of church and schools who publicly strayed from biblical doctrines. Obedient to, if critical of, government censorship, he was less circumspect with regard to the jealous orthodoxy of academicians and theologians. His *Streit der Facultaten* [Conflict of the Faculties] (1798), for instance, is an open denunciation of university biblical theologians implicated in attempts to impede or proscribe heterodox inquiries into religion and philosophy.

35 Immanuel Kant, *Religion within the Limits of Reason Alone*, trans. Theodore M. Greene and Hoyt H. Hudson (New York: Harper and Brothers, 1960), 46, 47.

36 Ibid., 47.

37 Cf. Martha Nussbaum, *The Fragility of Goodness: Luck and Ethics in Greek*

Tragedy and Philosophy (Cambridge: Cambridge University Press, 1986), 5: "That I am an agent, but also a plant; that much that I did not make goes towards making me whatever I shall be praised or blamed for being; that I must constantly choose among competing and apparently incommensurable goods and that circumstances may force me to a position in which I cannot help being false to something or doing some wrong; that an event that simply happens to me may, without my consent, alter my life; that it is equally problematic to entrust one's good to friends, lovers, or country and to try and have a good life without them—all these I take not just to be the material of tragedy, but everyday facts of lived practical reason."

38 Sandel, *Liberalism and the Limits of Justice*, 63. Cf. Alasdair MacIntyre, *After Virtue: A Study in Moral Theory*, 2d edn (London: Duckworth, 1997), 133–34: "I am brother, cousin and grandson, member of this household, that village, this tribe. These are not characteristics that belong to human beings accidentally, to be stripped away in order to discover 'the real me.' They are part and parcel of my substance, defining partially at least and sometimes wholly my obligations and my duties. Individuals inherit a particular space within an interlocking set of social relationships: lacking that space, they are nobody, or at best a stranger or an outcast."

39 Judith Butler, *Gender Trouble: Feminism and the Subversion of Identity* (New York: Routledge, 1990), 15.

40 Stuart Hall, *The Hard Road to Renewal: Thatcherism and the Crisis of the Left* (London: Verso, 1988), 282.

41 Paul Gilroy, *There Ain't No Black in the Union Jack: The Cultural Politics of Race and Nation* (London: Hutchinson, 1987), 227.

42 Edward Said, *Culture and Imperialism* (London: Chatto and Windus, 1993), 403.

43 In Rushdie's writing the hybrid subject is also immune, once again as in Kant, from the "extreme" passions of nationalism.

44 See Kant, *Religion within the Limits of Reason Alone*, 49.

45 Ibid., 48.

46 Ibid., 47.

47 Derrida, "Faith and Knowledge: The Two Sources of 'Religion' at the Limits of Reason Alone," *Religion* (Cambridge: Polity, 1998), ed. in Jacques Derrida and Giani Vattimo, 11.

48 Ibid., 37.

49 Ibid., 65.

50 Ibid., 64. Cf. Derrida, *Adieu to Immanuel Levinas*, trans. Pascale-Anne Brault and Michael Naas (Stanford: Stanford University Press, 1999), 8: "The 'unknown' is not the negative limit of a knowledge. This non-knowledge is the element of friendship or hospitality for the transcendence of the stranger, the infinite distance of the other."

51 Derrida, "Faith and Knowledge," 18.

52 Jacques Derrida, *Politics of Friendship*, trans. George Collins (London: Verso, 1997), 306.

53 Gilroy, *There Ain't No Black in the Union Jack*, 231, 233.

54 Colin MacCabe, *The New Republic*, 1997.

55 William James, *Essays in Radical Empiricism* (Lincoln: University of Nebraska Press, 1996), 39.

56 Ibid., 27.

57 James, *Essays in Radical Empiricism*, 37.

58 Ibid., 45.

59 Ibid., 180. James's conclusions here proceed from a reading of "To You," a poem by Walt Whitman. The most relevant lines, in context, are the following:

> There is no endowment in man or woman that is not tallied in you;
> There is no virtue, no beauty, in man or woman, but as is good in you;
> No pluck nor endurance in others, but as good is in you;
> No pleasure waiting for others, but an equal pleasure waits for you.

60 William James, *A Pluralistic Universe: Hibbert Lectures at Manchester College on the Present Situation in Philosophy* (Lincoln: University of Nebraska Press, 1996), 104–5.

61 Ibid., 321–22.

62 William James, *Pragmatism and Four Essays from the Meaning of Truth* (Cleveland: World, 1970), 187.

63 Nussbaum, *The Fragility of Goodness*, 7.

64 James, *Pragmatism*, 192.

65 Jacques Derrida, *The Gift of Death*, trans. David Wills (Chicago: University of Chicago Press, 1995), 47. For a sensitive commentary on the adieu in Derridean thought see Hent de Vries, *Philosophy and the Turn to Religion* (Baltimore: Johns Hopkins University Press, 1999), 26: "the formula *adieu* accentuates the fact that every discourse, even the most secular, profane, negative, or nihilistic of utterances, directs and redirects itself . . . unwittingly toward the alterity for which—historically, systematically, conceptually, and figuratively speaking—'God' is, perhaps and so far, the most proper name." For a different approach to the ideas being reviewed here see Ramachandra Gandhi, *The Availability of Religious Ideas* (London: Macmillan, 1976). Gandhi argues that self-consciousness, "itself . . . an imaginative recreation of the communicative form of human life," is informed and accompanied by "the possibility of exploratory communication, the possibility of calling upon God without being under an obligation to first establish his reality" (9). For Gandhi, as for the other thinkers under discussion, prayer and interpersonal communication are in effect the same activity or similar activities.

66 See James, *A Pluralistic Universe*, 31.

67 Ibid., 30.

68 Ibid., 43.

69 James, *Pragmatism*, 187.

70 James enthusiastically endorsed the founding of the British SPR in 1882 and played a leading role in the formation of an American branch of the London Society. In the course of his association with these societies he was involved in its various investigations into communication with the deceased. By 1885 he himself undertook research into the practices of a medium called Mrs. L. E. Piper. See Garner Murphy and Robert O. Ballou, eds., *William James on Psychical Research* (New York: Viking, 1960). For more on the SPR see Alan Gauld, *The Founders of Psychical Research* (London: Routledge, 1968), and Renee Haynes, *The Society for Psychical Research, 1882–1982: A History* (London: MacDonald, 1982). There is a vast secondary literature on late-nineteenth-century spiritualism. For a discussion of the links between British and American spiritualism see Peter Washington, *Madame Blavatsky's Baboon: A History of the Mystics, Mediums and Misfits Who Brought Spiritualism to America* (New York: Schocken, 1995). The most comprehensive study of the field is Janet Oppenheim, *The Other World: Spiritualism and Psychical Research in England, 1850–1914* (Cambridge: Cambridge University Press, 1985). For a provocative feminist reading see Alex Owen, *The Darkened Room: Women, Power and Spiritualism in Late Victorian England* (London: Virago, 1989).

71 See for example Murphy and Ballou, eds., *William James on Psychical Research*, 15: "The evidence furnished by Mrs Piper did not establish for William James any *prima facie* case for survival as such, but it indicated, as he said over and over again, a 'lightning stroke' of conviction that there were received by the medium's mind many items that she had never normally acquired."

72 For cross-gender, class, and race materializations see Owen, *The Darkened Room*, 216–21, 231–33. Frederic W. H. Myers's *Human Personality and Its Survival of Bodily Death* (New York: Longmans, Green, 1907) abounds with such examples.

73 Murphy and Ballou, eds., *William James on Psychical Research*, 17.

74 Gurney, "The Stages of Hypnotism," *Proceedings of the Society for Psychical Research* 2 (1884): 69–70, cited in Oppenheim, *The Other World*, 251.

75 Myers, "Multiplex Personality," *Nineteenth Century* 20 (November 1886): 648, cited in Oppenheim, *The Other World*, 256.

76 Owen, *The Darkened Room*, 226.

77 Myers, *Human Personality and Its Survival of Bodily Death*, 1, 15, 50.

78 Ibid., 56.

79 See Murphy and Ballou, eds., *William James on Psychical Research*, 237.

80 See Haynes, *The Society for Psychical Research*, 21; Owen, *The Darkened Room*, 230–31, and Vieda Skultans, "Mediums, Controls and Eminent Men,"

Women's Religious Experience: Cross-Cultural Perspectives, ed. Pat Holden (London: Croom Helm, 1983), 15–26.

81 Edward Carpenter, *My Days and Dreams, Being Autobiographical Notes* (London: George Allen and Unwin, 1916), 240.

82 Davidson urged Havelock Ellis in particular to "free himself from the last remnant of that terrible monism from which hardly any English thinker escapes." See W. H. G. Armytage, *Heavens Below: Utopia and Social Experiments in England, 1560–1960* (London: Routledge and Kegan Paul, 1961), 329. In 1875, while in Boston, Davidson was involved in a discussion group which included William James, who made significant efforts to draw him into the faculty at Harvard. James has a fictional portrait of Davidson in "The Knight Errant of the Intellectual Life," *Memories and Studies* (New York: Longmans, Green, 1911).

83 See William Knight, ed., *The Memorials of Thomas Davidson* (Boston: Ginn, 1907).

84 The prospectus for Davidson's educational community in the Adirondack Mountains, founded in 1888, defines culture itself as "Man's spiritual nature, his intelligence, his affections and the modes in which they express themselves." See Armytage, *Heavens Below*, 333.

85 Carpenter, *My Days and Dreams*, 225.

86 *Humane Review* 4 (1903): 171.

87 Carpenter, *My Days and Dreams*, 115.

88 Edward Carpenter, *The Teaching of the Upanishads, Being the Substance of Two Lectures to Popular Audiences* (London: George Allen and Unwin, 1920), 20.

89 Edward Carpenter, "A Note on 'Towards Democracy,'" *Towards Democracy* (1883; London: GMP, 1985), 410.

90 Edward Carpenter, *The Art of Creation: Essays on the Self and Its Powers* (London: George Allen, 1904), 98.

91 See Butler, *Gender Trouble*, 16, and James, *Pragmatism*, 97.

92 See Edward Carpenter, *Love's Coming-of-Age: A Series of Papers on the Relation of the Sexes* (1896; London: George Allen and Unwin, 1948), 54.

93 Carpenter's deep sympathies for the nonhuman world are eloquently expressed in the following excerpt from his *Towards Democracy*: "I saw deep in the eyes of the animals the human soul look out upon me. I saw where it was born under feathers and fur, or condemned for awhile to roam fourfooted among the brambles. I caught the clinging mute glance of the prisoner, and swore that I would be faithful" (146).

94 See Max Nordau, *Degeneration* (New York: D. Appleton, 1895), 1, and Friedrich Engels, *Socialism, from Utopia to Science*, trans. Edward Aveling (1892; New York: New York Labor Press, 1968), 21.

95 See Owen, *The Darkened Room*, 234–35.

96 Chakrabarty, *Provincializing Europe*, 13.

CHAPTER 6 Art

1 Oscar Wilde, "De Profundis," *The Soul of Man and Prison Writings*, ed. Isobel Murray (New York: Oxford University Press, 1990), 61–62.

2 Oscar Wilde, Review of *Primavera*, *Pall Mall Gazette*, 24 May 1890, 3.

3 Ibid.

4 See Matthew Sturgis, *Passionate Attitudes: The English Decadence of the 1890s* (London: Macmillan, 1995), 126–27.

5 Sri Aurobindo Ashram Archives, Manmohan Ghose Papers.

6 "Manmohan Ghose," *Collected Poems*, ed. Lotika Ghose (Calcutta: University of Calcutta, 1970), 1:225.

7 Oscar Wilde, *Collected Works of Oscar Wilde: The Plays, the Poems, the Stories and the Essays Including De Profundis* (Hertfordshire: Wordsworth, 1997), 35.

8 John Addington Symonds, *The Academy*, 9 August 1890, 103.

9 Wilde, *Collected Works*, 5.

10 Terry Eagleton, *Saint Oscar and Other Plays* (Oxford: Blackwell, 1997), 46.

11 Wilde, *Collected Works*, 92.

12 Ibid., 786.

13 Dipesh Chakrabarty, *Provincialising Europe: Postcolonial Thought and Historical Difference* (Princeton: Princeton University Press, 2000), 150, 153, 149.

14 Ibid., 149.

15 Jane Routh and Janet Wolff, Introduction, *The Sociology of Literature: Theoretical Approaches*, Sociological Review Monograph 25 (Keele: University of Keele, 1977): 3, are among those who express gratitude to the sociology of literature project for delivering unto sociology the gift of literature "*as a kind of sociology* . . . as a source of data, often data of a type which would not otherwise be accessible to a sociologist, and as a carrier of crystallised values and attitudes, as well as information about institutions."

16 See Stuart Hall, "A Critical Survey of the Theoretical and Political Achievements of the Last Ten Years," *Literature, Society and the Sociology of Literature*, ed. Francis Barker et al. (Colchester: University of Essex, 1976), 5: "every one of these developments has, in some way or another, been generated by Marxism. Since leaving the unsullied English reaches of *The Long Revolution* every subsequent transformation within the field has been a product of, or has claimed to be a product of, various versions of the Marxist problematic."

17 Cited in Pierre Macherey, "Problem of Reflection," *Literature, Society and the Sociology of Literature*, ed. Barker et al., 41.

18 Catherine Belsey, "The Politics of Meaning," *Confronting the Crisis: War, Politics, Culture in the Eighties*, ed. Francis Barker et al. (Colchester: University of Essex, 1984), 31.

19 Boyd Tonkin, "Right Approaches: Sources of the New Conservatism," *Confronting the Crisis*, ed. Barker et al., 4. Stephen Greenblatt's epochal *Renaissance Self-Fashioning* represents in many ways a characteristic critique of the myth of human autonomy. See for instance the reading of this book offered by Jonathan Dollimore and Alan Sinfield in *Political Shakespeare: New Essays in Cultural Materialism* (Manchester: Manchester University Press, 1985), 4: "In an epilogue Greenblatt tells how he began with an intention to explore 'the role of human autonomy in the construction of identity.' But as the work progressed the emphasis fell more and more on cultural institutions—family, religion and the State—and 'the human subject' itself began to seem remarkably unfree, the ideological product of the relations of power in a particular society."

20 Hall, "Title," 3.

21 Jan H. Birchall, "In Defence of Reductionism," *Europe and Its Others*, ed. Francis Baker et al. (Colchester: University of Essex, 1985), 1:107.

22 Belsey, "The Politics of Meaning," 29.

23 Edward Said, *Culture and Imperialism* (London: Chatto and Windus, 1993), 59.

24 Gauri Viswanathan's *Masks of Conquest: Literary Study and British Rule in India* (London: Faber and Faber, 1989), 20–21.

25 Said, *Culture and Imperialism*, 69.

26 Kai Hammermeister, *The German Aesthetic Tradition* (Cambridge: Cambridge University Press, 2002), 97.

27 Charles Taylor, *Hegel* (1975; Cambridge: Cambridge University Press, 1999), 33.

28 Immanuel Kant, *The Critique of Judgement*, trans. James Creed Meredith (Oxford: Clarendon, 1952), 23.

29 Ibid., 23–24, 25.

30 Ibid., 25, 27.

31 Ibid., 12.

32 See ibid.

33 Ibid., 28.

34 Ibid., 49.

35 See Friedrich Nietzsche, "The Genealogy of Morals," *The Birth of Tragedy and the Genealogy of Morals*, trans. Francis Golffing (Garden City: Doubleday, 1956), 238–40.

36 Giorgio Agamben, *The Man without Content*, trans. Giorgia Albert (Stanford: Stanford University Press, 1999), 43.

37 Terry Eagleton, *The Ideology of the Aesthetic* (Oxford: Basil Blackwell, 1990), 87, 80.

38 In this reading, which takes its cue from Bourdieu's critique of Kant, I am not pursuing Jacques Derrida's persuasive argument in *The Truth in Painting*, trans. Geoff Benington and Ian McLeod (Chicago: University of Chicago Press, 1987), 30–93, that the discourses of "disinterest" and "finality" are racked by self-contradictions liberating the subject of judgment into effects which we have identified with "the ethic of *domicilium*." What looks like autoaffection in the thematic of disinterest, Derrida argues, carries within itself the possibility of heteroaffection, or disposition toward pure alterity. For the extreme demands of pleasure without interest signal a bereaved relation to an object so radically absent in its nonexistence and nonpossessability as to constitute the pure objectivity of the entirely other. So too, Derrida claims, the project of finality disclosed in the third critique, far from turning the subject of judgment against the realm of the empirical (the order of difference), is sufficiently antipathetic to the teleology of "ending" as to separate—through a cognitive cut or wounding—the object of beauty from any determining or capturing concept, thus preserving its unimpeachable singularity. If compelling, Derrida's reading concedes so much to the self-critical action of the third critique as to render the corrective action of materialism and historicism entirely irrelevant. While I wish to point to the limits of a materialist critique of aesthetic autonomy, it is a distinctly historicist, even sociological, intervention that alerts us to the imperialist pitfalls of the discourse of disinterest.

39 Pierre Bourdieu, *Distinction: A Social Critique of the Judgment of Taste*, trans. Richard Nice (Cambridge: Harvard University Press, 2000), 3, 4.

40 See ibid., 5, 384, 179, 376.

41 See especially Bourdieu's critique of Derrida in *Distinction*, 493–500. See also Pierre Bourdieu, *The Rules of Art: Genesis and Structure of the Literary Field*, trans. Susan Emanuel (Stanford: Stanford University Press, 1996).

42 Georg Wilhelm Friedrich Hegel, *The Philosophy of History*, trans. J. Sibree (New York: Dover, 1956), 2.

43 Ibid., 161, 162.

44 See ibid., 111.

45 Ibid., 63.

46 Robert Young, *White Mythologies: Writing History and the West* (London: Routledge, 1990), 2.

47 See Mary Louise Pratt, *Imperial Eyes: Travel Writing and Transculturation* (London: Routledge, 1992), 7, 210–27, and Hélène Cixous and Catherine Clement, *The Newly Born Woman*, trans. Betty Wing (Manchester: Manchester University Press, 1986), 78.

48 G. F. W. Hegel, *Introduction to Aesthetics*, trans. T. M. Knox (Oxford: Clarendon, 1979), 31.

49 Ibid., 13.

50 Cixous and Clement, *The Newly Born Woman*, 70.

51 Hegel, *Introduction to Aesthetics*, 12.

52 See Taylor, *Hegel*, 472.

53 Hegel, *Introduction to Aesthetics*, 5, 47.

54 Ibid., 89.

55 Martin Heidegger, *Poetry, Language, Thought*, trans. Albert Hofstader (New York: Harper and Row, 1975), 130.

56 See Theodor Adorno, *Aesthetic Theory*, trans. Robert Hullot-Kentor (London: Athalone, 1997); Theodor Adorno, *Minima Moralia: Reflections from Damaged Life*, trans. E. F. N. Jephcott (1978; London: Verso, 2000); and Heidegger, *Poetry, Language, Thought*.

57 Cited in Peter Heehs, *Sri Aurobindo: A Brief Biography* (Oxford: Oxford University Press, 1989), 9.

58 Ghose, *Collected Poems*, 1:vii.

59 Ibid., 1:113–14.

60 Between 1895 and 1898 Binyon oversaw the publication of Elkin Matthews's Shilling Series, devoted to disseminating work by little-known contemporary poets to a general audience. Ghose's *Love Songs and Elegies* appeared as Garland no. 9 in the series in April 1898, and some of his poems were showcased alongside works by Victor Plarr, Selwyn Image, Romney Green, and Reginald Balfour in the commemorative anthology *The Garland of New Poetry by Various Writers*. In 1924 Binyon also secured the posthumous publication of Ghose's *Songs of Love and Death*.

61 Ghose, *Collected Poems*, 1:vii, 1:170–71.

62 For more on Binyon's view of "philistinism" see John Hatcher, *Laurence Binyon: Poet, Scholar of East and West* (Oxford: Clarendon, 1995), 7.

63 Ghose, *Collected Poems*, 1:vii.

64 *Rhythm* 4 (spring 1912): 1–2, Cited in Hatcher, *Laurence Binyon*, 155–56.

65 Hatcher, *Laurence Binyon*, 156.

66 Ghose, *Collected Poems*, 1:vii.

67 Ibid., 1:141.

68 Ibid., 1:138, 142.

69 Cited in Lotika Ghose, *Manmohan Ghose* (Sahitya Akademi: New Delhi, 1975), 56.

70 Laurence Binyon et al., *Primavera: Poems by Four Authors* (Oxford: B. H. Blackwell, 1890), 7.

71 Indeed Ghose all but loses faith in Swinburne after his public renunciation of Whitman, as he explains in another missive to Binyon in 1887: "By the way, have you seen Swinburne's brutal attack on Walt Whitman in the *Fortnightly* . . . ? After behaving so badly, turning renegade and worshipper of bloated bathos and female aristocracy . . . I think he might have spared us his swinish attack on a man greater in

most respects than himself . . . This has quite shaken my faith in Swinburne." See Ghose, *Collected Poems.* 1:134.

72 Where Binyon remains true to Arnold, Ghose finds it increasingly difficult to house him. "I have returned too," he writes in November 1890, "to our old admiration to Keats, and Byron, and Shelley—the only gods, surely, to worship! It is these *wonderful* beings of our century, *wonderful*, not merely cultured and graceful like Matthew Arnold . . . it is the *Personalities* that move, delight, and amaze me." See Ghose, *Collected Poems*, 1:248.

73 See Hatcher, *Laurence Binyon*, 6, 22.

74 Ghose, *Collected Poems*, 1:181.

75 In "De Profundis," *The Soul of Man and Prison Writings*, ed. Isobel Murray (Hertfordshire: Wordsworth, 1997), 102, Wilde famously describes Pater's *Renaissance*, which he discovered during his first term at Oxford, as "that book which has had such a strange influence over my life."

76 Cited in Hatcher, *Laurence Binyon*, 28.

77 Ghose, *Collected Poems*, 1:165.

78 Ibid., 1:165, 167, 170–71.

79 See Camille Paglia, *Sexual Personae: Art and Decadence from Nefertiti to Emily Dickinson* (London: Yale University Press, 1990), 512: "critics drift toward apologia, tediously extolling Wilde's humanity or morality, things utterly nonexistent in his best work. The time is past when it was necessary to defend a homosexual genius . . . In him we see that brilliant fusion of the aggressive western eye with aristocratic hierarchism, created by the Old Kingdom Pharaohs. Wilde was not a liberal, as his modern admirers think. He was a cold Late Romantic elitist, in the Baudelairean manner."

80 Regina Gagnier, *Idylls of the Marketplace: Oscar Wilde and the Victorian Public* (Stanford: Stanford University Press, 1986), 98. Matthew Sturgis, *Passionate Attitudes*, 115–16, makes a similar point, claiming that the "elaborate demands of dress, the scrupulous frivolities of the toilet, were a considered rebuke to the Victorian creeds of utility and seriousness."

81 Sri Aurobindo in A. B. Purani, *Evening Talks with Sri Aurobindo* (1959; 3d edn Pondicherry: Sri Aurobindo Ashram Trust, 1982), 603.

82 W. B. Yeats, "The Trembling of the Veil," *Autobiographies* (London: Macmillan, 1961), 300. Ghose's association with the Rhymers is confirmed by Ernest Dowson in a letter of 9 June 1891 to Victor Plarr. See Desmond Flower and Henry Maas, eds., *The Letters of Ernest Dowson* (Rutherford: Fairleigh Dickinson University Press, 1967), 203: "I write to you, an official exponent of the sentiments of the 'Rhymers' at their last meeting, and at their request, to ask, if we can count on you, as a contributor to 'The Book of the Rhymers Club' which it is proposed to issue, in an inexpensive manner in the autumn. The Rhymers to be represented in it are, pretty

much as follows: Yeats, Greene, Johnson, Dowson, Radford, Le Gallienne, Elis, Ghose, Symons, Rolleston, Todhunter, Rhys." Dowson adds that Ghose, Symons, Rolleston, and Rhys are among those "who have not yet *definitely* promised to join the scheme." Indeed, Ghose was not among the final list of contributors to the volume published in 1892 by Elkin Matthews, also publisher of the poetry series overseen by Laurence Binyon.

83 See Hatcher, *Laurence Binyon*, 27.

84 Book 42040, Rare Books Department, Huntington Library, San Marino, Calif., cited in Hatcher, *Laurence Binyon*, 32–33.

85 See Hatcher, *Laurence Binyon*, 48–49, and David Sweetman, *Explosive Acts: Toulouse-Lautrec, Oscar Wilde, Felix Fénéon and the Art and Anarchy of the Fin de Siècle* (New York: Simon and Schuster, 1999), 216–17.

86 See Richard Ellmann, *Oscar Wilde* (Harmondsworth: Penguin, 1987), 506–7.

87 *The Letters of Ernest Dowson*, 167, 177.

88 Ibid., 169.

89 Ghose, *Collected Poems*, 1:223.

90 Ibid., 238.

91 Ibid., 242, 239.

92 Ibid., 233.

93 Ibid., 233–34.

94 Gene H. Bell-Villada, *Art for Art's Sake and Literary Life: How Politics and Markets Helped Shape the Ideology and Culture of Aestheticism, 1790–1990* (Lincoln: University of Nebraska Press, 1996), 20. See also John Wilcox, "The Beginnings of L'Art pour L'Art," *Journal of Aesthetics and Art Criticism* 11 (1952–53): 360–77.

95 See Bell-Villada, *Art for Art's Sake and Literary Life*, 36–41.

96 See Ellmann, *Oscar Wilde*, 40.

97 See Gerald Monsman, "Pater, Hopkins, and Fichte's Ideal Student," *South Atlantic Quarterly* 70 (1971): 365–76.

98 One of the best studies of the close conjunction between French aestheticism and anarchism remains Sweetman's *Explosive Acts*.

99 See ibid., 212, 10–15.

100 Wilde, "De Profundis," 126.

101 Oscar Wilde, *Pall Mall Gazette*, 15 February 1889, repr. in Stanley Weintraub, *Literary Criticism of Oscar Wilde* (Lincoln: University of Nebraska Press, 1968), 109.

102 Cited in Ellmann, *Oscar Wilde*, 116.

103 Wilde, *Collected Works*, 909.

104 Wilde, *Collected Works*, 39, 787; "De Profundis," 71, 39.

105 Wilde, *Collected Works*, 56, 204.

106 Ibid., 92.

107 Ibid., 903.

108 Ibid., 917.

109 Ibid., 318.

110 Wilde, "De Profundis," 110.

111 Sri Aurobindo, "The Harmony of Virtue," *The Complete Works of Sri Aurobindo*, vol. 1, *Early Cultural Writings* (Pondicherry: Sri Aurobindo Ashram, 2003), 13.

112 Sri Aurobindo, *The Complete Works of Sri Aurobindo*, vol. 26, *The Future Poetry, with "On Quantitative Metre"* (Pondicherry: Sri Aurobindo Ashram, 1997), 6.

CHAPTER 7 An Immature Politics

1 J. H. Cousins and M. E. Cousins, *We Two Together* (Madras: Ganesh, 1950), 125.

2 George Orwell, *The Road to Wigan Pier* (1937; Harmondsworth: Penguin, 1967), 152.

3 Friedrich Engels, *Socialism, from Utopia to Science*, trans. Edward Aveling (1892; New York: New York Labor Press, 1968), 40; Robert Blantchford, *Merrie England* (1893; London: Journeyman, 1977), 44.

4 Max Nordau, *Degeneration* (Lincoln: University of Nebraska Press, 1993), 1.

5 Stephen Winsten, *Salt and His Circle* (London: Hutchinson, 1951), 64.

6 Cited in Lenin, *"Left-Wing" Communism: An Infantile Disorder: An Attempt at a Popular Discussion on Marxist Strategy and Tactics* (1920; rev. edn London: Martin Lawrence, 1934), 44.

7 Ibid., 9, 10, 11, 12, 61, 66.

8 Ibid., 22.

9 Immanuel Kant, *Foundation of the Metaphysics of Morals and What Is Enlightenment*, trans. Lewis White Beck (Indianapolis: Liberal Arts, 1959), 85, 90.

10 Martha Nussbaum, *The Fragility of Goodness: Luck and Ethics in Greek Tragedy and Philosophy* (Cambridge: Cambridge University Press, 1986), 5, 2.

11 Ernesto Laclau and Chantal Mouffe, *Hegemony and Socialist Strategy: Towards a Radical Democratic Politics*, trans. Winston Moore and Paul Cammack (London: Verso, 1985), 21.

12 Michel Foucault, *"Society Must Be Defended": Lectures at the Collège de France, 1975–76*, ed. Mauro Bertani and Alessandro Fontana, trans. David Macey (London: Allen Lane, 2003), 9–10.

13 Ibid., 10.

14 Ibid., 11.

15 For an exhaustive account of the creative theorization to which the politics of the event have been subject from Sartre through to Foucault see Robert Young, *White*

Mythologies: Writing History and the West (London: Routledge, 1995), 10–11, 34–37, 56, 80.

16 Alain Badiou, *Manifesto for Philosophy*, trans. Norman Madarasz (Albany: State University of New York Press, 1999), 67.

17 Alain Badiou, *Manifesto for Philosophy*, 6, 107; Alain Badiou, *Saint Paul: The Foundation of Universalism*, trans. Ray Brassier (Stanford: Stanford University Press, 2003), 42.

18 Badiou, *Manifesto for Philosophy*, 6.

19 Badiou, *Saint Paul*, 14.

20 Michel Foucault, *Language, Counter-Memory, Practice: Selected Essays and Interviews by Michel Foucault*, ed. Donald F. Bouchard (Ithaca: Cornell University Press, 1977), 177. Robert Young forcefully argues for the event's disposition toward alterity in his *White Mythologies*, 10: "This quest for the singular, the contingent event which by definition refuses all conceptualization, can clearly be related to the project of constructing a form of knowledge that respects the other without absorbing it into the same."

21 See the interview with Jacques Rancière, "Democracy Means Equality," *Radical Philosophy* 82 (March–April 1997): 33, also cited in Kristen Ross, *May '68 and Its Afterlives* (Chicago: University of Chicago Press, 2002), 25, 108. Further to the claim, above, that evental inclusiveness is best troped as Derridean *philoxenia*, it is important to note that Alain Badiou, whose theorization of eventality I draw on most directly in my argument, is vehemently opposed to identifying an evental politics with an ethics of alterity. For Badiou evental inclusiveness announces a form of universalism or constitutive indifference to difference best identified as a turn toward "the Same" rather than a "political opening toward the other." If compelling in its critique of the sentimentality and reification of victimhood that often accompanies formulaic renditions of an ethics of alterity, however, Badiou's own neo-Kantian allergy to "otherness" crucially contravenes the constitutive empiricism and materialism of "the event," postulating in the post-evental universalism of "the Same" a decisive movement of transcendence away from the contingencies of human existence, the complications of "interest," "affect," "attachment." So, for example, in his *Ethics: An Essay on the Understanding of Evil*, trans. Peter Hallward (London: Verso, 2002), 49, 131, Badiou's defense of universalism and accompanying critique of the ethics of alterity are typically posed as the need for flight from affective contingency, a desire to be "that excess beyond myself induced by the passing through me of a truth"; or, as an "effort to distinguish an immortal truth from the corruption of the flesh, of temptation, of desires and interests that are no more, no less worthy than those of moles." Against this view it is my contention that eventality, albeit flawed, can only maintain its own defining radical empiricism, in William James's sense, if it surrenders to the conjuncture of alterity, resisting the will-to-transcen-

dence postulated by the order of the Same. No less, conceived as the name for relation, otherness is also the sign under which affect, that crucial component of the utopianism under survey in this book, can be imported into the realm of the political with a view to disrupting therein the austere regulations of Kantian ethics and scientific socialism.

22 Giorgio Agamben, *Homo Sacer: Sovereign Power and Bare Life*, trans. Daniel Heller-Roazen (Stanford: Stanford University Press, 1998), 109–10.

23 See ibid., 126–34. Agamben's critique of predicating citizenship upon the eviction of the refugee to the desert of "bare life" draws upon Hannah Arendt's earlier disclosure of this paradox in *The Origins of Totalitarianism* (New York: Harcourt, Brace, 1966), 299, 300: "The conception of human rights, based upon the assumed existence of a human being as such, broke down at the very moment when those who professed to believe in it were for the first time confronted with people who had indeed lost all other qualities and specific relationships—except that they were still human. The world found nothing sacred in the abstract nakedness of being human . . . It seems that a man who is nothing but a man has lost the very qualities which make it possible for other people to treat him as a fellow-man."

24 Foucault, *"Society Must Be Defended,"* 254, 255, 256.

25 Arendt, *The Origins of Totalitarianism*, 474.

26 See Diana Burfield, "Theosophy and Feminism: Some Explorations in Nineteenth-Century Biography," *Women's Religious Experience: Cross-Cultural Perspectives*, ed. Pat Holden (London: Croom Helm, 1983), 31; Keith Nield, "Edward Carpenter: The Uses of Utopia," *Edward Carpenter and Late Victorian Radicalism*, ed. Tony Brown (London: Frank Cass, 1990), 24; Alain Touraine, *The May Movement: Revolt and Reform: May 1968—The Student Rebellion and Workers Strikes—The Birth of a Social Movement*, trans. Leonard F. X. Mayhew (New York: Random House, 1971), 26, 45.

27 Touraine, *The May Movement*, 352.

28 Jean-Paul Sartre and Daniel Cohn-Bendit, Untitled interview, *The Activists Speak*, ed. Hervé Bourges, trans. B. R. Brewster (London: Jonathan Cape, 1968), 103.

29 Daniel Cohn-Bendit and Gabriel Cohn-Bendit, *Obsolete Communism: The Left-Wing Alternative*, trans. Arnold Pomerans (London: A. Deutsch, 1968), 253–54.

30 Naomi Klein, *No Logo* (London: Flamingo, 2000), 457–58.

31 See Patrick Seale and Maureen McConville, *French Revolution 1968* (Harmondsworth: Penguin, 1968), 130–69.

32 See Ross, *May '68 and Its Afterlives*, 25.

33 Bourges, ed., *The Activists Speak*, 18–19. A comprehensive account of the profound anticolonial motivations of May 1968 is offered in Ross, *May '68 and Its Afterlives*.

34 Ross, *May '68 and Its Afterlives*, 69.

35 See especially Naomi Klein, *Fences and Windows: Dispatches from the Front Lines of the Globalisation Debate* (New York: Picador, 2002), and Arundhati Roy, *The Ordinary Person's Guide to Empire* (London: Flamingo, 2004).

36 Klein, *Fences and Windows*, 30, 101.

37 See Daniel Singer, *Prelude to Revolution: France in May 1968* (New York: Hill and Wang, 1968), 403. May 1968, it is worth noting, also fell prey to the charge of "immaturity" leveled against fin-de-siècle utopian socialism. After a brief and strategic exile in Romania, General de Gaulle returned to France on 18 May even as the Great Strike was continuing to spread unabated: millions of workers had abandoned their tools; banks, postal services, and transport were all at a standstill. Advised to maintain his silence in the surrounding sirocco, the indefatigable general nonetheless let a single jeering remark leak into Paris: *"Oui à la réforme, non à la chienlit"* (Reform, yes, bed-messing, no), attaching, once again, the tedious charge of infantilism to a certain style of politics.

38 Giorgio Agamben, *Means without End: Notes on Politics*, trans. Vincenzo Binetti and Cesare Casarino (Minneapolis: University of Minnesota Press, 2000), 57.

INDEX

Adorno, Theodor, 161, 173, 219 n. 1, 230 n. 56

aesthetics, aestheticism, 62, 146, 153–55, 157, 163, 231 n. 80; aesthetic autonomy, 146, 148–62, 167, 168, 171, 173, 229 n. 38; anti-imperialism and, 12, 144–45, 170; (anti)colonialism and, 150–51, 156, 161, 168; difference and, 154, 160, 173; homosexuality and, 168, 169; "interested autonomy" and, 161, 171; Kantian, 151–52, 153–55; materialism and, 157; politics and, 148–49, 167, 172, 177, 232 n. 94; sacrifice and, 174; spiritualism and, 122

affect, 14, 17, 29, 45, 60, 103, 134, 162, 235 n. 21; affective affiliation, 25, 99, 177; affective singularity, 20; animal welfare and, 100, 103, 104, 113, 114; difference and, 174; governmentality and, 100, 112–13; homosexuality and, 59, 141; human experience and, 21, 117; self-denial and, 105; socialism and, 178

affiliation, 199 n. 57

Agamben, Giorgio, 20, 26, 29, 54, 155, 159, 189, 206 n. 81; citizenship and, 184, 235 n. 23

agency, 5, 21, 31, 191 n. 12; autonomy and, 126; consumerism and, 23; ethico-political, 24, 117, 125–27; inclusiveness and, 141; individualism and, 22; relationality and, 133

ahimsa, 63, 85–86, 97, 114

AIDS, 39

Alfassa, Mirra (the Mother), 11, 12, 220 n. 3, 221 n. 13, 222 n. 26; anticolonialism of, 120–21, 182; socialism and, 124–25; spiritualism of, 118, 119–21, 124, 141; Sri Aurobindo and, 119

alienation, 22

Althusser, Louis, 148

Almonds and Raisins, 80, 83

alterity, 38, 134, 156, 234 n. 21; anti-imperialism and, 7

American Civil War, 8

American Sex Problems (Gadiali), 15

anarchism, 113, 123, 192 n. 18, 218 n. 159; aestheticism and, 169, 171, 172, 174; evolution and, 114, 218 n. 156; as sociality, 112. *See also* radicalism

Andrews, Charles Freer, 20, 194 n. 22; friendship and, 14, 15–18, 194 n. 18; Indian anticolonialism and, 13; theosophy and, 195 n. 24

animal liberation: radical thought and, 74; utilitarianism and, 89, 99

Animal Rights (H. Salt), 113

Animal's Friend, 102, 108
animal welfare, 8, 75, 88, 102, 107, 174, 215 n. 111; *ahimsa* and, 86, 114; anarchism and, 87, 113; anti-colonialism and, 11, 35, 85, 97, 192 n. 21; class and, 92–94, 105–6, 109; cranks and eccentrics and, 87, 104; cruelty and, 84, 92–94, 105; eastern customs and, 80; love and, 104, 108; "mainstream," 87; poetry and, 103; publications, 80, 83–85, 101, 102, 113; radical causes and, 77–78, 101, 104,114; utilitarianism and, 74, 89–92, 96–97, 100; working poor and, 92–94, 97, 108. *See also* Gandhi, M. K.
"Anomaly," 60
anthropocentrism, 76, 89–90, 101
anthropology: evolutionary, 10, 36; social, 47
anticolonialism, 2, 9, 14, 16, 63, 64, 73, 192 n. 17; art and, 144–46; (literary) autonomy and, 146, 151, 156; love for animals and, 101; relationality and, 101; socialism and, 123; of South Asians, 10, 83, 85; theism and, 11, 17; western, 9, 10, 13, 79. *See also* anti-imperialism
anti-communitarianism, 26, 29, 32
anticorporatism, 185, 186, 188
anti-imperialism, 10, 71, 121, 176, 177; community and, 8; cultural boundaries and, 2, 14; utopianism and, 7, 8; western, 1–2, 5–6, 7, 8, 11, 34–35, 62, 189, 192 n. 21
anti-vivisection, 78–79, 104, 106, 138, 139; class and, 108; spiritualism and, 122. *See also* animal welfare
Appiah, K. Anthony, 25
Arabian Nights (trans. Burton), 52
Arendt, Hannah, 184, 235 n. 23
Aristotle, 28, 29, 199 n. 64
Armytage, W. H. G., 226 n. 82
Arnold, Matthew, 166, 231 n. 72
Aron, Raymond, 197 n. 38
art, 171; alterity and, 161; autonomy and, 146, 151, 161, 166, 173; history and, 158, 160; imperialism and, 145, 173, 176; "orientalism" and, 145; the real and, 146, 161, 173. *See also* aesthetics, aestheticism; literature; poetry
Art of Creation, The (Carpenter), 139
Arya, 119
asceticism, 68–69. *See also askesis*
askesis, 55, 57, 60, 61, 125
asylum seekers. *See* outcasts, outsiders
Aurobindo, Sri, 11, 12, 121, 125, 162, 176, 220 n. 3, 220 n. 8, 221 n. 13; in England, 163, 175; Indian nationalism and, 118, 119, 220 n. 8
Autobiography (J. S. Mill), 99
autonomy, 23, 24, 126, 141, 228 n. 19; materialism and, 148; as separation, 153, 154–55, 158–59. *See also* self-sufficiency

Badiou, Alain, 183, 234 n. 21
Bakshi, Parminder Kaur, 205 n. 73
Bakunin, Mikhail, 218 n. 159
Bakunist International, 218 n. 159
Baldick, Chris, 148
Balibar, Etienne, 221 n. 19
Ballou, Robert O., 225 n. 70
Barrow, Logie, 121
Bataille, Georges, 21, 53, 55, 196 n. 36, 197 n. 45

Baudelaire, Charles, 41, 42
Beast and Man in India (J. Kipling), 100
beauty. *See* aesthetics, aestheticism
beef. *See* meat eating
Beehive, 9
Beer, Gillian, 47
Beesley, E. S., 8, 9
being-in-common, 19, 28, 32
Beith, Gilbert, 37
Bell-Villada, Gene H., 171
belonging, 7, 17; uniformity and, 25
Belsey, Catherine, 148, 149
benevolence: affinity and, 100; rights and, 91
Bentham, Jeremy, 68–69, 89–100. *See also* utilitarianism
Bersani, Leo, 38, 203 n. 33
Besant, Annie, 80, 122
Bhabha, Homi, 3–4, 5–6, 149, 191 n. 12
Bhagavad Gita, 139
biculturalism, 71
Binyon, Laurence, 142, 162–70, 173, 175, 230 n. 60, 230 n. 62, 231 n. 72
Birchall, Jan H., 228 n. 21
bisexuality, 59, 63
Blanchot, Maurice, 23, 24, 31, 54, 198 n. 50
Bland, Lucy, 51
Blantchford, Robert, 122–23, 178–79
Blavatsky, H. P., 124
Blaythwayt, Raymond, 80
Bloch, Iwan, 49, 50, 51, 53
Book of the Rhymers Club, 168, 232 n. 82
Boone, Joseph A., 205 n. 73
border crossing, 7
Bose, Rasbehari, 121
Bourdieu, Pierre, 149, 151, 152, 153, 155, 157, 161, 229 n. 38
Bourges, Hervé, 187
Breckenridge, Carol A., 201 n. 76
Briggs, Asa, 94
Britain, 1–2, 9, 60, 67
Browne, Janet, 109
Brutalitarian, 84, 102
Buber, Martin, 195 nn. 29–30
Bullock, Arthur Broderick, 216 n. 119
Burfield, Diana, 186
Burton, Sir Richard, 52–53
Butler, Josephine, 138
Butler, Judith, 31, 42, 46, 54, 56, 58, 128, 197 n. 39, 207 n. 84

Cannadine, David, 1
capitalism, 139
Carpenter, Edward, 11, 12, 44, 47, 55, 64, 107, 113, 135, 138, 172, 177, 208 n. 99; animal rights and, 140, 226 n. 93; anti-imperialism of, 34–35, 43, 58, 62, 78, 182, 185, 201 n. 4; Fellowship of the New Life and, 138; homosexuality of, 35–36, 43, 58–61, 63, 65, 118, 139; sexual evasiveness of, 37, 39, 40; socialism and, 138–39, 140, 178, 179, 217 n. 129; spiritualism of, 115, 118, 140
Carr, E. H., 192 n. 18
Chakrabarty, Dipesh, 117, 141, 146, 147, 151, 193 n. 7
Chamberlin, J. Edward, 205 n. 63
Chants of Labour (Carpenter), 172
Chartism, 8
Christianity, 17, 18, 129, 135. *See also* religion
citizenship, 10, 184, 235 n. 23
Civilisation (Carpenter), 62, 63, 64

civilization (western), "civilized" community, 34 53, 62, 63, 66, 94, 98, 165; evils of, 76; margins of, 36, 49, 50; "native" races and, 109–10; obedience and, 95, 109; sexuality and, 49, 51, 58. *See also* evolution
Cixous, Hélène, 159, 160
Clement, Catherine, 159–60
Cobbe, Frances Power, 78–79, 103, 104, 105, 212 n. 45
Coetzee, J. M., 216 n. 111
Cohn-Bendit, Daniel, 185, 186, 187, 188
Cohn-Bendit, Gabriel, 185, 186
collaboration, 20, 177; anticolonial, 114; crosscultural, 6, 10; divine–human, 141; spiritual, 11; transnational, 8
colonial encounter, 1, 2, 3, 4, 14; art and, 145
colonialism, 31, 95; alienation and, 101; animal welfare and, 96–97; as anthropocentrism, 211 n. 31; difference and, 159; division and, 2–3, 4, 5, 7, 14; homosexuality and, 53; literature and, 151; vegetarianism and, 82
Common-Sense Vegetarianism (Light), 83–84, 105
communication, 18, 24
communism, 179
communitarianism, 24, 25, 30; anti-, 26, 29, 32
community, 5, 18–19, 24, 46, 73, 195 nn. 28–29, 198 n. 50, 199 n. 56, 223 n. 38; affective, 196 n. 36; anticolonialism and, 8, 74; of descent, 111; difference and, 54, 156; exclusion and, 19, 53, 55, 61–62; human–animal, 74, 111; "negative," 53, 54, 55, 66; radicalism and, 9; sex and, 203 n. 33, 207 n. 88; similitude and, 25, 26, 31, 54, 111; solipsistic, 152; utopian, 19, 20, 208 n. 99. *See also* affect; sociality
Companion Species Manifesto, The (Haraway), 211 n. 33, 216 n. 115
compearance, 19–20
conatus, 18, 24
Constantinou, Marios, 200 n. 68
consumerism, 22–23, 197 n. 45
contingency, 135
contrapuntality, 3, 6
cooperation. *See* collaboration
Cornell, Drucilla, 20
cosmopolitanism, 8, 10, 31–32, 193 n. 7, 200 n. 76
Cousin, Victor, 171
Cousins, J. H., 124, 177
Cousins, M. E., 177
Cracow uprising, 8
Creed of Kinship, The (H. Salt), 111
Cripps, Arthur, 142
Critique of Judgement (Kant), 146, 151, 153, 158, 171
Critique of Practical Reason (Kant), 126
Critique of Pure Reason (Kant), 126
Crosby, Ernest, 84
Cruelties of Civilisation (H. Salt), 101
Cry of Nature, The (Oswald), 75
culture, 3, 192 n. 13, 226 n. 84; cultural insularity, 71; diet and, 82–84; history and, 158; imperialism and, 145, 162, 175; myths of, 4; nonwestern, 52, 59; the real and, 148; western, 117, 152

Culture and Imperialism (Said), 2, 150, 152
"cyborg economy," 31, 101

Darwin, Charles, 36, 47–49, 50, 53, 55, 101, 110–11, 131, 204 n. 44; colonialism and, 109. *See also* evolution
David-Neel, Alexandra, 124, 220 n. 8
Davidson, Thomas, 138, 177, 226 n. 82
da Vinci, Leonardo, 65
Deane, Seamus, 198 n. 48
Debord, Guy, 187
decadence, 161, 168
de Certeau, Michel, 23
de Gaulle, Charles, 236 n. 37
degeneration, 51, 205 n. 63
Degeneration (Nordau), 18, 179
democracy, 130
deontology, 23, 158, 159
De Profundis (Wilde), 172, 174, 231 n. 75
Derrida, Jacques, 10, 27, 28, 117, 128–29, 134, 174, 184, 220 n. 6, 229 n. 38; friendship and, 19, 30, 130; hospitality and, 73, 74, 130, 223 n. 50; risk and, 32
Descartes, René, 90
Descent of Man, The (Darwin), 47–49, 53, 55, 204 n. 44
desire, 23, 46, 59, 62, 129, 135, 198 n. 46; destruction and, 22; difference and, 17, 54; homosexual, 38, 57; hybridity and, 21, 128, 130
determinism, 5, 191 n. 12
deviancy, 25; sexual, 38
de Vries, Hent, 224 n. 65
Dial, 169
dialecticism, 5
difference, 30, 133, 155, 159; cultural, 7, 32, 145; desire and, 17, 54; ethics and, 25; nonwestern, 4; sexual, 49, 50, 55, 58, 59, 65
disciplinarity, 97–98, 99, 100, 109; politics and, 181
disinterest, 155–57, 159, 161, 174, 229 n. 38
dissent, 2, 76, 97
Distinction, La (Bourdieu), 149, 151, 153, 157
Doane, Laura, 204 n. 56
Dollimore, Jonathan, 228 n. 19
Douglas, Alfred, Lord, 142, 168, 173
Dowson, Ernest, 169, 231 n. 82
Drayton, Richard, 214 n. 88
Drew, John, 212 n. 37

Eagleton, Terry, 144, 156, 228 n. 37
East, 52–53, 62; ethics and, 79; religion and, 79. *See also* India; orientalism
Edward Carpenter (Beith), 37
Ellis, Havelock, 44, 50, 226 n. 82
Ellmann, Richard, 169
Elwin, Verrier, 6
émigrés. *See* outcasts, outsiders
empire, 1–2; the "citizen" and, 10; collusion and collaboration in, 5; hierarchies of, 14; India and, 115
Empire (Hardt and Negri), 10
empiricism, the empirical, 117, 122, 126, 128, 130, 132, 221 n. 19; agency and, 127; radical, 188, 234 n. 21
Engels, Friedrich, 12, 18, 140, 178, 179, 181
England for All (Hyndman), 139

English studies: (anti)colonialism and, 12, 151; empire and, 4, 162. *See also* literature
Epicurianism, 29, 30, 200 n. 68
equality, 25
Erskine, Thomas, Lord, 90, 93
Essays in Radical Empiricism (W. James), 131
ethics, 117, 131, 153, 158, 220 n. 6; animals and, 89–90, 102, 103; of "beyond," 20; community and, 24; of *domicilium*, 154, 156, 157, 161, 229 n. 38; as hospitality, 30; hybridity and, 127; legislation and, 91; materialist, 132; multiple personality and, 137; the other and, 7, 111, 234 n. 21; rationality and, 116, 126; relationality and, 133–34; religion and, 121, 126–27. *See also* Kant, Immanuel; politics
Ethics (Badiou), 234 n. 21
Ethics of Diet, The (H. Williams), 70, 106
ethos, 206 n. 81
Europe and Its Others, 149
evolution, 10, 47, 112, 131; animal welfare and, 111; "civilization" and, 47–48; immutability of species and, 110; kinship and, 109, 111; sexuality and, 51, 58
exclusion, 29, 184
exiles. *See* outcasts, outsiders
experience, 117, 126, 131; rationality and, 132
Experiments with Truth, My (M. K. Gandhi), 70
Explosive Acts (Sweetman), 232 n. 98

faith. *See* religion
False Beasts and True (Cobbe), 103
Fane, Violet, 76
feeling. *See* sentiment
Fellowship of the New Life, 138, 177
feminism, 6, 196 n. 35
Fénéon, Félix, 172
Ferrero, William, 205 n. 61
Ferry, Luc, 196 n. 38
Fichte, J. G., 171
First International, 8–9, 218 n. 159
First Step, The (Tolstoy), 106
"Florence *Pietà*" (Michelangelo), 43, 44–46
Flower, Desmond, 231 n. 82
Forel, August, 50, 51
forgiveness, 10
Forster, E. M., 10, 30, 31, 37–38, 51, 73
Forster, Michael, 108
Foster, William Z., 192 n. 17
Foucault, Michel, 40–41, 42, 49, 55, 183, 203 nn. 33–34, 220 n. 6; homosexuality and, 56–57, 61; knowledge and, 181–82; power and, 18, 86, 92, 97–98, 184
foundationalism, 19
Fragment on Government (Bentham), 98
Francis of Assisi, Saint, 192 n. 21
Fraternal Democrats and International Association, 8
freedom. *See* autonomy
Freud, Sigmund, 64–66; homosexuality and, 203 n. 35, 209 n. 122
Friedman, Marilyn, 25
Friedman, Susan Stanford, 192 n. 13
Friend of Man, The (Cobbe), 103
friendship, 6, 10, 19, 28, 51, 61; anticolonial thought and, 14, 16–17, 64, 73; art and, 162–67; cross-cultural, 162, 163, 164; Indian

nationalism and, 14; *philia* and, 28, 29; as *philoxenia*, 29, 31, 189; politics and, 27, 28; risk and, 29–30, 31, 200 n. 68; similarity and, 28; singularity and, 26; utopic community and, 20. *See also* politics: of friendship
From Adam's Peak to Elephanta (Carpenter), 62
Fundamental Principles of the Metaphysics of Morals (Kant), 126
"fusion," 31, 200 n. 72
Future Poetry, The (Aurobindo), 176

Gadiali, Dinshah, 15
Gagnier, Regina, 168
Gallacher, W., 179
Gandhi, Devdas, 120, 221 n. 13
Gandhi, Leela, 222 n. 33
Gandhi, M. K., 14, 15, 16, 18, 64, 117; *ahimsa* and, 63, 85–86, 114, 120; animal welfare and, 86–87, 97, 114; anticolonialism of, 63, 83, 96, 193 n. 5; in England, 67–73, 76, 77, 79, 80, 111; vegetarianism and, 67, 68, 69–76, 79, 82, 83, 210 n. 16, 211 n. 33
Gandhi, Rajmohan, 72
Gandhi, Ramachandra, 224 n. 65
Garber, Marjorie, 207 n. 87
Gauba, Kanhaya Lal, 15
Gauchisme, Le (D. and G. Cohn-Bendit), 185, 186
Gauld, Alan, 221 n. 19
Gautier, Théophile, 149, 166, 171
Geddes, Patrick, 50
gender, 17–18, 45, 48, 49, 64; division and, 125; gender binarization, 39, 207 n. 84
Gender Trouble (Butler), 207 n. 84
German Ideology, The (Marx), 148
Ghosal, Sarala, 82
Ghose, Aurobindo. *See* Aurobindo, Sri
Ghose, Benoybhushan, 162
Ghose, Kristo Dhone, 163
Ghose, Manmohan, 12, 151, 161; aestheticism of, 162, 164–65, 167–71, 173, 175, 230 n. 60, 230 n. 71, 231 n. 72, 231 n. 82; as poet, 142, 143, 144, 145, 146, 163; politics and, 166–67
Gilman, Sander L., 205 n. 63
Gilroy, Paul, 128, 130
God, 126, 134–35, 137
Godse, Nathuram, 209 n. 117
Goldmann, Lucien, 148
Good Shepherd, The (Andrews), 17
governmentality, 86, 91, 92, 97, 98, 112, 113; animal welfare and, 97, 101, 108; art and, 173–74; civilization and, 95, 110; colonialism and, 96, 215 n. 102; "improvement" and, 94–95; sentiment and, 104, 113
Gray, John, 211 n. 31
Greenblatt, Stephen, 228 n. 19
"guest-friendship," 31, 32, 111
Guha, Ramachandra, 6
Guha, Ranajit, 215 n. 102
Gurney, Edmund, 136, 138
gurus, 219 n. 2

Halevy, Elie, 91
Hall, John, 147
Hall, Stuart, 128, 148, 227 n. 16
Hammermeister, Kai, 152
Haraway, Donna, 31, 74, 100–101, 111, 211 n. 33, 216 n. 115
Hardt, Michael, 10, 11, 12, 23
Hatcher, John, 230 n. 62

Hay, Stephen, 71
Haynes, Renee, 225 n. 70
Heehs, Peter, 220 n. 8, 220 n. 12
Hegel, G. W. F., 21, 22, 24, 25, 31, 54, 132, 135, 159, 171, 196 n. 34; aesthetics and, 152, 157–58, 160, 161, 173
Hegel (Nancy), 206 n. 82
Heidegger, Martin, 161, 207 n. 82, 230 n. 55
heteronormativity, 49, 52, 58
heterosexuality, 49, 51, 56, 207 n. 84, 207 n. 88; imperialism and, 60
heterosociality, 46
Hilliard, David, 51
Hills, Arnold, 75
Hind Swaraj (M. K. Gandhi), 18, 63, 117
Hinduism, 75, 209 n. 117; colonialism and, 81–82
Hints to Workers (Monro), 93–94
Hippolyte, Jean, 21
Hirschfeld, Magnus, 53, 60, 206 n. 77
historicism, 152, 158, 160, 161, 173
history: colonialism and, 160; difference and, 157, 159; freedom and, 158, 159
History of British India (James Mill), 95
History of Sexuality, The (Foucault), 40–41, 42, 49, 55
homesickness, 67–68
homophobia, 39
Homos (Bersani), 38, 203 n. 33
homosexual exceptionalism, 39, 43, 59, 64–65, 139–40, 177; spiritualism and, 122
homosexuality, 37–42, 47, 51, 55, 56, 60–62, 65–66, 84, 143, 168, 201 n. 13; anti-imperialism and anticolonialism and, 10–11, 35, 49, 58–59, 62; crosscultural affinity and, 11, 35, 36, 58–59, 140; as friendship, 61; hybridity and, 140; lifestyle and, 42, 57; Michelangelo and, 44; in Nazi Germany, 53, 206 n. 77; orientalism and, 53, 205 n. 73; "savagery" and, 51–52, 55; scrutiny and, 60. *See also* sexuality
hospitality, 10, 30, 31; anticolonial, 72–73, 111, 114
Housman, Lawrence, 37, 39
Hughes, Langston, 6
Humane Review, 78
humanism, 100, 146
Humanitarian, 102
humanitarianism, 101, 106
Humanitarian League, 35, 77–78, 105–6
human nature: the empirical and, 117, 122, 126, 127, 128, 130; the metaphysical and, 117, 127, 128, 130
Human Personality (Myers), 135, 136, 137, 225 n. 72
Hutter, Horst, 27, 28
Huysmans, J. K., 171
hybridity, 6, 21, 22–23, 62, 121, 128, 130, 131, 137; affect and, 127; agency and, 191 n. 12; anticolonialism and, 118; ethics and, 117; hybrid subject and, 22, 23, 139, 198 n. 46, 223 n. 43; religion and, 128–29, 135; social reconstruction and, 22, 140; utopian socialism and, 177
Hyndman, H. M., 34, 35, 123, 138, 139, 179
hysteria, 137

identity, 3, 17, 128; homosexual, 38, 39; the other and, 55; privilege and, 31
imperialism, 1–2, 58, 60, 96, 163; Christianity and, 17; culture and, 158; dissidence and, 34; division and, 6, 7; hierarchies and, 7; imperial binarism, 3, 5; imperial manicheanism, 4, 5; imperial periphery, 7; inequity and, 9; nature management and, 214 n. 88; power and, 86; relationality and, 184–85
"improvement," 94–95
In Another Country (Joshi), 151
Independent Labour Party (ILP), 179
India, 82; Andrewsganj, 13; animal rights and, 75–76; colonial government and, 95–96, 165; culture and customs of, 95–96, 100, 158; freedom and, 86; independence of, 121; marriage in, 64; morality and, 15; Pondicherry, 118, 119, 120, 121, 220 n. 8; spirituality and, 115–20; western anti-imperialism and, 6–7, 13, 114. *See also* nationalism
Indian Eye on English Life, The (Malabari), 81
individualism, individuality, 25, 26, 113, 196 n. 34
Inoperative Community, The (Nancy), 19, 198 n. 50
Institute for Sexual Science, 206 n. 77
insufficiency, 24, 31, 54, 206 n. 82
Intermediate Sex, The (Carpenter), 44, 58, 63, 140
Intermediate Types among Primitive Folk (Carpenter), 59
internationalism, 9
International Working Men's Association, 8–9, 218 n. 159
Intimate Enemy, The (Nandy), 6–7
Introduction to Aesthetics (Hegel), 158, 159
Introduction to the Principles of Morals and Legislation, An (Bentham), 89–90, 99
inventiveness, 41; of homosexuality, 42
inversion. *See* homosexuality
Invert, The (Anomaly), 60
invulnerability, 29, 32
Ioläus (Carpenter), 61

Jallianwala Bagh tragedy, 14–15, 193 n. 5
James, William, 53, 118, 132–38, 140, 226 n. 82; relationality and, 141, 188; Society for Psychical Research and, 225 n. 70; spiritualism and, 131, 136, 225 n. 71
Jameson, Fredric, 158
Jayawardene, Kumari, 6, 116
Johnson, Lionel, 142, 168
Joll, James, 192 n. 17
Jones, Greta, 205 n. 63
Joshi, Priya, 151
Journal of Researches (Darwin), 109
judgment, 153–55
Jungle Books, The (Kipling), 96
justice: conceptions of, 117; risk and, 134, 141
Justice, 34–35

Kant, Immanuel, 21, 23, 24, 25, 31 118, 132, 134, 146, 159, 196 n. 34, 200 n. 76; aesthetics and, 151–55,

Kant (*continued*)
157, 158, 161, 171, 173; animals and, 90; ethics and, 117, 125–27, 128, 131, 222 n. 33, 235 n. 21; rationality and, 180–81; religion and, 126–27, 129–30, 141, 222 n. 34
Kensworthy, John, 78
Killing for Sport (H. Salt), 85
Kingsford, Anna, 70, 79, 83, 104, 106, 108
kinship, 43, 45, 46, 61, 104, 114, 184, 203 n. 33; the other and, 174–75
Kipling, John, 100
Kipling, Rudyard, 96
Klein, Naomi, 186, 236 n. 35
Knight, William, 226 n. 83
knowledge(s), 117, 149, 150; desire and, 154; hierarchies of, 181–82; oriental, 164
Kojeve, Alexandre, 21, 22
Krafft-Ebing, R. von, 49–50
kreophagy. *See* meat eating
Krishnaswamy, Revathy, 209 n. 117
Kropotkin, Peter, 112–13, 172, 218 n. 159

Labouchere Amendment, 60
Labour Church movement, 122
Laclau, Ernesto, 181
Lane, Christopher, 205 n. 73
Leask, Nigel, 212 n. 37
Leavis, F. R., 89
"Left-Wing" Communism (Lenin), 178, 179, 181, 185
Lenin, Vladimir, 12, 178, 179–80, 181, 185
Levinas, Emmanuel, 27, 129, 200 n. 72, 220 n. 6
liberalism, 196 n. 34
Liberalism and the Limits of Justice (Sandel), 222 n. 33
libertarianism, 148
Life of Michelangelo, The (Symonds), 44
Light, Henry, 83–84, 105
literature, 142; autonomy and, 148, 151; imperialism and, 150; pluralism and, 149; sociology of, 147
Lombroso, Cesare, 205 n. 61
love: animal welfare and, 104; as sacrifice, 105, 108
Love's Coming of Age (Carpenter), 58, 60–61, 63, 140
Love Songs and Elegies (M. Ghose), 164, 230 n. 60
Lukács, Georg, 21–22, 148
Lyotard, Jean-François, 220 n. 6

Macaulay, T. B., 82, 94
McCabe, Colin, 130
McConville, Maureen, 235 n. 31
Macherey, Pierre, 227 n. 17
MacIntyre, Alasdair, 24, 196 n. 34, 223 n. 38
Mahabharata, 105
Maitland, Edward, 79
Malabari, Behramji, 81
"man": evolution and, 47; as producer, 21
Mani, Lata, 149
Mansell, Thomas, 217 n. 140
marriage, 63; violence and, 64
Martin, Sir Richard, 88, 89
Marx, Karl, 4, 21–2, 23, 148; First International and, 9, 218 n. 159
Marxism, 9, 21, 139, 196 n. 34
masculinity, 63, 84–85, 209 n. 117
Masks of Conquest (Viswanathan), 150

materialism, 131, 152, 158; aestheticism and, 149, 155, 161; autonomy and, 148
Matthews, Elkin, 230 n. 60
Maurice (Forster), 37–38
May 1968, 18, 185–87, 197 n. 38, 235 n. 33, 236 n. 37
Mayo, Katherine, 15
meat eating, 68, 69, 75–76, 213 n. 55; cruelty and, 84; as exploitation, 106; imperialism and, 78, 84–85
Meat Fetish, The (Reclus and Crosby), 113
Merrie England (Blantchford), 178–79
metaphysics, the metaphysical, 117, 127, 128, 130, 137, 139, 141
Michelangelo, 43, 44–46, 55; homosexuality of, 44, 203 n. 35
Mill, James, 95, 96
Mill, John Stuart, 94, 99, 221 n. 19; colonialism and, 95, 96
minorities, 63
Mitchell, Timothy, 215 n. 102
Mitsis, Phillip, 200 n. 68
modernity, 7, 41; the political and, 146, 147; sexuality and, 40, 43; western, 5, 99
monism, 138
Monro, S. S., 93–94
Moonje, B. S., 120
Moore, Arthur, 169
Moore, Howard J., 111
morality, 47, 91, 134; Kantian, 126, 129, 130
Morris, William, 34, 123
Moss, Arthur, 214 n. 73
Mother India (Mayo), 15
Mouffe, Chantal, 22, 181, 196 n. 34
Murphy, Garner, 225 n. 70
Mutual Aid (Kropotkin), 112–13
Myers, Frederic, 135, 136, 137, 140, 141, 225 n. 72
mysticism, 116, 118, 138, 175; as degeneration, 140; pluralism and, 135; radicalism and, 137
mythology, 59

Nahar, Sujata, 220 n. 9
Nancy, Jean-Luc, 19, 20, 22, 54, 195 n. 28, 195 n. 30, 196 n. 36, 197 n. 45, 198 n. 50, 206 n. 82
Nandy, Ashis, 6–7, 63, 116, 219 n. 3
Naoroji, Dadabhai, 79–80
nationalism, 2; anticolonial, 1, 4, 5, 13, 15, 63; colonial, 5; "derivative discourse" and, 5; in India, 15, 35, 63, 115, 116, 119–20, 193 n. 7, 209 n. 117; "invention of tradition" and, 5
nation-states, 5, 41
natural selection. *See* evolution
negativity, 53, 54–55, 206 n. 82
Negri, Antonio, 10, 11, 12, 23
neoliberalism, 25
Nesbit, E., 106–7
neurosis, 65
Neve, Michael, 109
New Treasure Seekers (Nesbit), 106–7
Nichomachean Ethics (Aristotle), 28, 199 n. 64
Nield, Keith, 186
Nietzsche, Friedrich, 155, 159
nihilism, 22, 153, 197 n. 38–39
Nirodbaran, 221 n. 13
Nivedita, Sister (Margaret Noble), 115–16, 219 n. 1; anticolonialism of, 115

No Logo (Klein), 186
Nordau, Max, 18, 140, 179
Nussbaum, Martha, 134, 181, 222 n. 37

obedience, 92; civilization and, 95–96; the poor and, 94
Okawa, Shumei, 121
Oldfield, Josiah, 70, 72
Oliver, Hermia, 218 n. 159
On the Basis of Morality (Schopenhauer), 102
Oppenheim, Janet, 225 n. 70
orientalism, 115, 149, 150; homosexuality and, 53, 205 n. 73; romantic, 76, 212 n. 37
Orientalism (Said), 2, 3, 149
Origin of Species, The (Darwin), 47, 110–11, 112
Origins of Totalitarianism, The (Arendt), 235 n. 23
Orwell, George, 178
Oswald, John, 75
other, 3, 7, 141; other-directedness, 20; risk and, 31
outcasts, outsiders, 8, 26–27, 36, 55, 79, 184, 235 n. 23; homosexuality and, 57, 61
Owen, Alex, 137
Owen, Robert, 122

Paglia, Camille, 168, 231 n. 79
Panopticon, 97–98
Passage to India, A (Forster), 31
Passionate Attitudes (Sturgis), 143
Pater, Walter, 167, 171, 231 n. 75
Perfect Way in Diet, The (Kingsford), 70, 79, 83, 106
Perpetual Peace (Beck), 200 n. 76
Peters, John Durham, 99
Phenomenology of Mind (Hegel), 22, 54
Phillips, Stephen, 142
philosophy, 29, 132, 171; history and, 160; political, 27; western, 117
Philosophy of History (Hegel), 158
philoxenia, 29, 31, 184, 189, 234 n. 21
Pick, Daniel, 205 n. 63
Picture of Dorian Gray, The (Wilde), 144, 173
Plato, 57
Plea For Vegetarianism (H. Salt), 69
pluralism, 132, 133
Podmore, Frank, 138
poetry, 142, 143, 163–64; anticolonialism and, 145, 146, 164–65; *askesis* and, 103; imagination and, 160; "prose" and, 164–65, 167, 175
polis, 30; exclusion and, 29
political thought: friendship and, 27, 28; humanism and, 146; secularism and, 117; western, 12, 30, 117
politics, 31, 211 n. 33, 220 n. 6; "adulthood" and, 180–81; aesthetics and, 157, 161, 175; anarchist, 20; desire and, 198 n. 46; of the "event," 183, 186, 233 n. 15, 234 n. 20; exclusion and, 29, 184; failures of, 123; as friendship, 28; of friendship, 9–10, 12, 26–27; of hybridity, 131, 132, 140; identity politics, 177; imagination and, 147; immature, 12, 182–88, 236 n. 37; imperialism and, 12, 184–85; knowledge and, 150, 181–82; literature and, 148–49, 153; the other and, 7, 183; parliamentary, 179; poetry and, 176; realism and, 146–47, 151, 180; sexual, 37, 38, 39, 202

n. 31; similarity and, 28–29; singularity and, 147, 181; spiritualism and, 115, 116, 121, 123; of transgression, 15; transnational, 12. *See also* ethics; homosexuality; radicalism; utopianism
Politics (Aristotle), 28
Politics as Friendship (Hutter), 27
postcolonialism, 1, 7, 143, 149; aesthetic autonomy and, 152; determinism and, 5; hybridity and, 128; imperialism and, 4, 150, 162; literature and, 146, 147, 157; postcolonial theory, 2, 3, 4, 145; realism and, 147; spiritualism and, 115, 116
Postcolonial Theory (L. Gandhi), 222 n. 33
postmodernism, 20, 29–30, 196 n. 38, 197 n. 39, 220 n. 6; community and, 26; essentialism and, 21, 23
power, 20, 41, 98, 184; governmentality and, 92; homosexuality and, 40, 42
pragmatism, 132
Pratt, Mary Louise, 159
prayer, 117, 126, 127, 130, 224 n. 65; desire and, 129, 135. *See also* religion
Prescott, Mary, 172
present, transformation of, 20
Primate Visions (Haraway), 211 n. 31
Primavera (Binyon, Cripps, Ghose, and Phillips), 142–43, 144, 153, 163, 166, 169
Principles of Political Economy (J. S. Mill), 94
Promise and a Way of Life, A (Thompson), 6
Provincialising Europe (Chakrabarty), 146
provisionality, 186–87
psychoanalysis, 65
psychology, 36, 131, 135; abnormal, 137
Psychopathia Sexualis (Krafft-Ebing), 49–50
Pultney, William, 92, 93
Purani, A. B., 221 n. 13
Pyarelal, 77
Pythagoras, 76

queer theory, 128, 202 n. 33

race, racism, 58, 125; politics of, 128
radicalism, 102, 141, 179, 183, 192 n. 18; anarchism and, 219 n. 159; anticolonialism and, 2, 7, 8, 76; art and, 166, 172; heterodoxy and, 121–22; heterogeneity of, 115, 123, 138; hybridity and, 118; as politics, 12; sexuality and, 63; socialism and, 137; theism and, 125; transnationalism and, 9, 10; vegetarianism and, 77, 106
Rait, Suzanne, 210 n. 122
Ramakrishna, Sri, 209 n. 117
Rancière, Jacques, 183
rationalism, 103, 127; politics and, 180; religion and, 129, 221 n. 19
Rawls, John, 127
realism, 173
Reclus, Elisée, 113, 218 n. 159
recognition, 54, 55, 159, 160, 199 n. 53
Redesdale, Lord, 93
refugees. *See* outcasts, outsiders
relationality, 6, 32, 45, 55, 99, 131, 174; anarchist, 20; difference and, 54, 56, 125; ethics and, 133; homosexuality and, 42, 43, 57, 61, 202 n. 33; human–animal, 97, 100, 102,

relationality (*continued*)
111, 211 n. 33, 216 n. 115; the other and, 129; politics and, 184, 185, 187, 188; power and, 20, 97; sex and, 62
religion, 126–27, 129, 141, 160, 221 n. 19; cooperation and, 134; eastern, 11, 122; ethics and justice and, 117, 127–130; pluralism and, 141; religious heterodoxy, 122, 125; science and, 122; socialism and, 123, 140. *See also* spiritualism, spirituality
Religion within the Limits of Reason Alone (Kant), 126–27, 129
Remember Me to Harlem (Bernard), 6
Renaissance, The (Pater), 167, 231 n. 75
Renaissance Self-Fashioning (Greenblatt), 228 n. 19
Renault, Alain, 196 n. 38
resistance: to boundaries, 11; homosexual, 42, 55, 56; inventiveness and, 43; to power, 40–41
revolutions of 1848, 8
Revue de la Grande Synthèse, 119
Rhymers, 231 n. 82
Richard, Paul, 118, 119, 120, 222 n. 27. *See also* Alfassa, Mirra
Rickett, Charles, 169
risk, 29–30, 31, 32
Risorgimento, 8
Ritvo, Harriet, 79
Road to Wigan Pier, The (Orwell), 178
Ross, Kristen, 187–88
Rosselli, John, 82
Rousseau, Jean-Jacques, 25, 207 n. 88
Routh, Jane, 227 n. 15
Rowbotham, Sheila, 217 n. 129
Roy, Arundhati, 236 n. 35
Roy, Evelyn, 116
Roy, Nirendranath, 165
Roy, Parama, 115
Royal Society for the Prevention of Cruelty to Animals (RSPCA), 87, 107; "vigilance" and, 93, 214 n. 93; working poor and, 93–94
Rubin, Gayle, 38
Rudra, S. K., 16
Rules of Art, The (Bourdieu), 157
Rushdie, Salman, 128, 223 n. 43
Russett, Cynthia, 204 n. 54

Said, Edward, 2, 3, 28, 128, 149,150, 151, 152, 199 n. 57; art and, 161
Saint Oscar (Eagleton), 144
Salt, Henry, 11, 12, 64, 70, 71, 85, 87–88, 101, 102, 106, 216 n. 122; animal welfare and, 77, 111, 140, 177, 208 n. 99; anti-imperialism and, 113, 114, 182; Fellowship of the New Life and, 138, 177; socialism and, 217 n. 129; vegetarianism and, 69; working poor and, 107, 113
Salt, Kate, 138
sameness, 30
Sandel, Michael, 24, 117, 127, 130, 222 n. 33
Sartre, Jean-Paul, 183
"savages," 49, 50, 62, 204 n. 61; civilization and, 94–95, 98; homosexuality linked to, 51–52, 53, 59, 61, 66
Savaging the Civilised (Guha), 6
Sayle, Charles, 169
Schneer, Jonathan, 1, 2
Schopenhauer, Arthur, 102
science, 109; anti-vivisection and, 108

Seale, Patrick, 235 n. 31
Second International, 192 n. 17, 218 n. 159
Sedgwick, Eve Kosofsky, 39, 201 n. 13
self, 125, 180, 206 n. 82; affect and, 17; conscience and, 91; division and, 153; others and, 125; self-estrangement, 189; variegated, 118, 136–37, 139. *See also* subject
self-sufficiency, 23, 25, 29
sentient life: kinship of, 112; as web of affinities, 111
sentiment, 99, 103; animal welfare and, 215 n. 111; humanitarianism and, 101–2
Seth, Vikram, 32–33
sex, 40, 42, 55, 57, 202 n. 33, 207 n. 85; binarism and, 208 n. 99; categories of, 56, 58, 59, 62, 65; community and, 43; power and, 43; sexual repression, 40; transvestitism, 207 n. 87. *See also* gender
sexology, 10, 39, 47, 49–51, 204 n. 56, 205 n. 61
sexual dissidence, 8, 10; anti-imperialism and, 11, 39
Sexual Inversion (Ellis), 44
sexuality, 36, 38, 40, 64; "civilization" and, 49–50; defined, 39; racism and, 53; reproduction and, 48; systems of alliance and, 42–43, 61
sexual selection, 48–49
Shannon, Charles, 169
Sheehan, James J., 218 n. 151
Shelley, Percy Bysshe, 76
Sidgwick, Henry, 138
Sidney, Sir Phillip, 42
Simians, Cyborgs and Women (Haraway), 74
similitude, 28, 29, 159
Sinfield, Alan, 228 n. 19
Singer, Daniel, 236 n. 37
Singer, Peter, 89, 215 n. 111
singularity, 26; division and, 125
Sinha, Mrinalini, 209 n. 117
Sister India, 15
Skultans, Vieda, 225 n. 80
slavery, 8
socialism, 8, 97, 108, 114, 135, 137, 181, 185–86, 218 n. 159; affective, 101, 113, 138; anticolonialism and, 123, 141; art and, 166, 171, 172; scientific, 12, 179–80, 181–82, 185, 235 n. 21; spiritualism and, 118, 122–23; utopian, 12, 18, 20, 105, 123, 138, 140, 177, 178–80, 183, 185, 217 n. 129. *See also* utopianism
Socialism, from Utopia to Science (Engels), 18, 140, 178
sociality, 31, 36, 42, 68, 73, 203 n. 33; human–animal, 103, 109, 111, 113, 211 n. 31; as problem, 96, 97, 99
social justice, 219 n. 2; subjectivity and, 139
Social Mission of English Criticism, The (Baldick), 148
society, disciplinary, 92, 96
Society for Prevention of Cruelty to Animals, 89
Society for Psychical Research (SPR), 118, 136, 137–38, 140
sociology: aestheticism and, 151; literature and, 147–49, 150–51, 227 n. 15; postcolonialism and, 149
solidarity, 9, 29, 31; human–animal, 74; transnational, 8, 10
solipsism, 29, 30
Songs of Love and Death (M. Ghose), 230 n. 60

Sophocles, 46
Sosna, Morton, 218 n. 151
speciesism, 18, 74, 125
spirit possession, 136
spiritualism, spirituality, 8, 79, 219 n. 2, 225 n. 70; agency and, 125; anti-imperialism and, 11, 116, 120–21, 123–24, 175; art and, 176; critiques of western civilization and, 122; decline of, 140; God and, 135; hybridity and, 131, 139; non-Christian, 115; plurality of the self and, 118; psychology and, 136–37; radicalism and, 122; socialism and, 122, 123, 124, 140, 177; western political thought and, 117. *See also* West
Spivak, Gayatri, 149
Sri Aurobindo Ashram, 116, 121
Staël, Anna Louise Germaine de, 171
state: friendship and, 28, 29–30; power and, 20; racism and, 184. *See also* governmentality
Steevens, G. W., 84
Stendhal, 155
Stokes, Eric, 96
Storr, Anthony, 219 n. 2
Straight Mind, The (Wittig), 56
Straw Dogs (Gray), 211 n. 31
Streit der Facultaten (Kant), 222 n. 34
Sturgis, Matthew, 143
Subaltern Studies collective, 5
subject: autonomy and, 153, 159, 180–81; desire and, 22, 26; difference and, 174; ethics and, 91; judgment and, 153–54, 156, 157, 229 n. 38; privilege and, 23; self-sufficient, 117, 127, 148
subjectivity, 133, 136, 180; ego and, 156; female, 196 n. 35; inter-, 139; transformation of, 125, 188–89
Sulloway, Frank, 48
Sweetman, David, 172, 232 n. 98
Swinburne, Algernon Charles, 166, 230 n. 71
Symonds, John Addington, 44, 60, 61, 65, 142, 144, 166
Symposium (Plato), 57
System of Logic, A (J. S. Mill), 221 n. 19

Tagore, Rabindranath, 16; desire and, 194 n. 17; nationalism of, 147
Taylor, Charles, 23, 24–25, 131, 197 n. 41
Taylor, J., 34
Taylor, Thomas, 91
Teltscher, Kate, 209 n. 117
theism, 131, 135; the other and, 141. *See also* religion; spiritualism, spirituality
Théon, Max, 124
Theosophy, 79, 122, 138; in France, 124; radicalism and, 221 n. 20; spiritualism and, 123
Thomas, Keith, 75, 89
Thompson, Becky, 6
Thomson, J. Arthur, 50
Thoreau, Henry David, 87
Tolstoy, Leo, 106, 113
Tonkin, Boyd, 148
Toulouse-Lautrec, Henri de, 172
Touraine, Alain, 186
Towards Democracy (Carpenter), 34, 139
transcendence, 19
Trembling of the Veil, The (Yeats), 168

True India, The (Andrews), 15–16
Two Cheers for Democracy (Forster), 10, 30, 51

Ulrichs, Karl Heinrich, 57
Unavowable Community, The (Blanchot), 23
Uncle Sham (Gauba), 15
Universal Kinship, The (H. Moore), 111
Urania, 208 n. 99
"urning," 57
utilitarianism, 68–69; animal welfare and, 74, 89–91, 92, 96–97, 103–4; colonialism and, 94, 95–96, 215 n. 102; governmentality and, 91, 92; sentiment and, 99
utopianism, 7, 12, 19, 31, 58, 66, 179, 235 n. 21; anarchism and, 9; anticolonialism and, 178; culture and, 165; fin-de-siècle, 18, 26, 182; immaturity and, 12, 178–79, 180, 182, 183, 185–86, 236 n. 37; inclusiveness and, 130. *See also* politics; socialism

Van Vechten, Carl, 6
Van Vrekhem, Georges, 220 n. 8
Vegetarian, 71, 72, 79, 80, 107
vegetarianism, 68, 69–71, 82–84, 138, 212 n. 35, 212 n. 41; anticolonialism and, 11, 73–76, 80, 84–85; class and, 107–8; hospitality and, 72–74; meat eating and, 106; orientalist, 79; radicalism and, 76–77, 106, 123, 189; spiritualism and, 122; subordination and, 83; vegetarian cuisine, 80–81, 107; working poor and, 107; xenophilia and, 73
Vegetarian Messenger, 107
vegetarian societies: in London, 70, 71, 72, 75; in Manchester, 76, 89, 107
Vera (Wilde), 172
Vindication of Natural Diet, A (Shelley), 76
Vindication of the Rights of Brutes, A (T. Taylor), 91
Visram, Rosina, 211 n. 26
Visvanathan, Susan, 14
Viswanathan, Gauri, 145, 150, 151
Vivekananda, Swami, 82, 116, 209 n. 117

Walzer, Michael, 24
Warner, Michael, 203 n. 33
Washington, Peter, 225 n. 70
"web of affinities," 112, 218 n. 156; human–animal relationality and, 111
Weber, Eugen, 222 n. 25
Weeks, Jefferey, 217 n. 129
Weintraub, Stanley, 232 n. 101
West: anthropocentrism and, 76; colonialism and, 5; search for spirituality and, 115–19, 121, 124
Westcott, Brooke Foss, 18
White Woman's Other Burden, The (Jayawardene), 6
Whitman, Walt, 61, 166, 224 n. 59, 230 n. 71
Wilberforce, William, 93, 100
Wilcox, John, 232 n. 94
Wilde, Oscar, 12, 76–77, 161, 162, 167, 173, 174, 231 n. 75, 231 n. 79; aestheticism of, 144–45, 146, 166, 168, 169–75, 177; anarchism and, 172; anticolonialism of, 144–45, 146, 151, 153, 175, 176, 182; philoso-

Wilde (*continued*)
phy and, 171; poetry and, 142–43; trials of, 60
Williams, Howard, 70, 106
Williams, Raymond, 148
Windham, William, 92, 94
Wittig, Monique, 39, 55, 56, 201 n. 13, 207 n. 84, 207 n. 86
Wolff, Janet, 227 n. 15
Woman's Freedom League, 140, 208 n. 99
women, 49, 138, 168, 204 n. 54; male homosexuals and, 140, 189, 208 n. 99; obedience and, 92; ordination and, 17; spiritualism and, 115–16; vivisection and, 108; women's suffrage, 123, 140, 189
Woomera detention center (South Australia), 26
working poor: animal welfare and, 92–94, 97, 108; legislative control and, 92–94; vegetarianism and, 107
World Trade Organization (WTO), 185, 188

xenophilia, 73, 111; anti-imperialism and, 144

Yeats, W. B., 168
Yeo, Stephen, 221 n. 23
Young, Robert, 158

Zastoupil, Lynn, 215 n. 102
Žižek, Slavoj, 40–41, 197 n. 39, 197 n. 46
zoophilia, 86, 101, 111, 114; colonialism and, 177; as sacrifice, 105, 109
Zoophile, Le, 79
Zoophilist, 79, 108

LEELA GANDHI
teaches in the school of English
at La Trobe University.

CPSIA information can be obtained
at www.ICGtesting.com
Printed in the USA
LVHW051648201120
672268LV00011B/1411

9 780822 337157